S0-BZB-623

Reading the Old Testament in Antioch

Bible in Ancient Christianity

General Editor
D. Jeffrey Bingham

Editorial Board
Brian E. Daley
Robin M. Jensen
Christoph Markschies
Maureen A. Tilley
Robert L. Wilken
Frances M. Young

VOLUME 5

Reading the
Old Testament in
Antioch

by

Robert C. Hill

BRILL

LEIDEN • BOSTON

2005

BS
1171.3
.H55
2005

Cover design: Jeannet Leendertse
Cover art: Adapted from Greek New Testament, with Erasmus's translation into Latin.
Special Collections Division, Georgetown University Library.

This book is printed on acid-free paper.

Library of Congress Cataloging-in-Publication Data

Hill, Robert C. (Robert Charles), 1931–
 Reading the Old Testament in Antioch / by Robert C. Hill.
  p. cm. — (Bible in ancient Christianity, ISSN 1542-1295 ; v. 5)
 Includes bibliographical references and indexes.
 ISBN 90-04-14538-9 (hard : alk. paper)
 1. Bible. O.T.—Criticism, interpretation, etc. 2. Antioch (Turkey)—Church history.
 3. Christianity—Origin. 4. Church history—Primitive and early church, ca. 30–600.
 I. Title. II. Series.

 BS1171.3.H55 2005
 221.6'0939'43—dc22

                                                                    2005047111

ISSN 1542-1295
ISBN 90 04 14538 9

© Copyright 2005 by Koninklijke Brill NV, Leiden, The Netherlands.
Koninklijke Brill NV incorporates the imprints Brill Academic
Publishers, Martinus Nijhoff Publishers and VSP.

All rights reserved. No part of this publication may be reproduced, translated,
stored in a retrieval system, or transmitted in any form or by any means,
electronic, mechanical, photocopying, recording or otherwise, without prior
written permission from the publisher.

Authorization to photocopy items for internal or personal use is
granted by Brill provided that the appropriate fees are paid directly to
The Copyright Clearance Center, 222 Rosewood Drive,
Suite 910, Danvers, MA 01923, USA.
Fees are subject to change.

PRINTED IN THE NETHERLANDS

For Louis J. Swift,
in friendship and esteem

CONTENTS

PREFACE

In his second sermon on Genesis given in Antioch in 386, midway through the period studied in this volume that begins with the council of Nicea in 325 and extends to the council of Chalcedon in 451, John Chrysostom makes an admission to his congregation about the Jewish origins of the Old Testament, that "though the books are from them, the books and their meaning belong to us." He is perhaps assuring himself, at the outset of a long career of commentary on these works, that it is a Christian endeavor he is commencing, as he is also assuring his listeners that when they take the books in hand at home (as he urges them to do), that practice also befits a Christian family.

Both activities, reading and commentary, are the object of study here, particularly as practiced at Antioch, though evidence bears especially on the latter, thanks to the degree of survival both of written works and of homilies delivered orally in its churches. The Old Testament commentaries composed by Theodoret towards the end of our period, in fact, have survived entirely, their relative bulk suggesting that this ancient and obscure material represented a more urgent and more challenging demand on a pastor's ministry than the New. Initiation of the faithful into Antioch's theological mindset rested also on an appreciation of the Old, less familiar though it may be; its very obscurity and diversity made it more incarnational and for that reason, one might say, susceptible of an Antiochene approach.

Mention of Theodoret, appointed bishop of Cyrus (Cyrrhus) in 423, is a reminder that Antioch is not used here as a univocal term in the sense of the city founded by Seleucus on the river Orontes. By the period under consideration here, the name stood also for a vast *dioikêsis* comprising fifteen provinces of the empire and an ecclesiastical district with jurisdiction over many sees such as Tarsus, Mopsuestia and Cyrus. In the interests of precision it should be noted as well that this is not a comparative study, evaluating the approach of the Antiochenes by contrasting it with that of commentators elsewhere in that period or with modern western approaches to the Bible. Such an exercise attempted in the past has generally proven to be unhelpful. We intend to take the commentators and their works as we find them; they have suffered enough from prejudice, as the paucity of extant works of some of them demonstrates.

What, in fact, is aimed at here is an examination of the text of the commentaries of the leading Antiochene figures, who flourished in the period roughly from the council of Nicea in 325 to Chalcedon in 451 (Theodoret dying a decade later), for the benefit of those scholars less familiar with them. Such textual examination will hopefully throw light on aspects of Antioch's approach to the Old Testament, and lead to recognition of the distinctive worldview that accounts for it. The writer, coming from a biblical background, has been interested in reading and translating their Old Testament works, less well known than the New but (with the exception of Chrysostom's) better represented in extant remains in Greek. In the course of analysis of these many commentaries and the reading strategies they illustrate, abundant reference is made to the text to help conclusions be more cogent. If this is achieved, light will be thrown on a significant if sometimes misrepresented chapter in the history of Christian reading and biblical commentary, of which modern commentators and general readers might well take account.

In expressing appreciation to the general editor of *Bible in Ancient Christianity*, D. Jeffrey Bingham, for inclusion of this work in the series and for his patience, the author also regrets having had to complete it before the appearance of Charles Kannengiesser's opening volumes.

ABBREVIATIONS

AAS	*Acta Apostolicae Sedis*
AB	Anchor Bible
AnBib	Analecta biblica, Roma: Pontificio Istituto Biblico
ASE	*Annali di storia dell' esegesi*
Aug	*Augustinianum*
BAC	Bible in Ancient Christianity, Leiden-Boston: Brill
Bib	*Biblica*
BJRL	*Bulletin of the John Rylands University Library of Manchester*
CCG	Corpus Christianorum: Series graeca, Turnhout: Brepols
CCL	Corpus Christianorum: Series latina, Turnhout: Brepols
CPG	Clavis patrum graecorum, Turnhout: Brepols
DBSup	*Dictionnaire de la Bible. Supplément*, Paris: Librairie Letouzey et Ané
DS	*Enchiridion Symbolorum, Definitionum et Declarationum*, 34th ed., edd. H. Denzinger, A. Schönmetzer, Freiburg: Herder, 1967
DTC	*Dictionnaire de théologie catholique*, Paris: Librairie Letouzey et Ané
ECS	Early Christian Sudies, Brisbane: Australian Catholic University
ETL	*Ephemerides Theologicae Lovanienses*
EstBib	*Estudios Bíblicos*
FOTC	Fathers of the Church, Washington DC: Catholic University of America Press
GO	Göttinger Orientforschungen, Wiesbaden: Otto Harrassowtiz
GOTR	*Greek Orthodox Theological Review*
HeyJ	*The Heythrop Journal*
ICC	International Critical Commentary, Edinburgh: T&T Clark
ITQ	*Irish Theological Quarterly*
JAC	*Jahrbuch für Antike und Christentums*
JECS	*Journal of Early Christian Studies*
JTS	*Journal of Theological Studies*
KlT	Kleine Texte für Vorlesungen und Übungen, Bonn: A. Marcus und E. Weber's Verlag
LEC	Library of Early Christianity, Washington DC: Catholic University of America Press
LXX	Septuagint

MSU	Mitteilungen des Septuaginta-Unternehmens, Göttingen: Vandenhoeck & Ruprecht
NJBC	*New Jerome Biblical Commentary*, eds. Raymond E. Brown et al., Englewood Cliffs NJ: Prentice Hall, 1990
NS	new series
ÖBS	Österreichische Biblische Studien, Frankfurt am Main: Peter Lang
OCA	*Orientalia Christiana Analecta*
OCP	*Orientalia Christiana Periodica*
OTL	Old Testament Library, London: SCM
PG	Patrologia graeca
PL	Patrologia latina
RB	*Revue biblique*
RHT	*Revue d'Histoire des Textes*
RSPT	*Revue des sciences philosophiques et théologiques*
SBL	Society of Biblical Literature
SC	Sources chrétiennes, Paris: Du Cerf
ST	Studi e Testi, Città del Vaticano: Biblioteca Apostolica Vaticana
StudP	*Studia Patristica*
SVTQ	*St Vladimir's Theological Quarterly*
TGl	*Theologie und Glaube*
TS	*Theological Studies*
TRE	Theologische Realenzyklopädie
VC	*Vigiliae Christianae*
VTS	*Vetus Testamentum*, Supplement, Leiden: Brill
WGRW	Writings from the Greco-Roman World, Atlanta: SBL

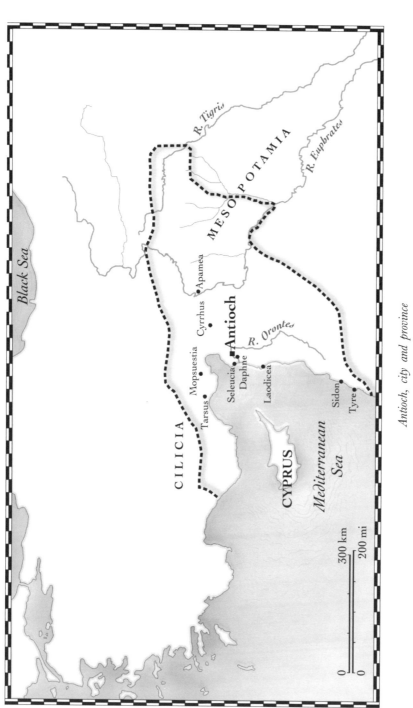

Antioch, city and province

CHAPTER ONE

TRADITION OF THE FAITH IN ANTIOCH

"Faith comes through hearing," Paul assures his Roman converts (Rom 10:17); and by citation of Isaiah 52:7 and Psalm 19:5 he argues that to everyone, Jews included, the opportunity has been given to hear the εὐαγγέλιον. Evangelization, however, is not enough; the Church of his day and ours realizes that communities and individuals must be brought to experience constantly God's action in Jesus for that faith to be nourished. It may not be the direct experience of the Jesus of the public ministry enjoyed by eyewitnesses, as it was not in Paul's own case; he and we others after him have depended on a range of forms of transmission, or tradition, to allow us to tap into the original experience and to share in a life-giving κοινωνία. Hence his letter to the Romans, and hence also the other Christian scriptures, which by being read out and distributed to a growing number of communities nourished the faith of believers in the early Church. The Jewish scriptures, too, fulfilled—and still fulfil—that function in the case of the Jewish people: "Listen, Israel" (cf. Deuteronomy 5:1; 6:4) was and is a life-giving injunction for their faith, Jesus himself sharing in that traditional process. Paul's citation of the Jewish texts to his converts in Rome shows that their faith, too, could be nourished by attending to the Word both old and new.

These scriptures, Old and New, describe both peoples, old and new, celebrating and confirming their faith in God, making their confession and deepening their commitment in still other ways—by liturgical and sacramental anamnesis, by homiletic commentary and development, by catechetical initiation and explication, by familial example and demonstration, by moral suasion and encouragement, and in other traditional ways. And the literature that has come into our possession from the words and writings of early Christian commentators, catechists, celebrants, homilists and mentors of various kinds testify to this fertile process of tradition of the faith that operated in the burgeoning community. One such traditional form of faith development, of course, was the reading and explication of the community's scriptures, the Old and the New; evidence of its exercise is happily quite abundant.

A. ANTIOCH A PRIVILEGED COMMUNITY

Believers in the church of Antioch, the first to be called Christians (Acts 11:26 tells us),[1] were also beneficiaries of this manifold process of faith development. In fact, Luke presents them in his history as the initial exception to the general rule of proclaiming the Lord Jesus "to no one except Jews" (11:19). As well, this first Gentile community had the advantage of being not only evangelized but also of having Paul (and Barnabas) spend a year (perhaps 44–45) meeting with them and "teaching (διδάξαι) a great number of them."[2] This year-long course in faith development doubtless involved not only mediating to them what Paul himself had learnt from his mentors about the Lord Jesus[3] and catechesis in the Lord's teachings, but also commentary on the Jewish scriptures (in which he claimed particular expertise: Gal 1:14) and eucharistic celebration of "the Lord's death" of which he speaks to another such community (1 Cor 11:23–29). In other words, the young church of Antioch enjoyed a uniquely sustained period of traditional formation in the faith by leading apostolic figures.

This privilege was not without justification. Antioch, by dint of its foundation by Alexander's general Seleucus, its position on the commercial highway reaching from Asia to the Mediterranean through its nearby port of Seleucia, its status as capital of Syria and a military and diplomatic centre in the empire, and its architectural splendor, had become by Paul's time a jewel in the Roman crown.[4] It

---

[1] For Wayne A. Meeks and Robert L. Wilken, *Jews and Christians in Antioch in the First Four Centuries of the Common Era*, 16, the phrase in Acts means that "it was in Antioch that (the Christians) first stood out from Judaism as a distinct sect."

[2] It was later in that decade that the incident occurred of Paul's difference with Peter in Antioch over the extent of table fellowship between Jews and Gentiles (Gal 2:11–18)—a further indication of the Gentile character of this sect of Judaism in that city. Cf. J. D. G. Dunn, "The incident at Antioch (Gal 2:11–18)."

[3] Cf. Gal 1:18, where the purpose of Paul's fifteen-day stay with Peter was (as suggested by the term ἱστορῆσαι) "to get information from him about Jesus' ministry," in the view of J. A. Fitzmyer, "Galatians," *NJBC*, 783.

[4] Cf. G. Downey, *A History of Antioch in Syria from Seleucus to the Arab Conquest*; D. S. Wallace-Hadrill, *Christian Antioch*, 1–5.

was also a city well-provided with facilities for public enjoyment of games, races, wild beast hunts, orgiastic festivals and a range of other amusements, thanks to the liberality of emperors and governors, that would prove the bugbear of Christian pastors and draw their criticism. On the other hand, this liberality also extended to provision of fine church buildings: Constantine began the construction of an octagonal Great Church on the island in the river Orontes on which the imperial palace stood, his son Constantius completing the structure, which was dedicated in 341.[5] By that time Antioch had become the capital of the vast διοίκησις of Oriens comprising fifteen provinces of the empire extending from Mesopotamia to the borders of Egypt.[6]

B. Antioch in fourth and fifth centuries

By the time of the council of Nicea in 325—which may appropriately mark the beginning of the period of this study of Antioch,[7] a period concluding with the death of Theodoret of Cyrus around 460—this city, centre of a vast civil region and an ecclesiastical diocese that stretched from Tyre and Damascus in the south to the minor sees of Tarsus, Mopsuestia and Edessa in the north and west,

---

[5] In the town proper there were three or four parish churches, including the Old Church, built in the third century, destroyed during the Diocletian persecution and rebuilt between 313 and 324; cf. Downey, *The History*, 342–50. There were also martyrs' shrines, the most notable being one at Daphne containing the relics of St Babylas, to which Chrysostom refers in commenting on Ps 111 (PG 55.285). The number of churches is debated by W. Mayer, "John Chrysostom: extraordinary preacher, ordinary audience," in M. B. Cunningham, P. Allen (eds), *Preacher and Audience. Studies in Early Christian and Byzantine Homiletics*, 126–27.

[6] J. N. D. Kelly, *Golden Mouth. The Story of St John Chrysostom, Ascetic, Preacher, Bishop*, 1. Theodoret at different times in his career registers the general appreciation felt in the region of Antioch for the *Pax Romana* and regret at its disruption, the Persians nominated as the villains of the piece. While in his Commentary on Daniel he associates Roman rule with "submission, good order and the rule of law" (and taxes), and sees it continuing from its inception under Augustus till the Second Coming ("The Roman kingdom remained in power under him, and has lasted even to this day"), it has begun to deteriorate by his next work, on Ezekiel, and the later Psalms Commentary laments the assault of the Persians in 441.

[7] Only a year later Eustathius was deposed as bishop of Antioch by the Arians after having been the first to speak at the council. His sole surviving work, attacking Origen's homily on the witch of Endor (1 Sam 28), was nevertheless a signature statement of Antioch's approach to biblical texts. Critically edited by E. Klostermann (KlT 83), Quasten, *Patrology* 3, 303, dates it before the beginning of the Arian controversy, and puts the death of Eustathius before 337.

had attained such prominence as to be recognized by that council as enjoying a precedence accorded also to the sees of Rome and Alexandria. At that time the New Rome of Constantine to the north was still some years from inauguration to replace the old Byzantium on the Bosphorus. Its population and importance grew so rapidly, however, that it was to a city of some 200,000 or more people (much the size of Antioch) that Theodosius I summoned the second ecumenical council in 381, which declared the bishop of Constantinople to have precedence next after the bishop of Rome, now uncontested by Antioch or by that other ancient seat of learning more to the west and south, Alexandria.

If it was at Antioch that the preference given by Jesus and his followers to the evangelizing of Jews was first rescinded in favor of Gentiles, the city's numerous Jewish community knew they had suffered discrimination since the time of Antiochus IV Epiphanes, the ill-feeling spilling over into rioting that went on for the next seven centuries. Anti-Jewish sentiment surfaces frequently in the works of the biblical commentators under consideration here, testifying to the influence Jews wielded and the perceived dangers of syncretism.[8] And yet this Jewish community's tradition of Old Testament exegesis left its mark on a Christian commentator like Theodore, perhaps responsible for earning him a second sobriquet, *Ioudaiophrōn*.[9]

Pagan cults of semitic, Hellenistic and Roman origin also abounded in Syria; Daphne a few miles to the west of Antioch became the site of shrines and temples built there by Epiphanes and a succession of Roman emperors.[10] Julian the Apostate endeavoured to sub-

---

[8] R. L. Wilken, *John Chrysostom and the Jews. Rhetoric and Reality in the Later Fourth Century*, 57, 60, notes that though Libanius in his letters testified to the wealth of the Jews, this is not the basis for any criticism of them by Chrysostom. More to the point may have been the Jews' claim to have been in Antioch longer than the Christians, a boast made by Porphyry and Julian (79).

[9] M. Wiles, "Theodore of Mopsuestia as representative of the Antiochene school," 498.

[10] It could be that a statue erected at Daphne to the *tyche* of Rome under Julius Caesar prompted Theodoret's Question 88 on Genesis, *Theodoreti Cyrensis Quaestiones in Octateuchum*, 78–79, "Why does Scripture mention τύχη?" (in reference to Leah's choosing Gad—LXX εὐτύχηκα—as a name in 30:11). Theodoret is clearly on the defensive: "The expression 'I am in luck' was not Jacob's but Leah's, a woman, as I remarked, raised in irreligion and schooled only briefly in divine things; her father likewise said, 'I took omens,' whereas the divine Law forbids recourse to omens. So let no one think such words are those of the divine Scripture: the author includes what is said by those who are not religious because he is relaying facts."

ject Christianity to such pagan worship, but his failure was due less to the brevity of his stay in Antioch in 362–63 than to Antioch's having become by then a predominantly Christian city (if rent by internal ecclesiastical divisions).[11] Gnostic groups of various hues were also rife, resisted earlier by Ignatius but still promoting docetic and Valentinian views in the period under discussion. Marcion's dualism and consequent assault on the Old Testament was a related aberration that earned the ire of Antiochene Fathers, as did Manichean depiction of a world divided between the powers of Light and Darkness and their denying moral freedom in human beings.[12] Though Antioch hosted none of the early ecumenical councils, trinitarian and Christological debate was in the air, in which the key figures in focus here took part, as we shall see in Chapter Nine; at least Diodore and Theodoret are on record as taking conspicuous roles in the second and fourth of those councils, respectively. In short, in this diverse religious environment there was plenty of scope for the multi-pronged faith formation of Antioch Christians provided by catechetical, biblical, liturgical and other forms of tradition in the community.

C. Pastors of the Antioch churches

Fortunately for these believers, their introduction and nourishment in the faith through such traditions were in that period in the charge of outstanding pastors, some of whom have bequeathed to us the

---

[11] R. Wilken, *John Chrysostom and the Jews*, 30, speaks of Antioch as "a competitive religious environment, in which the loyalties and allegiances of Christians were constantly shifting." Chrysostom in commentary on Ps 111:4 (PG 55.285) speaks of the ups-and-downs of life in Antioch with the rise and fall of rulers like Julian: "How many marvels occurred in the time of Julian, who surpassed everyone for impiety, despite the Church's resistance? How many in the time of Maximin? How many before those awful emperors? If you prefer, however, there were those happening in our generation, like the crosses suddenly engraved on the garments, the razing of the temple of Apollo by a thunderbolt, the translation of the holy martyr Babylas who was in Daphne, the conspicuous victory over the demon, the surprising death of the imperial treasurer, the actual removal of the emperor Julian himself, who surpassed everyone for impiety."

[12] Marcion and Mani regularly feature in the rogues gallery Chrysostom parades before his classes in the διδασκαλεῖον in Antioch in the course of his treatment of (fifty eight) Psalms (e.g., Pss 110, 144, 145, 148). It may be a conventional listing (Didymus often has recourse to a similar one); Chrysostom's exegetical homilies do not develop into full scale theological polemic.

literary remains that are the object of study here. Though bishop of
the city itself for only a short period before deposition by an Arian
synod in 326, Eustathius had been the first to speak at Nicea, and
left the influential tractate against Origen's approach to Scripture
that summed up the approach that would be adopted by later
Antiochenes.[13] The work was clearly a factor in the biblical formation of the Antiochene Diodore, the man who would be responsible
(after Lucian, martyred in 312) for developing the distinctive exegetical and hermeneutical method subsequently associated with Antioch;
he had also studied philosophy and rhetoric in Athens. Diodore,
endorsing Eustathius's uncritical rejection of Origen-style scriptural
interpretation, played a key role in the biblical education of budding churchmen in his seminary, or ἀσκητήριον, before appointment
in 378 as bishop in one of the sees in the district of Antioch, Tarsus
in Cilicia. His orthodoxy is attested to by his conspicuous resistance
to Julian the Apostate during the latter's residence in Antioch in
362–63, and by his participation in the council of Constantinope in
381, which won him a glowing tribute from the emperor Theodosius.[14]
The loss after his death before 394 of most of his vast commentary
on the Old Testament is due to implied involvement in the doctrines of Nestorius.

Diodore's most famous students in the Antioch asketerion were
John (later spoken of as Chrysostom for his oratorical gifts) and
Theodore (later appointed bishop in Mopsuestia, another see in the
district of Antioch). Also contributing to their education was Antioch's
official rhetorician, the pagan sophist Libanius, who saw in the former student his ideal successor.[15] Instead, John was ordained to the
diaconate by the bishop Meletius and to the priesthood by his successor Flavian, and conducted a busy ministry of the liturgy and the
Word in Antioch before his consecration as bishop of Constantinople
in 398. His extant homilies and treatises delivered to the faithful in
these churches are unsurpassed in number by those of any other
Greek Father, his immunity from theological criticism being partly

---

[13] Cf. note 7 above.
[14] Cf. C. Schäublin, "Diodor von Tarsus," 764–65.
[15] Sozomen, *Historia Ecclesiastica* 8, 2 (PG 67.113). Chrysostom did not return the
compliment, taking occasion in his works to criticize Libanius along with emperor
Julian for attacks on the Church; cf. D. G. Hunter, "Libanius and John Chrysostom:
New thoughts on an old problem," *StudP 22* (1989) 129–35.

responsible for their survival.[16] Theodore's works did not enjoy the same fate; though ordained priest and bishop about the same time as his friend Chrysostom, and in his pastoral career likewise producing a vast amount of biblical commentary and dogmatic exposition as "a teacher of the whole Church in battle against every heretical column,"[17] he was condemned at the fifth ecumenical council of 553 and most of his works were lost. To the Syriac Church in that same century, however, he became known as The Interpreter, *Mephasqana*.[18]

In the next generation, as John and Theodore were moving to the pastoral care of the churches of Constantinople and Mopsuestia, respectively, Antioch became the birthplace also of Theodoret. He would hardly have known these predecessors (John dying in 407, Theodore in 428), though sometimes credited with close association with Theodore and Nestorius. Having experienced monastic life at Apamea on the Euphrates to the north east of Antioch, and enjoying a distinctive introduction to principles of biblical commentary held in Alexandria,[19] he was appointed bishop of nearby Cyrus (Cyrrhus) in 423. Despite active involvement in theological debate and participation in the council of Ephesus in 431, he could claim in a letter in 448 that he had commented on "all the prophets, the psalter and the apostle."[20] He would proceed to compose other biblical, dogmatic and historical works; despite his deposition, he was rapidly reinstated and involved in the convocation of the council of Chalcedon in 451. He died around 460,[21] the last of these four great Antiochene biblical commentators, his death closing the period of this study.

D. Literary and philosophical education in Antioch

In the period under discussion, at least city dwellers of Antioch spoke Greek; Syriac was spoken by peasants, a dialect of Aramaic acquired

---

[16] Cf. J.-M. Leroux, "Johannes Chrysostomus," 118–27.
[17] The view is that of Theodoret, *Church History* 5.40 (PG 82.1277).
[18] Cf. P. Bruns, "Theodor von Mopsuestia," 240–46.
[19] In his first exegetical work, on the Song of Songs, for instance, Theodoret has no qualms about admitting familiarity with "the norms of allegory" (PG 81.40), which Diodore's students would not have enjoyed. His works on Psalms and Prophets also show influence of Cyril and Eusebius of Caesarea, as we shall see below.
[20] *Ep* 82, to Eusebius of Ancyra (SC 98.202).
[21] Cf. J.-N. Guinot, "Theodoret von Kyrrhos," 250–54.

by Theodoret at his mother's knee,[22] and an asset in trying to wrestle with Hebrew terms lying behind his Greek biblical text, but an unfamiliar language to Theodore and despised by him. The Antioch Fathers in their tradition of the faith show little explicit indebtedness to philosophy, though often credited with being Aristotelian. David Wallace-Hadrill concludes,

> Antiochene Christianity was in its essence unphilosophical . . . It is only in a general sense that the Christian writers of Antioch can be called Aristotelian. The sense in which the term is admissible is that which credits them with an Aristotelian frame of mind or outlook, and this is probably true of many of them even when they had little knowledge of Aristotle's works . . . The Antiochene characteristically thought in terms of history and Scripture . . . We may look in vain for an attempt to base their historical or scriptural standpoint upon a logical or metaphysical foundation derived from Aristotle. The Antiochenes appear to have been unaware of the possibility of such support or uninterested in making use of it.[23]

The question is of relevance for us in our stated intention of accounting for the distinctive approach to the Old Testament found in Antiochene commentators, which we shall see (in Chapter Eleven) is but part of a much more comprehensive—and distinctive—mindset.

Wallace-Hadrill further claims that Alexandria, putatively indebted especially to Plato through Philo, contributed more to the study of Aristotle than did Antioch. Certainly an Alexandrian commentator like Didymus the Blind in his Commentary on Zechariah invokes the terminology and categories of Aristotle along with Peripatetics, Stoics, Pythagoreans and Philo.[24] None of this is acknowledged or utilized in Antioch by Theodore and Theodoret in their later works on this prophet composed with Didymus open before them.[25] On

---

[22] Cf. P. Canivet, *Histoire d'une entreprise apologétique au Ve siècle*, 26–27. We shall note in Chapter Four that the Antioch Fathers shared the general patristic ignorance of Hebrew.

[23] *Christian Antioch*, 96, 102–103. Wallace-Hadrill also cites the claim of R. Walzer, "Arabic transmission of Greek thought to Medieval Europe," *Bulletin of John Rylands Library* 29 (1945) 169, that the eastern church as a whole abandoned philosophy during the fourth and fifth centuries—the period under discussion here.

[24] For these influences evident in the work of Didymus, see L. Doutreleau, *Didymus l'Aveugle. Sur Zacharie*, I, 101–102, 108, 112–114.

[25] In response to Q.4 on 1 Kings (*Theodoreti Cyrensis Quaestiones in Reges et Paralipomena*, 129) in reference to Solomon's wisdom and that of the Egyptians, Theodoret will mention a range of Greek philosophers likewise indebted to the Egyptians: "Recourse

the other hand, it is not to be regretted that we do not find in them the flawed numerology that Didymus derives from Philo to account for the dating of the prophet's visions based on the erroneous version he is using of Zech 1:7.

If Antiochene education in this period did not have a strongly philosophical basis, it was not uninfluenced by grammarians, rhetoricians and historians of a kind. "Antiochene exegesis is grounded in the exegetical activities of the rhetorical schools," Frances Young maintains,[26] seeing in such schools the source of the accent to be found in Diodore (and Eustathius before him) and his pupils Theodore and John Chrysostom and later in Theodoret on the *skopos* (or purpose) of the author in composing his biblical work, its ὑπόθεσις (theme, or narrative setting), διάνοια (its thrust, or overall meaning), ἑρμηνεία (its interpretation), λέξις (the biblical text), τὸ ἱστορικόν (the factual element), and θεωρία (discernment by the reader of a further level of meaning). These are the terms and categories of traditional education, παιδεία, in the rhetorical schools, and in Chapter 7 we shall see the Antiochenes adopting them in their commentaries.

In the case of Chrysostom and Theodore we know from the historian Socrates that it was in the classes of the city's official rhetorician, the pagan Libanius, friend of Julian, that they were introduced to these canons.[27] This rhetorical education under Libanius we see reflected in Chrysostom's homilies (Edwin Hatch assures us), explaining the complimentary reference to them by Photius in the ninth century as ὁμιλίαι rather than mere λόγοι because of the homilist's engagement with the listeners.[28] It is to Greek rhetoric, Hatch also claims, that we owe not just the early Christian homily but also

> such an exegesis of the sacred books as the Sophists gave of Homer, or such elaborated discourses as they also gave upon the speculative and ehtical aspects of religion.[29]

As a further guidance to their reading of the sacred writings they would (claims Christoph Schäublin)[30] have been introduced to the

---

to them was had by Pherecydes the Syrian, Pythagoras of Samos, Anaxagoras of Klazomene and Plato the Athenian in the hope of gaining from them a more precise knowledge of theology and natural philosophy."

[26] *Biblical Exegesis and the Formation of Christian Culture*, 175.
[27] *Historia Ecclesiastica* 6, 3 (PG 67.665–668).
[28] *Bibliotheca* 172 ed. R. Henry II, 168.
[29] *The Influence of Greek Ideas on Christianity*, 109–113.
[30] *Untersuchungen zu Methode und Herkunft der Antiochenischen Exegese*, 158–70. Schäublin

hermeneutical principles of Aristarchus, Porphyry, Plutarch, Strabo and Eratosthenes. As a result, the biblical tradition of Christianity that was mediated to the faithful in Antioch in these decades at the hands of distinguished pastors came colored by the education they themselves had received.[31] The accents they gave to Psalms and Prophets, for example, and particularly the hermeneutical perspective they adopted in interpreting them, can be traced to these pagan authors.[32]

If the ministerial formation at Antioch did not reflect the more philosophical approach favored in that other seat of learning, Alexandria, and evident in the biblical commentaries of its exponents, the ultimate purpose did not differ, namely, the faith formation of the communities for which they as Christian pastors would be responsible. "The most important thing these so-called schools had in common was a desire to foster the life of faith."[33] If that aim was not shared by Libanius in his rhetoric classes, it would have been pre-eminent in the institutions of spiritual formation, like the asketerion presided over by Diodore that John Chrysostom and Theodore attended,[34] and the monastery Theodoret joined at Apamea. All of these men were prepared in this rounded way for ministry in churches within the larger Antioch jurisdiction.

E. Faith formation in Antioch

Comprehensive ministry to the faithful requires exercise of all those forms of tradition itemized at the beginning of this chapter: liturgi-

---

takes Theodore as a case in point, claiming, "Theodor sein Rüstzeug als Interpret der paganen Grammatik verdankt" (158). For other views on the extent of pagan influence on the Antiochenes' education, see A. Viciano, "Das formale Verfahren der antiochenischen Schriftauslegung," 404–405.

[31] It is a fact reminiscent of the insistence of Augustine's mother, the pious Monica, on his receiving a good grounding in the pagan classics as a preparation for his becoming one day a good Christian.

[32] Theodore's extant Old Testament commentaries being those on the Twelve Prophets and the Psalms, Schäublin takes these to illustrate the influence on him of Porphyry, Plutarch, Eratosthenes and Aristarchus in particular (*Untersuchungen*, 162–167).

[33] Young, *Biblical Exegesis*, 185.

[34] Kelly, *Golden Mouth*, 19, does not see the asketerion simply as a monastery: "It seems more realistic to envisage Diodore's pupils as a close-knit fellowship of dedicated Christians who, while staying in their separate homes and living in the world, accepted self-imposed rules of rigorous self-denial and met together, probably in some private house, to pray, study the bible and hear expositions on it, and be counselled by the master in ascetic withdrawal."

cal, biblical, homiletic, moral, doctrinal, catechetical (not to mention the lived experience of Christians in families and parishes). Though liturgy may claim to be *prima theologia*, and though Paul's letters to his communities show them already being nourished in their faith by the anamnesis and celebration of the Christian Passover before his writings became Holy Writ for them, the pastors of these communities regarded it as a principal role to familiarize them with the *magnalia Dei* to be found in the scriptures Old and New. As a result we have—despite the ravages of time and the flames of prejudice—voluminous remains of biblical commentary from pastors in the churches of Antioch as of other centres, remains that betray both the common adherence to the faith of the apostles as well as the influence on the commentators of differing educational and philosophical positions and processes.

In the case of an orator like Chrysostom we have—thanks to the remarkable resources of stenography in the ancient world recorded for us by Eusebius, for instance, in regard to Origen's dictation and preaching[35]—over eight hundred homilies extant, of which the bulk deal with Old and New Testament works or pericopes. While most of them were delivered in churches during liturgical or paraliturgical ceremonies (as distinct from a classroom venue, like the διδασκαλεῖον he mentions in the course of his large series of homilies on the Psalter), we are not in possession of the lectionaries of the period that would allow us always to pinpoint the particular occasion when some scriptural text was set down for homiletic explication in the liturgy of the Word in a church.[36] The custom of preaching on

---

[35] Cf. Eusebius, *H.E.* 6, 23 (SC 41.123.2): "As he dictated, he had available more than seven shorthand writers (ταχύγραφοι), who interchanged with one another at set intervals, and copyists (βιβλιόγραφοι) no fewer in number, as well as girls trained in penmanship (καλλιγραφεῖν)." Similar banks of stenographers were available to Origen in his preaching, as also to other orators even from classical antiquity; cf. J. De Ghellinck, *Patristique et moyen age: études d'histoire littéraire et doctrinale*, II *Introductions et complément à l'étude de la patristique*, 217; A. Hamman, "Stenography," in A. Di Berardino, ed., *Encyclopedia of the Eary Church* 2, 794; R. C. Hill, "Chrysostom's *Commentary on the Psalms*: homilies or tracts?"

[36] Cf. M. Aubineau, "Restitution de quartorze folios du codex hierosolymitain, Photios 47, au codex Saint-Sabas 32. Prédication de Chrysostome à Constantinople et notamment à Saint-Irène," *JTS* 43 (1992) 537: "Un *système* de lectures, couvrant l'ensemble de l'année litrurique, n'avait pas encore été élaboré et généralisé à Constantinople, dès le temps de Chrysostome." Aubineau admits (537, n. 28) "l'ignorance où sommes au sujet du lectionnaire biblique dans la liturgie byzantine, à très haute époque," also claiming that "un système de lectures, couvrant l'ensemble de l'année liturgique, n'avait pas encore été élaboré et généralisé à Constantinople dès le temps de Chrysostome."

Genesis in (the eight week) Lent, which yields us three sets of homilies on that book by Chrysostom,[37] would be an exception to our ignorance in that regard.

On the other hand, while Diodore, Theodore and Theodoret exercized their pastoral ministry in the sees of Tarsus, Mopsuestia and Cyrus, respectively, and thus preached regularly to their flock on the scriptural texts prescribed in a church lectionary, it is not homilies they have left us so much as formal commentaries on whole books of the Bible, written at their desks and distributed to individual readers as an important contribution of their faith development. In this process, as we shall see in Chapter Six, Antiochene commentators broke the bread of the Word for their flock from the Law and the Prophets, from the Psalms and some other of the Writings, if less widely from Israel's sages.

Did all members of these communities benefit equally from this form of scriptural tradition of the faith? Were they all, for instance, in a position to acquire and read the commentaries on the sacred books written by their pastors, or are the "brethren," ἀδελφοί, Diodore speaks of as the readers for whom he is writing his commentary on the Psalms simply the students in his asketerion?[38] We know that for Theodore the Scriptures are for reading aloud in church and also being kept at home;[39] Chrysostom envisages his listeners returning home and "taking the sacred books in hand, to gain benefit from them and provide spiritual nourishment for their soul."[40] Presumably, therefore, these same Bible owners were in a position to acquire and read also written commentaries, which we shall see in Chapter Four were readily available. But they were surely a minority of the community of the faithful;[41] Chrysostom urges his (affluent) congregation

---

[37] The eight "sermons" (possibly in 386), the score or so of Homilies on the Statues in 387, and the sixty seven homilies (some time before Chrysostom's move to Constantinople in 397).

[38] Cf. *Diodori Tarsensis commentarii in psalmos*, I *Commentarii in psalmos I–L*, prol. (CCG 6.4).

[39] Cf. his commentary on Zeph 1:4–6: "All of us, having come to faith in Christ the Lord from the nations, received the Scriptures from (the apostles) and now enjoy them, reading them aloud in the churches and keeping them at home" (H. N. Sprenger, *Theodori Mopsuesteni commentarius in XII prophetas*, 284).

[40] Homily 2 and 10 on Gen (PG 53.31,90).

[41] So argues E. A. Clark, *Reading Renunciation. Asceticism and Scripture in Early Christianity*, 49, who sees only a small proportion of Chrysostom's congregation being in a position to respond to his directive, while she also contests the view that only

listening in church to his sermon on Genesis not to neglect the appeals of the poor waiting outside.[42]

If both poor and rich, illiterate and well-educated attended the liturgy and profited from the celebrant's homilies, did they include both men and women? Today's reader of Antiochene homilies and commentaries from the period under discussion can gain the impression that preacher and writer had men particularly in mind—not just from the frequent reference to males, ἄνδρες (ἀδελφοί), in address, and substitution of this term where a biblical author may have had rather the non-committal term ἄνθρωποι in mind, but also from pejorative remarks about women and from citation of biblical texts inappropriate in the case of a mixed congregation or readership.[43] On the other hand, the case has been mounted that Antioch churches made particular provision for women worshipers, and that women are sometimes directly (if rhetorically?) addressed by Chrysostom, for example.[44]

---

a small fraction of people in the Roman empire at this time were literate. H. Gamble, *Books and Readers in the Early Church*, 231, limits literacy to 20 percent of Christians.

[42] Cf. the close of the fifth sermon on Genesis (SC 433.270.2): "It is the time of fasting, such close attention and much instruction in salutary doctrines, constant praying, daily assemblies—and the outcome of such devotion? Nil. From here we go off, seeing the clusters of the poor drawn up on all sides; with a glance at them as though they were pillars and not human bodies we pass them by pitilessly; with a glance at them as though they were lifeless statues and not breathing human beings we hurry off home." R. MacMullen, "The preacher's audience AD 35–400," *JTS* N.S. 40 (1989) 504–506, cites instances of patristic preachers' congregations being affluent, though not specifically of Antioch.

[43] At the beginning of his Commentary on the Psalms Theodoret (perhaps taking a lead from Diodore's similar comment on Ps 45:15) notes that Ps 1 begins, "Blessed the man" (ἀνήρ in his LXX, and masculine also in the Heb., though the latter predictably escapes him). He observes, "Now, no one seeing only a man declared blessed here should think that womankind is excluded from this beatitude. I mean, Christ the Lord in delivering the beatitudes in the masculine did not exclude women from possessing virtue: his words include women." But from that point on, his usage gives the lie to this inclusive attitude. Chrysostom likewise thinks of the people left "hope-filled and secure" by the Lord in Ps 4:8 as including "your wives, your friends, anyone at all," and he reminds his listeners to commentary on Ps 148:10 that "desire, when managed with moderation, makes you a father."

[44] Cf. W. Mayer, "John Chrysostom: extraordinary preacher, ordinary audience," 123; "Who came to hear John Chrysostom preach? Recovering a late fourth century preacher's audience," *ETL* 76 (2000) 80. Did Jews occasionally attend Chrysostom's homilies? A reader of his first homily on the obscurity of the Old Testament delivered in Antioch (S. Zincone, *Omelie sull' oscurità delle profezie*, 62–105) senses he is rather defensive because of the presence of "unfriendly" listeners.

As the liturgy of the Eucharist celebrated in the churches of Antioch re-enacted the passion, death and resurrection of Jesus for the communities' nourishment and development of the faith, so the liturgy of the Word gave scope for the exercise of its homiletic tradition. From Chrysostom principally, as has been noted, comes our evidence of it in this period—and it is abundant. Scholars have combed the text of his homilies for evidence of the particular church in Antioch (and later in Constantinople) where each was delivered, whether the Great Church of Constantine and Constantius, the Old Church, the shrine of St Babylas or some other, and the architectural provision for preacher and congregation within.[45] There is also evidence of Chrysostom as sole preacher,[46] as opening speaker when Bishop Flavian is also present to preside and preach (as with the first sermon on Genesis), and (after transfer as bishop to Constantinople) as second speaker.[47] He can congratulate his audience on their attention and rapturous applause (if we are to believe the text we have).[48] He can also chide them for inattention (like the celebrated rebuke for being distracted by the lamplighter in sermon four on Genesis)[49] and even for absenting themselves to frequent places of enjoyment, like the horse races and theatre,[50] with which the city was liberally

---

[45] The rebuke in Homily Six on Gen for his congregation's inattention because rapt in "this wonderful ceiling" suggests Chrysostom is preaching on that occasion in the Great Church. Cf. Mayer, "The dynamics of liturgical: Aspects of the interaction between St John Chrysostom and his audiences," *Ephemerides Liturgicae* 111 (1997) 108–109.

[46] Cf. his homily on Jer 10:23 (PG 56:153–62), a reading apparently presented to him by the lectionary for the day, though susceptible of development to rebut popular irresponsibility in quoting texts at random. Cf. Hill, "'Norms, definitions, and unalterable doctrines': Chrysostom on Jeremiah."

[47] Cf. the homily on Isa 45:6–7 (PG 56.141–52), where Bishop Chrysostom is faced with a text for which he is unprepared, and in course of delivery exemplifies the neglect of the very principles spelt out by him in the Jer homily cited in the previous footnote. Also the second homily on Ps 49:16 (PG 55.511–18; not part of the large series on the Psalter), where as bishop in Constantinople he congratulates the first speaker.

[48] In beginning the seventh sermon on Genesis (SC 433.302.1) Chrysostom refers to "the applause for my words, the commendation for my teaching: when I said yesterday, Let each of you turn your home into a church, you burst into loud applause, indicating satisfaction with what was said."

[49] (SC 433.238–40.3). For text of the rebuke, see below, p. 101.

[50] In Homily Six on Genesis Chrysostom is too dejected by his congregation's (or the absent members') infidelity to the spirit of Lent to the extent of attending horse races (with all the associated lewdness) to continue with his commentary. Finally he does return to Gen 1. Cf. his homily on Isa 45:6–7.

endowed. Though it was his ability to move his congregation that won Chrysostom his sobriquet in the next century, presumably bishops Diodore, Theodore and Theodoret exercised a similar ministry, though its fruits are not so celebrated or so well documented.

The pulpit of the churches of Antioch proved a means, not only of commenting on the Scriptures, but also of exercizing the community's doctrinal and moral tradition. That sixth homily on Genesis, where Chrysostom is furious at the absence of some of the congregation at the races, is an abrasive condemnation of such amusements, a theme he warmed to on many occasions. On a more serene note he delivers five homilies on the nature of God (followed by another similar series in Constantinople) against the Anomeans or Eunomians,[51] latterday Arians whose principal exponent Eunomius derided the talisman definition at Nicea of consubstantiality of Father and Son, ὁμοούσιος—hence "An-omean." Other polemical homilies could be directed at Christians frequenting synagogues and celebrating Jewish feasts;[52] his biblical homilies, however, beyond occasionally making a passing reference to a rogues gallery of Christian heresiarchs, do not develop into sustained theological polemic (by comparison, e.g., with his contemporary and *bête noir* in Constantinople, Severian of Gabala).[53] On the other hand, he can also compose treatises for individual or community reading, like his appeal to Theodore to return to the ascetical life,[54] or his very celebrated treatise on the priesthood.[55]

Diodore likewise, in addition to his sermons as a pastor and his commentaries on all the books of the Old Testament (we are told by Theodorus Lector in the sixth century,[56] those on the Psalms

---

[51] SC 28 bis. What also riles Chrysostom in Anomean teaching is their claim that God can be known by us as he knows himself—an infringment of divine transcendence that moves all the Antiochenes to lecture their listeners/readers on the dangers of anthropomorphisms in biblical texts.

[52] PG 48.843–942.

[53] Severian, bishop of Gabala near Laodicea, was made welcome at Constantinople by Chrysostom, but returned the compliment by exploiting the empress's favor to expedite his friend's exile and death. His six homilies on the Hexameron, once attributed to Chrysostom (CPG 4194; PG 56.429–500), reveal a much more literalistic and polemical commentator, Savile applying the analogy of iron compared with gold (429).

[54] PG 47.277–316.

[55] SC 272.

[56] According to the tenth century *Lexicon*, 1.1.1379, of Suidas, ed. A. Adler, *Lexicographi graeci* I, Leipzig, 1931, 103 (cited by Quasten, *Patrology* 3, 399).

alone being fully extant), composed a huge range of theological commentaries now lost. Responsibility attributed to him for the doctrines
of Nestorius ensured the destruction of this doctrinal output, as it
did most of his pupil Theodore's, fragments alone remaining of a
celebrated treatise on the Incarnation.[57] Theodoret attracted little of
this animosity, and so his contributions to the doctrinal tradition of
the faith have generally survived; towards the close of his life, in
introducing his Questions on Leviticus, he proudly lists his apolo-
getical works ("writings against the Greeks, against the heresies, and
of course against soothsayers")[58] but omits mention of works on the
Trinity[59] and the Incarnation[60] and his major Christological work,
the *Eranistes*.[61]

In short, the initiated in the churches under the jurisdiction of
Antioch were well instructed in the faith by these pastors. The catechetical tradition of Christianity, however, caters also to neophytes
preparing for baptism at Easter, a special responsibility for pastors.
Young remarks,

> The 'school' character of early Christianity appears again in the devel-
> opment of catechetical lectures delivered through Lent . . . The essen-
> tial purpose was to initiate converts into a learning community.[62]

A dozen such catechetical homilies of Chrysostom have come to
light, delivered in Antioch in 388 and shortly after,[63] as have six-
teen Antioch catechetical homilies of Theodore in a Syriac version,
dealing with the creed, the Our Father and the eucharist for the
benefit of neophytes before and immediately after baptism.[64] Such a
course in the faith for the recently evangelized in Antioch would
have paralleled that given by Paul and Barnabas around the year

---

[57] The Greek, Syriac and Latin fragments appearing in various editions are sum-
marized by R. Devreesse, *Essai sur Théodore de Mopsueste*, 44–48.
[58] *Theodoreti Cyrensis Quaestiones in Octateuchum*, 153.
[59] PG 75.1147–90.
[60] PG 75.1418–78.
[61] Ed. G. H. Ettlinger, Oxford: Clarendon, 1975.
[62] *Biblical Exegesis*, 243–44.
[63] A Wenger has edited eight of the homilies, *Huit catéchèses baptismales inédites*, 3rd
ed., 1985 (SC 50).
[64] A. Mingana, *Commentary of Theodore of Mopsuestia on the Nicene Creed*, Woodbrooke
Studies 5, Cambridge: W. Heffer & Sons Ltd, 1932; *Commentary of Theodore of Mopsuestia
on the Sacraments of Baptism and the Eucharist*, Woodbrooke Studies 6, 1933.

44. Though we are unsure of where, when and to whom he delivered his lectures on the Psalms, Chrysostom speaks of the venue as a classroom, διδασκαλεῖον, remarking of it,

> The classroom is more important than the courtroom. In the latter, after all, those due for punishment pay the penalty, whereas in the former everything is calculated not to punish the guilty but to correct the guilty through repentance.[65]

Theodoret reserves a special commendation for those pastors who have the ability to teach the faithful; in commenting on 1 Tim 5:17, "Let the elders who have presided well be accorded double honor, especially those engaged in preaching and teaching," he proceeds, "so praiseworthy is the profession of teaching."[66] He sees this didactic role as distinct from the kerygmatic ministry discharged in the pulpit for the benefit of the mature, itself a more challenging ministry than administration of (some) sacraments:

> Preaching is more important than baptizing: baptizing is easy for those thought worthy of priesthood, whereas preaching is proper to a few, who have received this good from a divine source.[67]

In short, at all the stages of Christian initiation and maturation, believers in Antioch received transmission of the faith through a range of ministries at the hands of zealous pastors.

Speaking of such pastors in the churches of both Antioch and Alexandria, Frances Young says, "All of them put their scholarly techniques to the service of preaching,"[68] to which we may add, "and of the other forms of tradition of the faith." For them, scholarship of one kind or another was not an end in itself; the faith development of the community was the goal being sought in every case. Reading of the Old Testament in Antioch in the fourth and fifth centuries was not an isolated pastoral exercise; it was but one of many traditions of the faith enjoyed by the faithful, thanks to their zealous pastors. Yet it was the exercise of the ministry of the Word that earned one of them his sobriquet Golden Mouth and

---

[65] On Ps 50:16 (PG 55.250).
[66] PG 82.820.
[67] PG 82.233.
[68] *Biblical Exegesis*, 185.

another The Interpreter.[69] In this volume, it is likewise the biblical
tradition that is at the focus of attention, though the other traditions
would also repay further examination. Fortunately, the exegetical
remains of these pastors bulk large, as biblical commentary formed
a major part of their pastoral ministry. Such commentary was shaped
not only by Christian beliefs and a sense of pastoral responsibility
for community faith formation in Antioch, but also by literary and
rhetorical canons formulated by pagan authors as far afield as Athens
and drilled into these Christian pastors by pagan rhetoricans. We
should now turn to examine the way the Antiochenes, under this
diverse influence, read and commented on the Old Testament in
particular according to the scriptural canon recognized in those
churches.

---

[69] Of the term "Chrysostom" Kelly remarks, *Golden Mouth*, 4, "The nickname
was applied to several admired orators, and to John, in the east and west generally, from the fifth century." The Syriac churches, to whom we owe much of our
information and remains of Theodore's work, applied to him the term *Mephasqana*
from the sixth century; it appears in a text of a synod of the Eastern Syriac churches
in 596 (cited from J. B. Chabot, *Synodicon Orientale*, by Mingana, *The Commentary of
Theodore of Mopsuestia on the Nicene Creed*, 459).

CHAPTER TWO

THE CANON OF THE OLD TESTAMENT IN ANTIOCH

For commentators on the Bible in our period, of course, Holy Writ includes both New and Old Testaments. To highlight its usefully moral character, Diodore begins his work on the Psalter by referring to 2 Tim 3:16:

> 'All Scripture is inspired by God,' according to blessed Paul, 'and useful for teaching, for reproving, for correcting, for training in righteousness.'[1]

And we shall see in Chapter Three the insistence of Antiochene commentators on the harmony and common origin of both testaments; each of these testaments is referred to as διαθήκη, both the Old and the New. Even though as we shall observe—for instance, in commentators' efforts to account for the acknowledged obscurity of the Old—that there is an assertion that the New is clearer because it "talks about more important things,"[2] the massive investment in commentary on the Old by Antiochene pastors is evidence enough that it is in no sense thought to be dépassé. Nor is the crassness of its narratives, that led to complete dismissal by a Marcion or denial of reality to incidents like Hosea's marriage by an Origen, sufficient to discourage total coverage by these commentators. They saw and appreciated in such texts the same human accents they would discern also in the humanity of Jesus, in the process of Christian salvation, in morality and the spiritual life. Their treatment of all these, including the Old Testament, we shall see, reflects an underlying worldview.

No debate is therefore considered necessary in that period about any inadequacy of the term "Old Testament."[3] Its Jewish character

---

[1] *Commentarii*, 3.

[2] Chrysostom in his first homily on the subject (*Omelie*, 74–76.3). Cf. Homily 3 on Gen (PG 53.29.3).

[3] The term derives (indirectly from 2 Cor 3–4 and) in its first extant usage by Christians in Melito of Sardis, ca. 170 (cf. F. F. Bruce, *The Canon of Scripture*, 71). Alternative terms like Hebrew Bible, Jewish Scriptures, First Testament are not

is conceded; when in discussion of the meaning of Gen 1:26 Chrysostom is rebutting a Jewish interpretation, he concedes the Jewish origin of the Old Testament while asserting the priority of a Christian hermeneutic:

> While the books are from them, the treasure of the books now belongs to us; if the text is from them, both text and meaning belong to us.[4]

A. A CHRISTIAN COLLECTION OF JEWISH BOOKS

Antiochene commentators do not debate the contents of the canon of the Old Testament on which they are commenting. They betray no knowledge of use of the word κανών in the sense of a closed and now authoritative collection of sacred writings, using the word simply in the sense of a norm.[5] In comment on Gen 1:13, where Chrysostom disputes a Jewish view that in the repeated mention of evening and morning in the opening verses of that chapter there is confirmation that "the evening is the beginning of the following day," he blurts out:

> But let them reap the reward of their own insanity. We, for our part, who have been fortunate enough to benefit from the rays of the sun, should obey the teaching of Sacred Scripture; let us follow its κανών, place its wholesome doctrines within the recesses of our mind, and with protection from it take good care of our own welfare, avoiding whatever impairs the health of our soul and abstaining from all such harmful notions in the same way as we would noxious drugs.[6]

While Christian and Jewish readers may not agree on when the day begins, for both parties the whole of Scripture represents the κανών

---

found in the Antioch commentaries; Christians are thought to have a claim on the writings without belittling their value. Cf. L. M. McDonald and J. A. Sanders, *The Canon Debate* (2002), a volume in which only Sanders uses such alternative terminology, even Jewish contributors employing the conventional terms Old and New Testament.

[4] Sermon 2 on Genesis (SC 433.188.1).

[5] Cf. B. S. Childs, *Introduction to the Old Testament as Scripture*, 50: "Although Origen used the term in an adjectival sense of *scripturae canonicae* (*De princ.* IV 33), the first application of the noun to the collection of holy scriptures appears in the last part of the fourth century and continued in common use from the time of Jerome. The use of the term canon to describe the scriptures was of Christian origin and not applied to classic Jewish literature."

[6] Homily 5 on Genesis (PG 53.53.5). Modern commentators (e.g., G. Von Rad, E. Speiser) differ on the respective interpretations of this phraseology in Gen 1.

of thought and living: it is simply the interpretation that differs. There is no discrepancy in the contents, nor do these Christian commentators in Antioch ever advert to any such.

Not that they were familiar with a Hebrew Bible and its traditional divisions; TaNaK is not a term found in their mouths. For one thing, as will emerge in Chapter Five, they had not sufficient Hebrew even to detect alphabetic structure of some psalms. Though doubtless familiar from New Testament usage with the phrase "the Law and the Prophets," they are not accustomed to speaking of a Pentateuch,[7] let alone Torah; Theodoret for all his knowledge of Judaism will pass in his Questions from Deuteronomy to Joshua without any acknowledgement of leaving one corpus for another or even any recognition of change of authorship. Likewise in commenting on Joshua-2 Kings they give no hint that they recognize a corpus of Former Prophets (let alone a Deuteronomist, of course). For them, as we shall see in Chapter Three, all Old Testament authors are προφῆται on the basis of their being divinely-inspired,[8] though ambiguously the term can be used also specifically of the Latter Prophets (another unfamiliar term to them) in reference to prospective prophecy, the only analogue of the charism recognized by the commentators.

In Antioch the Old Testament was read and commented on in the distinctive local Greek version (the Septuagint, if that term is not to be confined to the Greek form developed in Alexandria—a question we shall examine in Chapter Four), as their New Testament also contained distinctive readings.[9] The commentators in referring

---

[7] It is rather the term Octateuch that is known in the early Church, we are told by O. Eissfeldt, *The Old Testament. An Introduction*, 156; hence the title to Diodore's and Theodoret's *Quaestiones*.

[8] Cf. A. C. Sundberg, "The Protestant Old Testament canon," 199: "Soon (in the early Church) the Jewish categories of Law and Prophets were forgotten and the whole religious literature received from Judaism was treated as one, the Prophets." While such is the usage in early Church creeds ("He has spoken through the προφῆται:" DS 150), for our Antiochenes some biblical authors, such as sages and historians, can be accorded instead a different title, presumably for not sharing to the same degree in the gift of inspiration.

[9] Antioch commentators, even in the course of Old Testament commentary, are using a text of the New Testament we know as the Koine text, resulting from a major revision of Greek manuscripts at the end of the third century and the beginning of the fourth. On the testimony of Jerome, this Koine (or Byzantine) text, which spread widely with the spread of bishops from Antioch, was attributed to the scholar of Antioch, Lucian (cf. K. Aland, B. Aland, *The Text of the New Testament*, 51–71). Such attribution has come under recent scrutiny, Jerome's testimony being

in the course of their work to a copy of the Hexapla would be aware
that their local text differed at times from other forms of the LXX.
They may not have been equally aware that some books occurred
in their Old Testament in a different order from that found elsewhere in the LXX, such as the order of the Twelve Prophets, the
Antioch text following the order of the Hebrew Bible. Perhaps they
knew some books by different titles, too; Diodore refers to Genesis
as Κοσμοποιΐα and Theodore as Κτίσις. If they were aware that the
canon, or collection of normative writings, of the Old Testament in
use in their churches differed from others, they never advert to it,
even though it differs in various respects from the canons used in
western Christian communities today.

The Antiochene commentators never advert, either, to the development of different canons within Judaism, or to acceptance of a
canon within the Church different from one of these Jewish canons,
or to a ranking of books within the canon on the (supposed) basis
of differences in language of composition. They never advert, either,
to discrepancies between Jewish canons, to amendments to Jewish
lists such as Origen acknowledges in distinguishing between "their
Scriptures" and "our Scriptures," or Athanasius makes in admitting
2 Esdras to the canon and including under Jeremiah the books of
Baruch and Lamentations and the Epistle of Jeremiah, or Epiphanius
likewise does by including in his New Testament canon Sirach and
the Wisdom of Solomon excluded by other scholars from the Old.
They do not advert, either, to current disagreements over canon on
these lines occurring in the West between the likes of Hilary, Jerome,
Rufinus and Augustine, or to Church councils ruling on the canon
in our period. If it is true that "the Church was forced to determine her Old Testament for herself; the Old Testament thus is seen
to be a Christian canon,"[10] the Antioch commentators seem rather

---

now thought suspect. Theodore and Theodoret, who had before them in working
on Zechariah the commentary of the Alexandrian Didymus, whose New Testament
canon seems to have included The Shepherd of Hermas and the Epistle of Barnabas,
did not follow him in citing them.

[10] Sundberg, "The 'Old Testament': a Christian canon," 152. For details of the
views of these Fathers and councils, see Sundberg's article; they are also supplied
by Bruce, *The Canon of Scripture*, 70–80. Bruce proceeds to refer only to Theodore
of the Antiochenes ("the most illustrious exponent of the exegetical school of Antioch"—that common misconception), thus giving a skewed outline of the Antioch
canon.

to think that their canon is Jewish in origin and—rightly—that all the books came to them from Judaism. "The books are from them," Chrysostom tells his congregation in 386.

B. An Antioch canon

A critical factor in the recognition of the canon of Antioch is the inclusion by commentators at both ends of our period of 2 Esdras (IV Esdras in the Vulgate), containing in its chs 3–14 the Apocalypse of Ezra (commonly called 4 Ezra, a Jewish work originally in Aramaic or Hebrew from the second century CE) giving a non-biblical account of the loss of the Jewish Scriptures under Manasseh and their recomposition by Ezra in a vision. Diodore cites the story to support his view that the Psalms had to be collected anew in higgledy-piggledy fashion and that the psalm titles are not original.[11] Theodoret tells it to defend the inclusion in the canon of the Song, thought by some to be erotic, as a work of the Spirit:

> Blessed Ezra, remember, was filled with his grace, so we claim, when he rewrote the book; the blessed Fathers were aware of this in ranking it with the divine Scriptues.[12]

A notable omission from Antioch's canon (as it missing also from Qumran) is any form of the book of Esther, even the Greek "A-text" once thought to be a revision by Lucian; none of the commentators cite the text. Absence of evidence, of course, is not conclusive evidence of absence; but Theodore's reference to the story is more significant: in comment on Ps 66:3 he cites from Josephus almost verbatim the text of Esth 8:14–17, an unlikely citation if his Bible contained that book.[13] On the other hand, the Antioch Old Testament canon included books referred to today as deutero-canonical and apocryphal/pseudepigraphic: Sirach and the Wisdom of Solomon are

---

[11] *Commentarii*, 6. According to Childs, *Introduction*, 51, "this theory was widely accepted by Jews and Christians until the end of the nineteenth century."

[12] PG 81.32. The Church thus had a role in determining the canon in Theodoret's thinking.

[13] This is a significant datum that might well have been included in the lengthy discussions (by K. De Troyer and M. V. Fox) of the canonicity of Esther in S. White Crawford, L. J. Greenspoon, *The Book of Esther in Modern Research*, JSOT Supplement series 380, London-New York: T&T Clark, 2003.

freely cited, as are Baruch and 1 & 2 Maccabees, less so Tobit and
Judith. Theodoret, if only because the most extant commentator, is
seen to refer to such works (in addition to 2 Esdras) most often: to
1 Esdras three times and to 3 Maccabees; his Jeremiah Commentary
in the form we have it includes Baruch and Lamentations (but not
the Epistle of Jeremiah), while his text of Daniel (in the version of
Theodotion) comprises chapters 1–12 plus v.1 of the deuterocanon-
ical story of Bel and the Dragon (but not Susanna, though this story
is widely known by the Antiochenes); his Questions treat Chronicles
as two books, and of course they provide a unique patristic commentary on Ruth. The appearance of the queen in Dan 5 would
surely have evoked in Theodoret mention of Queen Vashti in Esther
had his Old Testament included that book; a local canon is surely
imposing real, if generous, limits.

C. A canon within the canon

If there is an official and relatively extensive canon operating in
Antioch, then, is it possible to discern "a canon within the canon"?
Diodore is credited with commenting on "all the books of the Old
Testament,"[14] and the Syriac catalogues of the thirteenth and four-
teenth centuries list a large number of such works by Theodore. The
greatest number of extant Antiochene exegetical works come from
Theodoret, so we may use him as a benchmark. At his death around
460, the end of our period, he had commented on Torah and
Nebi'im (Former and Latter) of the Hebrew Bible (as well as Baruch
as a codicil to Jeremiah); of the Writings he left works on the Song
of Songs, the Psalter, Ruth, the two books of Chronicles, Lamentations
and Daniel (a prophet in Theodoret's view). While the sapiential
books are a conspicuous omission from this list (the sages classed by
our commentators merely as "sages," σοφοί, not προφῆται), Chrysostom
is credited with works in note form on Job, Proverbs and Ecclesiastes
(as we mention in Chapter Six). Works that are more marginal to
the canon, like other deutero-canonical and apocryphal books, do
not attract sustained attention from Theodoret, as reference to them
in the above commentaries is also relatively sparse. In his Questions

---

[14] J. Quasten, *Patrology* 3, 399, citing the report of Theodorus Lector in the sixth
century.

we gain from this ageing commentator a sense that he is struggling to leave to his Antiochene community a complete legacy by "making clear to the readers what requires clarification in an effort not to leave incomplete" a coverage of vital elements in the scriptural canon known to them.[15] The Antioch church certainly received from their pastors a comprehensive introduction to this canonical collection of biblical texts.

---

[15] *Theodoreti Cyrensis Quaestiones in Reges et Paralipomena*, 3. There is also a sense of a considered judgement in Theodoret's not including the Gospels in his New Testament commentaries (Chrysostom already having left celebrated works on them), if we may depend on his claim in 448 to have commented on "all the prophets, the psalter and the apostle," and his listing of his works in opening comment on Leviticus in his Questions on the Octateuch.

CHAPTER THREE

ANTIOCH'S CONCEPT OF SCRIPTURAL REVELATION

Significance was found in our first chapter in the fact that, although the principal Antiochene pastors of the fourth and fifth centuries ministered to their flock also as celebrants, teachers, catechists, theologians and moral guides, it was for their eminence as biblical commentators that they gained particular recognition. And though the bulk of such commentary has been lost in the case of Diodore and Theodore, the criticism and condemnation heaped on them that resulted in the consignment of their works to the flames was primarily directed at theological positions which they were reputed to have held and transmitted to other notorious theologians, particularly Nestorius, who became bishop in Constantinople in 428, the year of Theodore's death.[1] The particular pastoral focus of these men, the master and the most devoted of his pupils,[2] as well as John Chrysostom and later Theodoret, was on reading and commenting on the sacred text, just as their flock expected this of them.[3] The education they had received in Antioch, we noted, while soundly

---

[1] Cyril of Alexandria, for example, had assailed both men in his *Contra Diodorum et Theodorum* (PG 76.1437–52); Diodore was condemned at a synod in Constantinople in 499, and Theodore's works at the fifth ecumenical council in 553 (DS 425–26, 433–37). Theodoret of Cyrus, *Church History* 5, 39 (PG 82.1277), on the other hand, has nothing but praise for them both.

[2] In the (jaundiced) view of Leontius of Byzantium, *Contra Nestor. et Eutych.* 3, 9 (PG 86.1364), in the sixth century, Diodore was Theodore's "father and leader in vice and impiety." Certainly the latter paid his master that sincerest form of flattery, imitation, at least as far as their approach to the Psalms is concerned (their only common extant work), where no doctrinal issues are developed. Cf. Hill, "His Master's Voice: Theodore of Mopsuestia on the Psalms."

[3] The so-called Liturgy of St John Chrysostom derives from a later period than the preacher of Antioch, and reasons for attributing it to him are "insecure" (Quasten, *Patrology* 3, 472). As to his doctrinal probity, later ages raised no quibble; Luther's dismissal of him as "worth nothing in my opinion, only a foolish babbler" (so C. Baur, *John Chrysosotm and His Time* 1, 374) may be due to his views (and Antioch's generally) on faith, grace and human effort, as outlined in Chapters Nine and Ten below. It was for his homiletic skills that Calvin admired him; cf. J. L. Thompson, "*Creata ad imaginem Dei, licet secundo gradu*: woman as the image of God according to John Calvin," *HTR* 81 (1988) 125–43.

rhetorical, was philosophical if at all—and Aristotelian only—in the sense that it shared that philosopher's "concentration of mind upon observable facts,"[4] and thus placed an emphasis on historical events, the Scriptures and the humanity of Christ. These pastors' biblical commentaries, including their Old Testament works, exemplify this emphasis, as shall be seen below in Chapter Eight.

Before turning to study their works, therefore, we should examine their understanding of the way God communicates with his people through the biblical authors and their works. In the process of distinguishing this divine influence from that predicated of seers by classical authors (in whom they are well versed, we saw), these commentators develop a profound theology of the revealing Word, if also an obscure Word, that is relevant to the Old Testament as well as to the New.

A. Revelation in word and writing

Predictably, the divine revelation that is mediated to humankind in the Old Testament is generally referred to by these commentators as coming via "the divine Scripture(s)," Γραφή/Γραφαί, less frequently "the Word/words," λόγος/λόγοι/λόγιοι/λόγια.[5] It is doubtless a conventional and widespread terminology, and not peculiar to Antioch. Yet one gains the impression that the commentators do think of revelation primarily in terms of Holy Writ, even in the case of the prophets; when Theodoret comes to the vision received by Zechariah on "the twenty fourth day of the twelfth month of Shebat in the second year of Darius" (Zech 1:7), he poses the question already posed by Theodore open before him as to the role of a prophet, whether visionary or recorder:

> The prophet's meaning is, then, In this month, when the second year had not yet expired, he received once again the impulse of divine grace, by *word*, or statement, or oracle, or hand, referring to the impulse

---

[4] Wallace-Hadrill, *Christian Antioch*, 96, 102.
[5] This is the usage also of a preacher like Chrysostom: in his Genesis homilies the former two terms occur 369 times, the latter only five; he also speaks of "Bible/book(s)," βιβλίον/βιβλία, three times. See Hill, "Chrysostom's terminology for the inspired Word."

of divine grace. Enlightened by it, and engaging in some discernment, he left it for us in writing in the following terms."[6]

Didymus in Alexandria, to whom they both had access, had raised the same question. For these Fathers, then, the biblical authors themselves are primarily written rather than oral transmitters of the revealing word; despite the credal article of the council of 381, "He has *spoken* through the inspired authors,"[7] they were not as convinced of "the fundamental orality of Scripture" as are some modern scholars.[8] For Diodore the Psalms are primarily a text to be read for our instruction (he begins his preface by citing 1 Tim 3:16–17), not songs to be sung. His dutiful pupil can be quoted to the same effect, but as in the case of Zechariah Theodore allows for both "listeners" and "readers" of David in introducing Ps 33.

> This is what we should consider most of all in the psalms, that (David) moves from development of a theme to catechetical exhortation, conducting this in particular also for the benefit of the listeners. The result is that it is necessary for us to recognise the themes with a view to knowledge of the psalms' force, on the one hand, while on the other hand it behoves us attend also to the other aspects which he employed with the readers' benefit in mind.[9]

Diodore, rationalist as he may be,[10] will also raise the question of the authorship of works attributed to composers like David, and of the role played by mere compilers, as we shall see in Chapter Seven.

An accent on the orality of biblical revelation would be expected to occur rather in the statement of a preacher in church, where the congregation are introduced to the inspired message in the context of a Liturgy of the Word by readings from a lector and a homily from the homilist. Though Chrysostom adopts the conventional terminology of "Scripture," ἡ Γραφή, it can suit his purposes to emphasize the orality of the message and the listeners' degree of readiness

---

[6] PG 81.1877.

[7] DS 150, τὸ λαλῆσαι.

[8] W. A. Graham, *Beyond the Written Word. Oral Aspects of Scripture in the History of Religions*, Cambridge: CUP, 1987, ix. Cf. Hill, "From Good News to Holy Writ. The share of the text in the saving purpose of the Word."

[9] R. Devreesse, *Le commentaire de Théodore de Mopsueste sur les psaumes*, 142. The quotations in English of the Antioch Fathers in this volume are translations by R. C. Hill.

[10] Gustave Bardy, "Diodore," 991, will baulk at the use of this term, preferring "raisonnable:" "Le mot rationaliste ne conviendrait ici."

to receive it. In his six homilies on Isaiah 6 (*In Oziam*), of which the opening verses were read out to the congregation and then commented on by himself as preacher, Chrysostom emphasizes both the orality of the prophet's message and the awesome revelation it contains. Consequently, he says, the congregation should attend carefully:

> The mouths of the inspired authors are the mouth of God, after all; such a mouth would say nothing idly—so let us not be idle in our listening, either . . . Pay precise attention, however: the reading out of the Scriptures is the opening of the heavens.[11]

As a corollary, in his first homily on the obscurity of the Old Testament, Chrysostom cites as one reason for such ἀσάφεια the listeners' inexperience and even resistance.

> It is possible, you see, that a text, simple by nature, becomes difficult through the inexperience of the listeners. I shall cite to you Paul as witness: after saying Christ became a high priest in the order of Melchizedek, and inquiring who Melchizedek was, he went on, "What I have to say to you is lengthy and difficult to interpret" (Heb 5:11). O blessed Paul, what are you saying? Is it difficult for you with your spiritual wisdom, having heard words beyond description, being snatched up to the third heaven? If it is difficult for you, to whom is it comprehensible? It is difficult for me, he is saying, not from an innate difficulty, but from the limitations of the listeners (τῶν ἀκούντων): after saying, "Difficult to interpret," he added, "Because you are hard of hearing." Do you see that it was not the nature of the text but the inexperience of the listeners that made difficult what was not difficult? Not only difficult, however: the same factor renders the short long— hence his saying it was not only difficult to interpret but also "lengthy," attributing the cause of its lengthiness and difficulty to the hardness of hearing.[12]

The listeners' "limitations," ἀσθένεια, hinder the process of reception: they are either unaccustomed to the sublimity of the message or even resistant to it.

---

[11] Homily Two *In Oziam* (SC 277.88.2). See Hill, "St John Chrysostom as biblical commentator: Six homilies on Isaiah 6."

[12] *Omelie*, 64–66.1.

B. Authors and works divinely-inspired

Faulty reception of revelation in this case, Chrysostom is saying, is primarily the fault of the listeners to the words of the authors. Even if it is also due to the words of the authors, however, as he will go on to concede of some instances, they are still authors in receipt of divine inspiration, and their works consequently are also inspired. God's revelation reaches its intended beneficiaries in a process and through agents and compositions that are all indebted to the inspiration of God/the Spirit. It is a conviction that is shared by Antioch with all other schools, as is the terminology they employ. From the outset of his Psalms Commentary, Diodore insists on this fact:

> The Holy Spirit, who guides all human affairs, gives voice through most blessed David to his own response to our sufferings so that through it the sufferers may be cured.

Chrysostom exploits the range of expressions available from the common deposit:

> The blessed Moses, inspired (ἐνηχούμενος) by the divine Spirit, teaches us . . .[13]
>
> (The Anthropomorphites) are not only unwilling to get any benefit from the teaching of the inspired (θεόπνευσται) Scriptures, but would derive great harm from it.[14]
>
> But if you do not believe these Old Testament authors (προφῆται), we can supply clear unmistakable signs which demonstrate above all that they were inspired (θεόπνευστοι) and that they told us nothing on their own account but with the inspiration (ἐπνεῖν) coming from that divine love which is higher than the heavens.[15]

In so far as they are inspired, the Old Testament authors are προφῆται, a term not applicable to New Testament authors, ἀποστολικοί; in commentary on the term "fountains of Israel" in Ps 68:26 Theodoret remarks,

> Now, it would be right for the inspired books of the Old Testament (προφητικοί) to be called *fountains of Israel*, because from them we offer hymn singing to God; but . . . in addition to the Old Testament books (προφητικοί) he regaled us also with the apostolic (ἀποστολικαί) fountains.[16]

---

[13] Hom. 7 on Gen 1:20 (PG 53.65.4).
[14] Hom. 8 on Gen 1:26 (PG 53.72.3).
[15] Hom. on Ps 4:8 (PG 55.57.11).
[16] PG 80.1392–93.

The distinction does not, on the other hand imply that inspiration is denied to New Testament authors. It is just that, composing in the wake of the Incarnation, they are not felt to be in such need of the special divine assistance that their less enlightened predecessors required.

Clearly, it is not only the Latter Prophets of the Hebrew Bible who are entitled to the term προφήτης. Moses and David as authors of Pentateuch and Psalms are likewise accorded it on the basis of divine inspiration. It is not accorded to the sages, however, presumably because sapiential material is thought to be (as it claims) the fruit of human experience; only the term σοφός is appropriate. When it comes to the composers responsible for the historical books, they are not regarded as προφῆται (even if styled Former Prophets in the Hebrew Bible—terminology unfamiliar to the Antiochenes, of course). Theodoret is clear about it in beginning his Questions (which immediately pass into mere commentary) on Chronicles:

> The composition of the book was done after the captivity: anyone composing a history mentions not later events but earlier or contemporary ones; it belongs to prophets to foretell the future."[17]

So, with their notion of prophecy as exclusively prospective, Antiochenes like Theodoret refer to composers like the Deuteronomist and the Chronicler as "historians, annalists," συγγραφεύς or ἱστοριογραφός—not that they (or the sages) are bereft of divine guidance, it would seem, but that they share to a lesser degree in the charism of inspiration.

C. Mantic possession or the Spirit's guidance?

This doctrine expounded by the Antiochenes of the fact of divine inspiration of the biblical authors in speaking or writing, however, is not novel; it was held by other Fathers of east and west.[18] But there is not such unanimity on the manner on this inspiration; as John N. D. Kelly observes, "Few, if any, of the fathers seem to have

---

[17] *Theodoreti Cyrensis Quaestiones in Reges et Paralipomena*, 247.

[18] Cf. Justin, *Apology I*, 36 (PG 6.385): "When you hear the expression of the prophets spoken in their own name, do not think they are spoken by the inspired men themselves but by the Word of God moving them;" Jerome, *In Mich.* 2, 7 (CCL 76.513): "The Scriptures are written and produced by the Holy Spirit."

tried to probe the deeper problems raised by their doctrine of inspiration."[19] The prophets, as has been said, are the prime analogues of biblical authors divinely-inspired,[20] conveying to us most dramatically the workings of the charism of inspiration. In his commentary on Zechariah (on which the five books of Origen's earlier partial treatment have been lost), Didymus speaks repeatedly of this prophet as θεοληπτούμενος, "divinely-possessed," an understanding of inspiration reminiscent of Plato's accounts of the pagan seers, μάντεις, possessed by a demon who supersedes the human faculties. It is not a notion to which Antioch would be expected to warm, with its accent both on Aristotle's "observable facts" and on the human element in moral accountability. Only Theodore will toy with it, with Didymus open before him, as in his commentary on the Twelve Prophets he comes upon the term for "oracle," λῆμμα, at the opening of Deutero-Zechariah (9:1) as well as Nahum, Habakkuk and Malachi. He correctly relates it to the verb "seize," λαμβάνω, and thus accepts—against the principles of his school—the notion of prophetic inspiration as ecstatic possession. He comments,

> It was by ecstasy, therefore, that in all likelihood they all received the knowledge of things beyond description, since it was possible for them in their minds to be quite removed from their normal condition and thus capable of devoting themselves to the contemplation of what was revealed."[21]

Theodoret will be less enthusiastic about the idea when he comes to The Twelve with his eye on Didymus and Theodore; the other Antiochenes are not extant. Fortunately, all Antiochenes and many others of the Greek (and Latin) Fathers have left us commentaries on the Psalter, where the opening to Ps 45 (in the LXX, "My heart belched a good word, I tell of my works to the king, my tongue the pen of a rapid scribe") prompted the commentators to develop their thinking on the manner of inspiration of the biblical author. The term "belch," ἐξερεύγομαι, for a hapax legomenon in the Hebrew, led a Cappadocian like Basil to see a suggestion of compulsion and lack of control by the author under the influence of the Spirit.[22]

---

[19] *Early Christian Doctrines*, 63.
[20] L. Alonso-Schökel, *The Inspired Word. Scripture in the Light of Language and Literature*, 92.
[21] *Theodori Mopsuesteni commentarius in XII prophetas*, 239.
[22] PG 29.393.3.

Perhaps persuaded by the argument of such predecessors, Chrysostom
in his διδασκαλεῖον at first acquiesces:

> We do not belch when we choose to; such and such a speech we utter
> when we want to, either speaking or holding it in; belching is not
> like that. The psalmist accordingly shows that what he says is not the
> result of human effort but of divine inspiration (ἐπίπνοια) guiding him
> (κινεῖν), and does this by calling his inspired authorship 'belching.'

But at once he is alarmed by the similarity of the notion to Plato's
thinking on the pagan seers,[23] which he rejects:

> The Holy Spirit, by contrast, does not act like that: he allows the heart
> to know what is being said; . . . being kindly and beneficent in his
> actions, he renders those who receive him sharers in his purposes, and
> reveals the things that are said with the understanding of the authors."[24]

Chrysostom would have been aware that Diodore had set the para-
meters for any such discussion on the respective roles of the Spirit
and the human author. For the master, the latter remains in control as far as this does not impugn divine transcendence:

> When he said, I utter the psalm from the depths of my mind, he
> means, I adjust my tongue, to the extent that this is possible, to respond
> to the movement of grace in the way a pen responds to the leading
> thought of a fluent writer.[25]

While contributing a further element to the discussion, namely, ink
to fill the pen ("the perceptions of revelation with which the Spirit
fills the human heart"), Theodore in this case typically respects his
master's accent on the human element:

> The Spirit, just like a perfect writer, fills, as it were with ink, the
> human heart with the perceptions of revelation, and from there allows
> the tongue to speak loud and clear and to formulate the sayings in
> letters and articulate them distinctly for those who are willing to receive
> the benefit which stems from them.[26]

---

[23] *Apology* 22C; *Meno* 99D.

[24] PG 55.183–84.1. Bruce Vawter, *Biblical Inspiration*, 38, evidently had Didymus
and Basil and not the Antiochenes in mind in attributing to the Fathers generally
"the prevalence of a concept of divine authorship that could lead to a practical for-
getting of the claims of human authorship."

[25] *Commentarii*, 269.

[26] *Le commentaire*, 282.

Chrysostom had no choice but to acquiesce; in fact, he went even further in maintaining Antiochene emphasis on authorial activity.

> "I tell of my works to the king"—or, in another manuscript, "my deeds." What works are referred to? Inspired composition (προφητεία). As it is the work of a smith to make a tool, a builder to build a house, a shipwright to build a ship, so it is an inspired composer's job to produce inspired composition.[27]

The preacher, for a time carried away, has come to heel: biblical composition is deliberate, workmanlike labor that can be worked at, where the activity of the Spirit is anything but that spontaneous irruption denoted before by "belching." Antioch's accents on biblical revelation have prevailed; Theodoret will not undermine them in later observing in his preface to the Psalter, "It is the role of an inspired composer to make his tongue available to the grace of the Spirit."[28]

D. A THEOLOGY OF THE REVEALING WORD

As inspired transmitters in word and writing of divine revelation, then, the biblical authors and the biblical text were highly esteemed by Antiochene readers and commentators, even if no philosophical school lay explicitly behind their commitment. It was enough that the text enjoyed divine authentication: despite the departure of the authors, the Scriptures are living images of them. In an isolated homily on Ps 146, Chrysostom seizes upon the reply of Abraham to the rich man in Hades in the parable in Luke 16:29:

> "They have Moses and the prophets." Actually, Moses and all the prophets were long dead in the body, but in their writings they had them. After all, if a person sets up a lifeless image of son or dear one and thinks that person, though dead, is present, and through the lifeless image he imagines him, much more do we enjoy the communion of the saints through the divine Scriptures, having in them images not of their bodies but of their souls, the words spoken by them being images of their very souls.[29]

---

[27] PG 55.184.1. Cf. Hill, "Psalm 45: a *locus classicus* for patristic thinking on biblical inspiration."

[28] PG 80.861.

[29] Homily on Ps 146:1, apparently delivered in Antioch outside the larger series of Psalm homilies (PG 55.521.2).

The reverence shown the Scriptures in eastern liturgies reflects the same esteem.

Yet this presentation of the Scriptures as living images of the biblical authors is by no means Antioch's most telling theological insight. In his six homilies on Isaiah 6, Chrysostom takes issue with the kataphatic theology of the Anomeans, "those who pry into the ineffable and blessed nature, who presume where presumption is illicit." Singling out as a figure of anomean temerity the King Uzziah of 2 Chr 26 who presumed to usurp high priestly functions and was punished with leprosy, Chrysostom expresses his own deep appreciation of scriptural κοινωνία. For him the biblical authors are the means by which communication (ὁμιλία) with God occurs, a communication which can be withheld; and (with a loose application of the situation obtaining rather in the time of Eli) he maintains that the people's unwillingness on that occasion to expel the leprous Uzziah resulted in such an interruption of this scriptural communication.

> Since they allowed him that liberty, therefore, God turned away from them and put a stop to the charism of inspiration (προφητεία)—and rightly so: in return for their breaking his law and being reluctant to expel the unclean one, he brought the charism of inspiration to a halt. "The word was precious at that time, and there was no inspired utterance" (1 Sam 3:1), that is, God was not speaking through the inspired authors: the Spirit through whom they made utterance was not inspiring them since they kept the unclean one, the Spirit's grace not being active in the case of unclean people. Hence he kept his distance, he did not reveal himself to the inspired authors; he was silent and remained hidden . . . You refuse? I shall have no dealings with you, either.[30]

The divine ὁμιλία occurring in scriptural discourse is a gift, one that can be withdrawn or suspended.

It is when the Old Testament is seen as one further instance of divine love for humankind, however, in which the Word comes clothed in the human limitations which the Word assumed in the Incarnation, that the heights of Antioch's concept of scriptural revelation are reached. The Scriptures, like the Incarnation, come to us as a gesture of divine considerateness, συγκατάβασις—a loving gesture, with nothing patronizing about it, nothing to suggest "con-

---

[30] Homily 4 *In Oziam* (SC 277.174.6). Cf. Hill, "St John Chrysostom's teaching on inspiration in 'Six Homilies on Isaiah.'"

descension" (though the term is often by a lazy calque thus rendered into English and other languages).[31] The Incarnation, after all, does not represent a patronizing gesture on God's part towards human beings—only love and concern. Perhaps Chrysostom's most profound explication of the relation between scriptural considerateness, συγκατάβασις, and the (other) Incarnation of the Word occurs in his commentary in his Genesis homilies. He comments on the vision accorded Jacob in his wrestling with the heavenly being and the consequent bestowal of the name Israel in 32:28 (the solecism in his grave remark, "'Israel' means seeing God," not negating the profundity of the thought). The continuing accent in this passage on considerateness, both in God's dealings with the patriarchs and in the Scriptures, and its cognate manifestation also in the Incarnation, makes it worth quoting at length.

> Do you see how the Lord shows considerateness for our human limitations in all he does and in arranging everything in a way that gives evidence of his characteristic love? Don't be surprised, dearly beloved, at the extent of his considerateness; rather, remember that with the patriarchs as well, when he was sitting by the oak tree, he came in human form as the good man's guest in the company of the angels, giving us a premonition from on high at the beginning that he would one day take human form to liberate all human nature by this means from the tyranny of the devil and lead us to salvation. At that time, however, since it was the very early stages, he appeared to each of them in the guise of an apparition, as he says himself through the inspired authors, "I multiplied visions and took various likenesses in the works of the inspired authors" (Hos 12:10).
>
> But when he deigned to take on the form of a slave and receive our first-fruits, he donned our flesh, not in appearance or in seeming, but in reality. He brought himself to undergo all our experiences, to be born of a woman, to become an infant, to be wrapped in swaddling clothes, to be fed at the breast, and to undergo everything for this purpose, that the truth of the divine plan might be given credence

---

[31] Such is the version suggested by M. H. Flanagan, *St John Chrysostom's Doctrine of Condescension and Accuracy in the Scriptures*, Napier NZ (private printing), 1948 (where "accuracy" also inadequately—and commonly—renders a key Antiochene term ἀκρίβεια); F. Fabbi, "La 'condiscendenza' divina nell' ispirazione biblica secondo S. Giovanni Crisostomo;" B. Vawter, *Biblical Inspiration*, 40, in comparing the term to Origen's συμπεριφορά; J.-M. Leroux, "Johannes Chrysostomus," 121, where the term is rendered "Herablassung." F. Asensio does better in his article, "El Crisóstomo y su visión de la escritura en la exposición homilética del Génesis." A monograph is being prepared on the term by David Rylaarsdam.

and the mouths of heretics be stopped . . . After all, if he had not taken on our flesh in reality, neither would he have been crucified, nor would he have died, been buried, and risen again. But if he had not risen, the whole purpose of the divine plan would have been thwarted. Do you see into what extreme absurdity those people fall who are unwilling to take their cue from the norm of Sacred Scripture but rather have complete confidence in their own reasoning?[32]

In this extended meditation the preacher, in documenting his theme of συγκατάβασις, moves from the Scriptures to the patriarchs and then to a sustained accent on the humanity of the Word incarnate.[33] In the process he demonstrates the typically Antiochene *Weltanschauung* incorporating salvation history, the Scriptures, the humanity of Jesus, soteriology—all betraying on their part that "concentration of mind upon observable facts" thought to be in some sense Aristotelian. The theological matrix, however, owes nothing to the philosopher; not surprisingly, it has received ecclesiastical endorsement in more recent times.[34]

In other Antiochene commentators, too, the notion of divine considerateness demonstrated in Old Testament texts is found, generally in reference to the allowance made for human weakness (in provisions of the Law, e.g.). Theodoret in particular thinks in these terms, though in one case approximating to Chrysostom's notion of the divinely-ordained style of scriptural discourse; when in his LXX text of Jer 9:9 the Lord says, "Shall my soul not be avenged on such a people?", Theodoret comments,

---

[32] Homily 58 on Gen (PG 54.509–510.3). This is but one of dozens of instances where Chrysostom develops the notion in reference to Old Testament texts. Calvin's indebtedness to Chryostom's thinking is outlined by D. F. Wright, "Calvin's accommodating God," in W. H. Neuser, B. G. Armstrong, eds, *Calvinus Sincerioris Religionis Vindex*, Sixth International Congress on Calvin Research, Kirksville MO: Sixteenth Cent. Journ. Publ., 1997, 3–19.

[33] Cf. the formulation of Chrysostom's thought in 1887 by F. H. Chase, *Chrysostom. A Study in the History of Biblical Interpretation*, 42: "The great principle expressed by the word *synkatabasis* is of deep and wide application. As in the historical Incarnation the Eternal Word became flesh, so in the Bible the glory of God veils itself in the fleshly garments of human thought and human language."

[34] Cf. the citation of Chrysostom to this effect by Pope Pius XII in his 1943 encyclical letter on biblical studies, *Divino Afflante Spiritu*, AAS 35 (1943) 316, and by the Second Vatican Council in 1965 in its *Dei Verbum* #11, AAS 58 (1966) 824. Chrysosom's biographer Kelly, on the other hand, is not so positive about the effect of his theology of the Word (*Golden Mouth*, 95): "This assumption (of divine inspiration) effectively blocked any open-minded examination of the Bible." The claim is not documented.

He used the phrase *my soul* in human fashion: the divine is not composed of body and soul, being simple, lacking composition and form. His words are adjusted to our capacity to receive.[35]

The principle thus formulated picks up but one of the many that Chrysostom in one place or another extrapolates from the rich notion of scriptural συγκατάβασις—that it is always a manifestation of divine φιλανθρωπία, that its purpose is to lead humankind from material things upward to spiritual realities, that the concreteness (παχύτης) of the language is required by the materialism of the listener/reader, that it was particularly necessary in the early stages of revelation history, that in Scripture God uses simple ways of speech to accommodate our limitations, that while the concern in such acts of considerateness is not primarily with the dignity proper to God, we should not remain at the level of banal vocabulary or think of God in human terms, and—eminently—that the prime analogue of divine considerateness is that (other) Incarnation of the Word in the person of Jesus.[36] Unspoken though this rich concept of scriptural revelation generally is in Antiochene commentators on the Old Testament, it lies behind their constant insistence on the danger of misconstruing anthropomorphisms in the text and the need to respond to the precision, ἀκρίβεια, of the text with a like precision in the commentator. We shall see both these dictates at work in the Antiochenes' approach to the task of commentary in Chapter Seven.

E. An obscure revelation

It is quite consistent with this acknowledgement and appreciation of God's loving gesture of considerateness in the language and literature of the Old Testament that the Antiochenes admitted as well its obscurity to reader/listener and commentator—a feature that preoccupied others as well.[37] The considerateness that marked God's dealing with humankind provided for a gradual revelation of himself.

---

[35] PG 81.561. It is a formulation of the incarnational principle of which Chrysostom would have been proud, and which the scholastic theologians will adopt in the form, *Quidquid recipitur, in modo recipientis recipitur.*

[36] Cf. Hill, "On looking again at *synkatabasis.*"

[37] Cf. M. Harl, "Origène et les interprétations patristiques grecques de l'obscurité biblique;" Zincone, "Le omelie di Giovanni Crisostomo 'De prophetiarum obscuritate.'"

Chrysostom in his Genesis homilies had developed a rationale for
this progress from obscurity to clarity:

> When Moses in the beginning took on the instruction of mankind, he
> taught his listeners the elements, whereas Paul and John, taking over
> from Moses, could at that later stage transmit more developed notions.[38]

However convincing the rationale, a challenge awaited the commentator on Old Testament texts to Antioch congregations/readers,
whose instinct was to focus on verifiable facts and who were less
interested in arcane speculation. The task was, as Theodore says in
beginning commentary on Haggai,[39] "by the grace of God to bring
clarity," or put another way, "to bring obscurity to clarity as far as
possible," as he says of his approach to the Song of Songs.[40] Chrysostom
and Theodoret both admit that many people recited or sang the
Psalms without understanding them, or at least no more than the
responsorium, ὑπακοή, sung by the congregation in the liturgy.[41]

These commentators came to their task with a less than perfect
preparation and without some skills necessary for exegesis of obscure
material. Necessary linguistic and paleographical attainments were
often not part of their formation, nor was a familiarity with some
literary genres. They were therefore not always well prepared for
the further task of interpreting biblical texts that were inadequately
critiqued (as we shall see in Chapters 6 & 8). It is understandable
that Theodoret, unfamiliar with apocalyptic, would find the book of
Daniel, which he took to be a statement of contemporary monar-
chies and a prophecy of future events, full of "riddles," αἰνίγματα;
the apocalyptic of Joel and Zechariah also bewildered himself and

---

[38] Homily 2 on Gen 1:1 (PG 53.29.3).
[39] *Theodori Mopsuesteni commentarius*, 304.
[40] On 4:12 (PG 81.212). Diodore in reference to Ps 47:7 had warned against
understanding the thought "superficially and at the level of the lips alone" (*Commentarii*, 4).
[41] In his διδασκαλεῖον Chrysostom regrets of Ps 141 that "those singing it daily
and uttering the words by mouth do not inquire about the force of the ideas underlying the words;" and Theodoret in the preface to his Commentary on the Psalter
hopes that the faithful "may sing its melodies and at the same time recognize the
sense of the words they sing." Of Ps 118, it was v.24, "This is the day the Lord
has made, let us rejoice and be glad in it," that was sung at Easter by the congregation in keeping with an ancient prescription, Chrysostom says, adding, "We,
on the contrary, must address ourselves to the whole psalm." Cf. Hill, "Psalm 41(42):
a classic text for Antiochene spirituality."

Theodore, as it had Didymus before them. Taking the fourth beast in Dan 7 to be the Roman empire, Theodoret admits the prophecy of it in the Old Testament to be less clear than his actual experience:

> While people in olden times came to know this in riddles, we have learnt it by experience, witnessing the outcome of the prophecy, the imposition of taxes, the poverty gripping most people and all the other things we observe happening every day.[42]

Antioch shared with Alexandria the problem of biblical eschatology, but predictably resolved it differently. Being unable to subscribe either to a naive millenarianism or to Origen's alternative of allegorizing eschatological language into the Christian's spiritual experience,[43] Antioch tended in some way to historicize it. Hence Theodoret's approach to Daniel and apocalyptic passages like chapters 38–39 in Ezekiel.

The problem of the obscurity of Old Testament texts, however, went beyond the apocalyptic genre found in Daniel, Ezekiel and some of The Twelve. Chrysostom chose to address it formally (if not quite logically) in two homilies in Antioch, beginning with the inexperience or even obduracy of the listeners/readers, as we saw above in his citing "Paul" in Heb 5:11 about Melchizedek. That is only a subjective reason, however; the problem lies deeper than that, he maintains.

> The Old Testament, in fact, resembles riddles (αἰνίγματα), there is much difficulty in it, and its books are hard to grasp, whereas the New is clearer and easier. Why is it, someone will ask, that they have this character, apart from the fact that the New talks about more important things, about the kingdom of heaven, resurrection of bodies and ineffable things that also surpass human understanding? So what is the reason why Old Testament works are obscure?[44]

---

[42] PG 81.1429. Though appreciative of the *Pax Romana* that was evidently still in force at this stage (the Daniel Commentary his second work, composed around 433), Theodoret understandably was not fully enamored of other aspects of Roman rule.

[43] Cf. R. P. C. Hanson, "Biblical exegesis in the early Church," 431–34. Brian E. Daley, "Apocalypticism in early Christian theology," 5, speaks of "a 'taming' of apocalyptic in order to integrate it into a larger picture of a Christian world order, a 'history of salvation' culminating in the redeeemed life of the disciples of the risen Christ."

[44] *Omelie*, 74–76.3.

There lies the objective reason that goes to the essence: the superiority of New Testament doctrines, even if these "surpass human understanding" (hardly clinching proof of greater clarity).

In addition, however, there is another reason for the obscurity that is more circumstantial: fear of reprisals being taken by the Jews against the Old Testament authors if the truth were plainly told. "In case the Jews should hear this clearly from the beginning and maltreat those saying so," Chrysostom says,

> they concealed the prophecies under the difficulty of interpretation and imparted to them great obscurity in the contents, ensuring by the obscurity of the reports the safety of the reporters.[45]

By way of proof he cites the treatment Jeremiah received for announcing to the court of Jehoiakim the impending catastrophe at the hands of the Babylonians as punishment for Jewish infidelity (Jer 36). Paul's astonishment in Rom 10:20 at Isaiah's blurting out the Good News of "our blessings and their troubles" is also quoted to this effect. And there is another circumstantial reason for the obscurity of the Old Testament, the fact of its being available to Antioch readers only in translation, with which the second homily begins.

> We do not have the Old Testament written for us in our native tongue: while it was composed in one language, we have it read out in another language. That is to say, it was written originally in the Hebrew tongue, whereas we received it in the language of the Greeks; and whenever a language is rendered into another language, great difficulty ensues. Everyone versed in many languages is aware of this, how it is not possible to transfer the clarity naturally contained in the words when moving to another language.[46]

Chrysostom's listeners would probably not need persuading of this difficulty; inspired though their Old Testament text assuredly was (and even its translation),[47] the revelation contained in its pages and "read out" to them was not always clear.

---

[45] *Omelie*, 76.3.

[46] *Omelie*, 114–16.2. In this second homily the preacher finally tires of the theme of obscurity, moving to parenesis on the subject of backbiting; and it is for this latter subject that the preacher at his next synaxis remembers the homily (PG 49.245.1), claiming that the congregation applauded him for it. Cf. Hill, "Chrysostom on the obscurity of the Old Testament."

[47] Chrysostom at this point proceeds to refer to the translation of the Hebrew Bible into Greek, without showing the uncritical acceptance of the legendary Letter

F. Revelation Old and New

If the Old Testament was so obscure—whether on account of listeners' limitations, the inherent inferiority of its contents, or the shortcomings of the Greek version—why would their pastors go to the trouble of mediating to them all the numerous books and expect them to read them instead of confining themselves to the "more important things" of the New Testament, "clearer and easier" as they were? This conundrum must have presented itself to Antiochene listeners and readers of their pastors' many commentaries, especially as things Jewish were objects of suspicion and hostility. Surely it would have been simpler merely to omit the Old Testament from consideration rather than labor its obscurity and the infidelity of Jews in Old (and New) Testament times. The lengthy catalogues we have of Diodore's and Theodore's Old Testament commentaries (if not the works themselves), and the happily extant coverage by Theodoret of so much of it (including unique Greek works on Ruth and Chronicles), show that the logic was not compelling. Chrysostom feels it necessary, however, to counter it even while lecturing on obscurity; if the Old Testament is obscure, it is not a total obscurity.

> Some things in the Old Testament are obscured, but not everything: if it was going to be totally obscure, there would be no point in things being said to the people of that time. After all, the inspired writings make mention of wars of the time, plagues and famines; they mention also things that are fulfilled today—the calling of the Church, the dismissal of the synagogue, the cancellation of the Law. These things, however, he did not want them to know—just the things happening in their own time. This is what I shall try to demonstrate, that he made only these things obscure—what had to do with us and the synagogue, present fulfilment, and the cancellation of the Law—which it was not necessary for them to know at the time. I mean, had they come to know from the beginning that the Law was temporary, they would have utterly scorned it.[48]

The "observable facts" prove the validity of the ancient writings, even if certain truths are obscure; after all, as Chrysostom goes on to say, there is a "kinship of the Law with grace." He had made the point frequently at other times in his Antioch ministry.

---

of Aristeas and even the divine inspiration of the Seventy translators shown by Theodore and Theodoret that we shall document in the next chapter.

[48] *Omelie*, 96.6.

What was said by the Old Testament authors about the Jews came true, and the fulfilment of it was clear to everyone; likewise what was said about Christ in the New Testament—which demonstrates above all the divine character of both Scriptures.

The New Testament and the Old come from the same Spirit, and the same Spirit who gave utterance in the New spoke also here.

Do you see the relationship of both testaments? Do you see the harmony in their teaching?

Do you see the consensus of Old Testament and New Testament statements?[49]

Theodoret, whose Questions on Exodus and Leviticus in particular show his familiarity with Old Testament Judaism, endorses this "harmony" and "consensus" of the testaments ("The same Spirit gave voice through both the Old Testament and the New Testament tongue"), and the progression from one to the other ("Through the inspired oracles we are led to the Gospel teaching to which they testify").[50] The same endorsement does not appear in the little we have of Diodore; and its absence from the two extant Old Testament commentaries of Theodore the *Ioudaiophrôn*[51] may be due to his reluctance in them to extend his hermeneutical perspective to the New Testament, there being no question of his esteem for psalmists or the Twelve.

At least Antiochene pastors were convinced that God revealed himself and his plan in Old Testament authors and their works as well as in the New—hence their giving themselves to the task of commentary on it generously; for Theodoret, in fact, commentary on the New Testament will be in a minor key.[52] Their commitment rested also on a profound theology of the inspired Word, in which the scriptural text is analogous to the person of Jesus in being also an incarnation of that Word. As with the person of Jesus, obscurity

---

[49] Homily on Ps 4:7 (PG 55.57.11); Homily on Ps 116:10 (PG 55.32.21); Sermon 1 on Gen (SC 433.154–56.2); Homily on Ps 110:1 (PG 55.268.3).

[50] Comm. on Ezekiel 34:15 (PG 81.1157); Comm. on Isaiah 8:13–14 (SC 276.310).

[51] A sobriquet suggesting his Jewish mentality applied to him by editor A. Mai in his 1832 preface to his edition of Theodore's Commentary on The Twelve (PG 66.121–202.II).

[52] Theodoret remarks in Letter 82 to Eusebius of Ancyra in 448 that he had commented on "all the prophets, the psalter and the apostle" (SC 98.202); and in the summary of work given at the beginning of his Questions on Leviticus in failing health five years later he makes no specific mention of Gospel commentary (*Theodoreti Cyrensis Quaestiones in Octateuchum*, 153).

in the Old Testament is but an implication of incarnation; and if there is a hierarchy in the two testaments in virtue of the superiority of teaching in the New, there is also the presence of the Spirit in the authors of each that calls for response. Though in Chapter Eight we shall not find Antiochene commentators endeavoring to find Christ in all biblical texts in the manner that Cyril is at least reputed to have done, they are none the less Christological in their incarnational understanding of the divine communication given in the text of the Old Testament. It is therefore time to examine the precise character of the text read by them.

CHAPTER FOUR

THE TEXT OF THE OLD TESTAMENT
READ IN ANTIOCH

For Christians in Antioch in the fourth and fifth centuries, like their fellows elsewhere, it was not a difficult matter to acquire and read in private a copy of the text of books of the Old Testament, those inspired if obscure scriptures. Chrysostom in Antioch, in fact, devotes a homily to the need to read the biblical text responsibly and not "mangle the limbs of Scripture" by lifting verses out of context, the verses in question including Jer 10:23; Hag 2:8; Pss 10:11,13; 14:1; 127:1, plus some Pauline texts. Some of these verses were "bandied about" from memory, as he says, and used to justify morally reprehensible behavior, such as the Jeremiah verse that formed the text for his homily that day, "Lord, people's ways are not their own, nor will human beings progress or direct their own going". But he criticizes also the incomplete reading of a biblical pericope, using a telling comparison to reinforce his point.

> No one, after all, would read out a royal law carelessly and in an offhand manner: unless they were to detail the time, mention the lawgiver and provide the text in its entirety, they would be punished and pay the ultimate penalty. In our case, on the contrary, in reading out not a human law but the one brought down from heaven, are we to treat it with such indifference as to tear it limb from limb? How could this merit excuse or pardon?[1]

If we are lucky enough to have a Bible, he is saying, let us read it responsibly so as to get the complete sense of individual passages. We have seen himself and Theodoret likewise lamenting incomplete understanding of some psalms through focusing on the single verse used as a responsorium.

---

[1] PG 56.158.2. See Hill, "Norms, definitions and unalterable doctrines': Chrysostom on Jeremiah." Henry Savile in the seventeenth century had come across in a library in Munich a full commentary on Jeremiah attributed to Chrysostom, Bernard de Montfaucon reports (PG 56.153–54), but judged it to have no claim to authenticity (*nugas meras et quisquilias*). Nothing of Diodore or Theodore is extant on the prophet; Theodoret's full commentary shows signs of transmission in the catenae.

A. Availability of a biblical text

The Antioch Fathers of that period will, like Didymus in Alexandria,[2] thus commend or at least acknowledge more studious readers of, or listeners to, their own commentaries who possess or have access to a Bible with a view to delving further into its contents. Theodoret counts on the readers of his Questions having a biblical text to check his information; to support his claim that a Deuteronomist or a Chronicler (terms not known to him, of course) drew on compositions of earlier authors, he says,

> The first book of the Kingdoms both in Hebrew and in Greek is called the inspired composition of Samuel, as is easy to realize for anyone willing to read that book.[3]

Speaking of this period, Harry Gamble agrees with Theodoret about the availability of Christian books like those of the Bible for people sufficiently (affluent and) willing to acquire copies:

> Apparently the problem was not that Christian books were especially difficult or expensive to procure for private use, but that few troubled to obtain them, and fewer still to read them.[4]

With the more convenient codex replacing the roll or scroll, books could be copied and distributed from the churches or monastic libraries where originals were held, even if we have little evidence of commercial distribution. While the Antiochenes do not describe this process of dissemination in the detail left us by Augustine in the west,[5] they do imply the existence of a literate readership[6] and of

---

[2] Didymus is confident that some readers of his Commentary on Zechariah (composed about 387) have read also his other biblical works; a reference to Matt 24:36 leads him to remark, "Sufficient reflections have been made about the Gospel passage in the work on Matthew in a previous composition, with which a studious reader will be familiar" (SC 85.1012.78). The Matthew Commentary is not extant.

[3] *Theodoreti Cyrensis Quaestiones in Reges et Paralipomena*, 4.

[4] *Books and Readers in the Early Church*, 233.

[5] Cf. Gamble, *Books and Readers*, 132–38.

[6] In Chapter 1 we saw E. A. Clark, *Reading Renunciation. Asceticism and Scripture in Early Christianity*, 49, contesting the view that only a small fraction of people in the Roman empire at this time were literate. Gamble, *Books and Readers*, 231, thinks of "a minority that probably never exceeded 15–20 percent."

available copies of both individual biblical books (like "some of the Psalters" Diodore mentions)[7] and their own commentaries.[8]

Chrysostom, on the other hand, while presumng this degree of literacy and availability, seems ambivalent about the value of a studious attitude in more diligent and better educated (and better off) listeners to his homilies on the Old Testament. At times he can flatter his congregation with the presumption of their ability to decide on variant readings of a text or its interpretation; after teasing out the drift of God's cryptic rebuke to Cain in Genesis 4:6–7 for his act of homicide and citing alternative views to his congregation in Homilies 18 and 19, he decides to "leave it to your judgement to choose for yourselves which view seems worth following."[9] At other times he can be quoted as referring somewhat pejoratively to well-educated readers (φιλομαθείς or φιλοπονώτεροι), as though these more scholarly people may venture to debate textual or hermeneutical issues with him to his discomfiture.[10] At still other times, by contrast, he will urge his listeners, on their return home from a synaxis, to peruse their family Bible in the company of their wife and children, and in this process to mediate to them something of the benefit they have gained from attendance at the golden-mouthed preacher's homilies.[11]

---

[7] In commentary on Ps 7:13 (*Commentarii*, 41). Bulk would have prevented assemblage of all biblical books in one volume.

[8] Eusebius in particular has left us ample evidence of the process of recording and producing copies of homilies delivered by preachers like Origen; see Hill, "Chrysostom's Commentary on the Psalms: homilies or tracts?" In some cases, we are told by Socrates (*Church History* 6,4; GCS N.F. 1, 316.12–13), Chrysostom's homilies were available both in the form he released them and in stenographic transcription.

[9] PG 53.159.1. In the homily on Isa 45:6–7 given in Constantinople he is likewise complimentary to studious listeners: "This every scholar (φιλόλογοι) knows, that everything happened as the prophets foretold against the false prophets" (PG 56.151.6).

[10] The attitude seems strange in one whom Libanius had hoped would succeed him as head of Antioch's rhetorical school, according to Sozomen, *Historia Ecclesiastica* 8, 2 (PG 67.1516). Chrysostom adopts a different tack in closing his homily on Ps 42 (outside the larger collection; PG 55.157.1): "Lest, however, I seem to bore you by prolonging the sermon, I shall leave the more studious (φιλοπονώτεροι) to choose individual refrains and examine the force contained in them. I shall thus close the sermon at this point by exhorting your good selves not to enter here to no effect, but to take up the refrains and make careful note of them as though they were pearls, meditate on them constantly at home and recite them all to your friends and your wives" (women not present, seemingly).

[11] The question as to whether men alone were in attendance at Chrysostom's

> It is better to conclude our sermon at this point, exhorting you in
> your goodness to remember what has been said and keep it ever in
> your mind; when you go home from here, lay out with your meal a
> spiritual meal as well. The father of the family might repeat some-
> thing of what was said here; his wife could then hear it, the children
> too could learn something, even the domestics might be instructed. In
> short, the household might become a church . . . We will be able while
> at home, before dining or after dining, by taking the sacred books in
> hand, to gain benefit from them and provide spiritual nourishment for
> our soul.[12]

Theodore, not disposed to see many of the Psalms referring to Jesus,
makes an exception (like master Diodore) in the case of Ps 110; taking issue with two Jewish interpretations that find reference in it to
David or Zerubbabel, he leaves it to his readers to decide how to
rebut them.

> Let us leave it up to each reader as to whether they choose to employ
> these arguments also against those who claimed this psalm refers to
> Zerubbabel . . . At all events, any of our brethren who are of a schol-
> arly bent will be able to equip themselves adequately with the same
> defense against both parties.[13]

B. The Hebrew text a closed book

Preachers and commentators on the Old Testament, studious readers of it and heads of families—all Greek speakers alike in Antioch
and Alexandria had available to them the biblical text in a Greek
version of the language of composition (as any native Syriac speakers, like Theodoret, could access the Peshitta in those centuries).[14]
Without such a version they would have been at a loss: none of

---

(and other preachers') homilies, or were the sole intended readers of written commentaries, was addressed in Chapter One. See also previous note.

[12] Homily 2 and 10 on Gen (PG 53.31.4; 90.8). Cf. Clark, *Reading Renunciation*,
49: "It appears that (Adolf) Harnack mistook prescription of Bible reading for
description of actual practices, and failed to note that those preachers who exhorted
to Bible reading, such as John Chrysostom, were addressing higher-class (i.e., more
literate) congregations, unlike the norm for Christians-in-general."

[13] *Le commentaire*, 8 (*studiosi* the fifth century Latin version, the Grk text not extant
at that point).

[14] On the basis also of work by J. Joosten, "The Old Testament quotations in
the Old Syriac and Peshitta Gospels," *Textus* 15 (1990), 55–76, and earlier work by
S. P. Brock, Michael Weitzman in his *The Syriac Version of the Old Testament*, 253,

them, even the preachers and commentators, had a knowledge of Hebrew—a serious handicap for exegetes and hermeneuts of the Old Testament. Amongst the Fathers, Jerome's drilling in Hebrew is exceptional, if not unique.[15] Though the Antiochenes will not concede this handicap, and some will—especially with youthful brashness—like to imply a familiarity with semitic usage, none will be so bold as to claim fluency in Hebrew. Their occasional ventures into linguistic and syntactic niceties of the Hebrew text can be fraught with unfortunate solecisms betraying their limitations. For this general ignorance, Diodore, the founder of the Antiochene method of exegesis[16] and director of the asketerion attended by Chrysostom and Theodore, bears much responsibility. Though one of these alumni will dutifully refer to "this wise father of ours,"[17] and on the basis of an extant fragment of comment on Gen 2:23 a modern commentator will commend Diodore for "his mostly accurate knowledge of the Hebrew text" and "erudition as an exegete,"[18] one has only to follow him through his sole fully extant work, the Commentary on the Psalms, to recognize his shortcomings. He is, for instance, unable to detect the alphabetic structure of certain psalms, despite sensing the effect this can have on the psalmist's movement of thought (e.g., in Pss 34; 37). Like many a teacher, unwilling to admit to

---

shows that the Peshitta version of Pentateuch, Latter Prophets and Psalms was available and had attained authoritative status by c. 170. By the early fourth century all the canonical books are quoted by Aphrahat from the Peshitta. For Theodoret's being a native Syriac speaker, see P. Canivet, *Histoire d'une entreprise apologétique au Ve siècle*, 26–27.

[15] Cf. J. Barr, "St Jerome's appreciation of Hebrew." Jerome's familiarity with Hebrew was due to time spent with a Jewish convert in Chalcis c. 375 (J. N. D. Kelly, *Jerome. His Life, Writings and Controversies*, 50). Origen's biographer, H. Crouzel, *Origen*, 12, concedes, "Certainly it would be wrong to credit Origen with a knowledge of Hebrew like Jerome's, but he must have had enough to direct the compilation of the *Hexapla*, even if the actual work was done by some assistant." N. Fernández Marcos, *The Septuagint in Context*, 204–206, assembles evidence on the degree of Origen's knowledge of Hebrew, beginning with the affirmative testimony of Eusebius and Jerome.

[16] Discussion of Diodore's claim to this title (ahead, say, of Lucian) and the legitimacy of use of the terms "school" and "exegesis" can be left to Chapter Seven.

[17] Chrysostom, *Laus Diodori* (PG 52.764.4).

[18] N. V. Harrison, "Women, human identity, and the image of God: Antiochene interpretations," *JECS* 9 (2001) 210–11. By contrast, the editor of Diodore's Psalms Commentary, J.-M. Olivier, *Commentarii*, xcviii, comes to the justified conclusion that "l'auteur du commentaire ne connaisait pas l'hebreu, mais avait à sa disposition un commentaire portant des indications sur le texte hébraique, ce que lui permet de faire parfois illusion."

imperfect knowledge, he will dogmatize on textual details when he should be more tentative (a habit Theodore will learn from him); when Ps 19 opens with the celebrated verse, "The heavens tell of the glory of God," Diodore assures his readers that the plural "heavens" is normal Hebrew usage, citing for contrast his (Greek) text of Ps 115:16, where—unfortunately for him—the Hebrew term is again in the plural.

> Stating singular things as plural is a Hebrew idiom, especially in the case of heavenly things, either on account of their importance or also by another custom. Elsewhere he illustrates this more clearly by speaking in this case not in the plural but in the singular, "The heaven is the Lord's heaven," in the sense of dedicated, and he goes on, "but the earth he has given to human beings."[19]

He is unable to detect the many shortcomings of the LXX in rendering the Hebrew text, and even to recognize a scribal error, such as occurs in Ps 48:9, where his local text reads, "We suspected, O God, your mercy in the midst of your people," a scribe obviously having copied ναοῦ, "temple," as λαοῦ, "people" (a solecism his pupils will replicate, Chrysostom even with a flourish of false erudition citing the Hebrew term *hecal*, "temple," to prove that the version "people" is correct!).[20]

Predictably, Diodore's student Theodore suffers his master's linguistic limitations—though again he has his modern champions.[21] As a young scholar, particularly in his first work, on the Psalms, clearly under Diodore's influence,[22] he claims a grasp of Hebrew syntax he did not in fact possess. And he is not far into his next work, on the Twelve Prophets, before encountering a confusion of past and future tenses by his Septuagint version in Hosea 9:2, "They did not inhabit the Lord's land," which he corrects to read "They will not inhabit" on the grounds that the Bible "expresses it as usual with a change

---

[19] *Commentarii*, 110.

[20] PG 55.219.2.

[21] Devreesse, *Le commentaire*, vi, speaks of Theodore's "uncommon knowledge of the Bible," but without presenting evidence of the kind L. Pirot, *L'Oeuvre exégètique de Théodore de Mopsueste*, 96–100, painstakingly assembles to the opposite conclusion. R. A. Greer, *Theodore of Mopsuestia. Exegete and Theologian*, 100, thinks "Theodore probably knew some Hebrew . . . He was not so proficient as Jerome." Theodore's editor Angelo Mai is unsure, thinking (on unconvincing grounds) that he did know Syriac (PG 66.121–22.II).

[22] Cf. Hill, "His Master's Voice: Theodore of Mopsuestia on the Psalms."

in tense, as was pointed out on many occasions in blessed David's usage." He wrongly detects the same reversal of tenses in Hos 12:9, "which I sufficiently demonstrated in the case of the Psalms as well." In other ways as well he shows his inability to appreciate the original. When he arrives at the mention of two astral deities in Amos 5:26 which his local text renders as Moloch and Remphan (Raiphan in other LXX forms), he admits his indebtedness to predecessors with more developed semitic lore:

> By *Moloch* he refers to the idol worshiped by them, and by *tent of Moloch* he means, You frequent the idol's shrine and care for it, and you are also involved in worship of a star, giving it the name of a god (commentators claiming that in the language of the Hebrews the morning star is given this name).[23]

As well as attributing confusion in tenses in his text to the Hebrew and not to its translators, he is forever fastening on examples of synecdoche as illustrative of "Hebrew parlance" rather than general literary expression. When he notes a double focus in the prophecy of Habakkuk, he compares it to the LXX Ps 9, which he is aware appears in Hebrew as two psalms, but unaware that the alphabetic structure in the Hebrew confirms the judgement of the Seventy to maintain it as one piece. And so on.

It is probably not necessary to proceed to demonstrate that the other two principal commentators on the Old Testament in Antioch, John Chrysostom and Theodoret, suffered the same limitation in approaching the biblical text. The former will admit it in his long series of homilies on Genesis; when he comes to the Hebrew plural form for "heaven" in Gen 1:1 that the LXX renders as the singular οὐρανός, he is more circumspect than his mentor in conceding the need for enlightenment in saying,

> Those with a precise knowledge of that language tell us that among the Hebrews the word 'heaven' is used in the plural, and those who know Syriac confirm this.[24]

Theodoret will enjoy the latter advantage of familiarity with that dialect of Aramaic to sense the force of a Heb. term; but (again despite modern commentators' willingness to concede him a knowledge

---

[23] *Theodori Mopsuesteni commentarius*, 136–37.
[24] Homily 4 (PG 53.43.4).

of Hebrew)[25] he will show the same inability as Chrysostom to detect the solecisms committed by the LXX in rendering the titles of the Psalms (which Diodore to his credit had dissuaded Theodore from taking seriously as being later insertions).[26] Like Chrysostom he accepts the confusion by the LXX of the musical direction for "flutes" (Heb. *nehiloth*) in the title to Ps 5 with the verb *nahal*, "inherit," though we do not get a subsequent discourse on inheritances to the length to which Chrysostom goes. The similar musical direction in the title to Ps 22, "The Deer of Dawn" (apparently a cue to a melody), from *'ayyelet*, "deer," is rendered as "on support at dawn," as though from *'eyalut*, "support;" likewise with Ps 45 the cue "For the Lilies," *shoshanim*, is rendered as "those to be changed," as though from *shanah*. In the title to Ps 46 the word for "maidens," *alamoth*, is read as "on the secrets" as though from *alam*, "conceal." And so on. As well, he frequently fails to recognize cases where the LXX has misread the tense of Hebrew verbs; and at the close of commentary on Ps 111 he has to take others' word for the fact that this psalm and the next have an alphabetic structure.

C. Antioch commentators' biblical text

Antiochene commentators on the Old Testament, then, were heavily dependent on the Greek version of the biblical text in common use in their church. Though it seems to be a fact of which many modern commentators on the Bible are unaware to their detriment,[27] the Antioch text differed significantly (if not in major proportions)

---

[25] M.-J. Rondeau, for example, in *Les commentaire patristiques du Psautier (III*[e]*–V*[e] *siècles)* 1, 136, may have been led by the term "bilingue" used by Canivet of Theodoret to conclude that Greek and Hebrew were his two languages. The evidence belies it.

[26] For Diodore the titles "are in most cases faulty, the compilers of the psalms mostly guessing at their connection and not placing them by meaning" (*Commentarii*, 6).

[27] While it is still possible to find a modern commentary on an Old Testament book which ignores the history of exegesis to the extent of failing to engage with patristic commentary, textual discrepancies between our Masoretic Heb. text and the Greek forms oblige a commentator in the case of Jeremiah, e.g., to acknowledge the history of the text. And yet even as eminent a commentator on Jer as W. McKane can speak of the Septuagint as though a univocal term and use simplistic phrases like "missing from the LXX" when a passage in fact is to be found in the Antioch form, as reference to one of the Göttingen volumes would reveal. See Hill, "*Orientale lumen:* Western biblical scholarship's unacknowledged debt."

from the Greek text used in other churches. Commentators in Antioch in the fourth and fifth centuries were alerted to this textual diversity if they took the trouble to consult a copy of that great resource compiled by Origen in Caesarea, the Hexapla,[28] which offered not only a Hebrew text (plus a transliteration) but also one (or more)[29] alternative forms (ἀντίγραφα) of the version known as the Septuagint as well as the versions associated with the names of the Jewish translators Aquila, Symmachus and Theodotion ("The Three," "Those of the company of Aquila").[30] The Antiochenes still believed, however, that their local form of the Greek text derived from the work of that original corps of translators, the Seventy, as outlined in the legendary *Letter of Aristeas (to Philocrates)*,[31] and because of these origins their version was both divinely inspired and superior to any subsequent version in another language. Theodoret, unaware that the *Letter* refers only to translation of the Torah, defends the text of the Psalter on the grounds that "the translators—not without divine inspiration—turned them into the Greek language."[32] For Theodore, who was also ignorant of the scope of the original translators, their version was preferable to any other (as he says in comment on Ps 56), inspiration predictably for him not being the key factor.

> If you have an eye to sequence and composition of the sense of the text, you would never prefer another version to that of the Seventy. Not that everything is translated better by them: there are places, in fact, where they offer the weaker version, and sometimes they fall short of the others, who said things more clearly and logically. But in general

---

[28] Jerome, *Comm. Titus* 3:9 (PL 26.594–95), *Comm. Ps* 1:4 (CCL 72.180.1), speaks of the Hexapla as widely available at one time in Palestine but later becoming defective.

[29] Twice in commentary on the Song of Songs (on 5:11; 6:12) Theodoret cites a "fifth edition," which owes its name to its appearance in the Hexapla as a fifth Greek version after those of the Three. Barthélemy, *Les devanciers d'Aquila*, 266–70, sees it as part of a Palestinian revision of the LXX. Jean-Noël Guinot, *L'Exégèse de Théodoret de Cyr*, 215, thinks it shows the influence of Origen, whose pioneering work on the Song Theodoret acknowledges in his preface.

[30] Theodoret also cites an obscure translator named Josephus (not the historian), as in replying to Q.28 on 2 Sam. Cf. Fernández Marcos, *The Septuagint in Context*, 169–72.

[31] Ed. A. Pelletier, SC 89, 1962.

[32] PG 80.864. Not that this belief made it immune to criticism; Theodoret judges the phrase "a wisp of smoke" in his text of 3:6 of the Song "a servile rendering of the Hebrew," probably by comparison with Aquila and Symmachus (PG 81.120); but our Heb. supports it.

by comparison with the others they are found far superior even if saying many things less competently. For the student there are many signs
of the greater attention to effect by the Seventy and the care for greater
clarity by Symmachus.[33]

It is a significant admission that Symmachus gives a "clearer" version than the LXX (perhaps a conventional concession, to be found
in these commentators repeatedly)—not that Theodore is capable of
a valid comparison. Chrysostom, too, concedes that the clarity of
Old Testament texts has suffered in the process of translation; it is
one of the reasons he gives for its obscurity in his two homilies on
the subject.

> We do not have the Old Testament written for us in our native tongue:
> while it was composed in one language, we have it read in another
> language. That it is to say, it was written originally in the Hebrew
> tongue, whereas we received it in the language of the Greeks; and
> whenever a language is rendered into another language, it involves
> great difficulty. All who are versed in many languages are aware of
> this, how it is not possible to transfer the clarity naturally contained
> in the words when moving to another language. Three hundred years
> before the coming of Christ, remember, when Ptolemy was still king
> of the Egyptians, the Old Testament was translated into Greek for
> pressing reasons of usefulness and necessity. You see, as long as it was
> addressed to one race of the Jews, it remained in the Hebrew tongue.[34]

Chrysostom, while likewise acknowledging the antiquity of his Greek
version, sees the process of translation to be in no way miraculous,
just pragmatically necessary for Greek-speakers. Theodore for his
part would want the LXX despite its faults to be preferred to a version in any other language; the Peshitta enjoyed no such credentials,
and was *a priori* rated inferior to the LXX. Predecessors who opted
for its rendering of Zeph 1:5 were obviously wrong.

> They ought to realise this before everything else, that whereas the con-
> tents of the divine Scripture are composed in Hebrew, they were trans-
> lated into Syriac by somebody or other (his identity is unknown to
> this day). The translation into Greek, on the other hand, was done by
> seventy men, elders of the people, possessing a precise knowledge of
> their own language and a knowledge of the divine Scriptures, approved
> of by the priest and all the Israelite people as particularly suited to

---

[33] *Le commentaire*, 365.
[34] Homily 2; *Omelie*, 114–16.2.

translating. Their translation and publication the blessed apostles clearly seem to have accepted, and to the believers from the nations who formerly had no access at all to the contents of the Old Testament they passed on the divine Scriptures written in Greek in the translation of the Seventy. All of us, having come to faith in Christ the Lord from the nations, received the Scriptures from them and now enjoy them, reading them aloud in the churches and keeping them at home.[35]

So the local Greek text was the *textus receptus* for the Gentile church in Antioch (the Hebrew text, it would seem from his argument and Chrysostom's, being redolent of Judaism).

D. ORIGIN AND CHARACTER OF THE ANTIOCH TEXT

These Antioch commentators are confident that the biblical text of their church stems directly from that original translation of the Hebrew text into Greek in Alexandria (purportedly in the third, but in fact) in the second century BCE, which came to be known as work of The Seventy, or Septuagint. By his time in the fourth century CE, however, a student of the history of the text like Jerome acknowledged three Greek texts that were current, respectively, in Alexandria, Constantinople-Antioch and "the provinces in-between," the second of these being

> another version which Origen and Eusebius of Caesarea and all the Greek commentators call the popular (κοινή) text, and which by most is now called the Lucianic text.[36]

"Greek commentators" in Antioch, however, did not seem to use that latter term—understandably, in view of Lucian's tarnished reputation;[37] we saw them tracing their text directly back to Alexandria (though not citing that city, either). What Lucian's role was in the development of the Antioch text, and whether such a text originated in Antioch, is the subject of debate; there are those who would

---

[35] *Theodori Mopsuesteni commentarius*, 283–84.

[36] *Praef. in Paral.* (PL 28.1324–25); *Ep. 106* (PL 22.838.2). Jerome was wrong in using the term, says Barthélemy, *Les devanciers d'Aquila*, 126–27, as the Antiochenes make no mention of Lucian.

[37] For Quasten, *Patrology* 2, 143, "Lucian was the father of Arianism;" but Wallace-Hadrill, *Christian Antioch*, 87, denies that this was his reputation in Antioch, while admitting "paucity of reference" to him.

support the development in Antioch of a distinct text,[38] even if only
for Lucian later to revise,[39] while others see simply reworkings of an
Ur-Septuagint that by Jerome's time constituted a family of texts.[40]

It would be fatuous to think that we might one day come across
a complete Antiochene Bible that illustrates Lucianic features throughout. Those who have given their attention to this form of the LXX
(if we are not, like P. Kahle, to restrict the term "Septuagint" to a
distinct version, that completed in the second century in Alexandria),
like R. Hanhart, N. Fernández Marcos, A. Sáenz-Badillos, J. R.
Busto Saiz, J. W. Wevers, and D. Barthélemy, suggest that the development of such distinctive features was more piecemeal. We are
warned that "there is no clear idea of what this recension consisted
nor whether it extended to the whole Bible or not."[41] Clarifying
these issues depends rather on our becoming acquainted with the
biblical commentaries of the Antioch Fathers, where the biblical text
is cited.

> One of the reasons for the uncertainty concerning the Lucianic recen-
> sion of the Octateuch was the lack of critical editions of the Antiochene
> Fathers,

Fernández Marcos came to believe,[42] and the same would be true
of the rest of the Old Testament.

Despite the length of the commentaries on Old Testament books
by these ancient preachers and writers, not to mention the loss of
so many to the flames of prejudice fanned against Antiochene figures
in particular, we are gradually amassing a collection of critical editions that throw such light on their local text. Because it was believed
that some parts of the Octateuch and much of Kingdoms would

---

[38] P. E. Kahle, *The Cairo Genizah*, 256–57, sees a translation developed in Antioch
and revised by Lucian.

[39] S. Jellicoe, *The Septuagint in Modern Study*, 160–161, denies Lucian the ability to
translate from the Hebrew. A revising role for Lucian is conceded by D. S. Wallace-
Hadrill, *Christian Antioch*, 30, B. Drewery, "Antiochien," 106, S. P. Brock, "Bibelüber-
setzungen I,2," *TRE* 6,166–67, whereas D. Barthélemy, *Les Devanciers d'Aquila*,
126–127, prefers to speak of a "texte Antiochien," and K. G. O'Connell, "Texts
and versions," 1092, would place the revision in Palestine.

[40] Fernández Marcos, *The Septuagint in Context*, 53–57, is not in favor of Kahle's
notion of a number of separate translations like the targums; yet he sees the LXX
as a "collection of translations" (xi, 22).

[41] Fernández Marcos, "The Lucianic text in the Books of Kingdoms," 102.

[42] "The Antiochene text of the Greek Bible," 28.

illustrate peculiarly Antiochene features, Fernández Marcos edited the happily extant *Questions on the Octateuch* of Theodoret (similar work by Diodore and Theodore only fragmentarily extant) in conjunction with A. Sáenz-Badillos, to which Chrysostom's collections of homilies (PG)[43] and sermons (crit. ed.)[44] on Genesis are relevant, and also the *Questions on Kingdoms and Chronicles* in conjunction with J. R. Busto Saiz. The evidence arising from the critical edition of the Octateuch *Questions* suggested that "at least a typically Antiochene text emerges in the last three books,"[45] viz, Joshua, Judges, Ruth. The critical edition of the Kgs & Chr *Questions* confirmed the impression of "a single, uniform text with very clear textual characteristics" in Kingdoms (1 Sam–2 Kgs).[46] Antiochene commentary on the Psalter is represented by complete works from Diodore and Theodoret,[47] the former in part available in a critical edition,[48] a collection of fifty eight homilies by Chrysostom,[49] and a critical edition of commentary on eighty one psalms by Theodore, partly in Greek and partly in early Latin translation.[50] The biblical text of the Psalter appearing in these commentaries reveals

> a textual phenomenon similar to that of the Greek New Testament: in books extensively used in the liturgy, the presence of different textual forms was particularly disturbing.[51]

The text of the prophets in Antioch shows evidence of a reworking that also can be called Lucianic;[52] we have a complete commentary

---

[43] PG 53, 54 contains the 67 homilies on Genesis.

[44] Eight sermons, ed. L. Brottier, SC 433. Of the text of Gen found in Chrysostom and Theodoret, Fernández Marcos can remark, *The Septuagint in Context*, 229, on the basis of work by Wevers that "if there had been a Lucianic recension in Genesis, (the Antiochenes) did not know it."

[45] *The Septuagint in Context*, 229.

[46] *The Septuagint in Context*, 230.

[47] PG 80.

[48] Ed. Olivier, *Diodori Tarsensis Commentarii in Psalmos* 1. *Commentarii in Psalmos I–L* (CCG 6).

[49] PG 55.

[50] Ed. Devreesse, *Le commentaire de Théodore de Mopsueste sur les psaumes I–LXXX*.

[51] Fernández Marcos, "Some reflections on the Antiochian text of the Septuagint," 221. In a review of Devreesse's work, Albert Vaccari had noted in Theodore's text what he calls "lezioni originali, genuine, conservate nel detto commento, perdutesi invece nel resto della tradizione" (*Bib* 21 [1941] 212).

[52] The conclusion is that of R. Hanhart, cited by Fernández Marcos, *The Septuagint in Context*, 236.

on Isaiah by Theodoret critically edited (containing a score of
distinctive readings),[53] and six homilies on Isaiah 6 by Chrysostom
also critically edited.[54] Theodoret's Commentary on Jeremiah in the
extant form shows signs of transmission in the catenae,[55] yet contains elements prematurely declared "missing from the LXX" by
modern commentators. His Ezekiel Commentary[56] incorporates over
a score of distinctively Antiochene readings; in the view of Leslie
McGregor, "the Greek translation of Ezekiel is not homogeneous,"
there being three different sections, not all by the one translator.[57]
In Theodoret's Commentary on Daniel[58] it is the Theodotion version that appears as the biblical text in preference to the LXX, as
usual with the Antiochenes. Both Theodore and Theodoret have left
us full commentaries on The Twelve Prophets (listed in the order
of the Heb., not the LXX), the former available in a critical edition;[59]
and we can see from a comparison of these with the earlier work
on Zechariah by Didymus known to both that the Antioch text incorporates other distinctive features.

In short, it can be said of the text of the Old Testament at Antioch—
whether interpreted by commentators oral and written, or read by
significant numbers of private readers—that it was distinctive and
able to be recognized by Jerome and others by the fourth century
as a widespread text, and by today's readers of the verse-by-verse
commentaries of the Antioch Fathers (to the extent that they have
survived prejudice and the passage of time). It was the result of revision or reworking, if not retranslation, and benefited from other such
recensions. The characteristics of such a distinctive text are still in

---

[53] By J.-N. Guinot, SC 276, 295, 315; 1980, 1982, 1984.

[54] By J. Dumortier, SC 277; 1981.

[55] PG 81. Discovery of a manuscript in Constantinople with an introduction to
the Jeremiah Commentary in a different form suggests that the PG text may owe
something to the catenae. Complete deterioration of this manuscript rules out the
possibility of further comparison.

[56] PG 81.

[57] *The Greek Test of Ezekiel*, 197. McGregor's conclusion is "that the multiple-trans-
lator theories as opposed to the translator-reviser theories cannot be rejected entirely."
This verdict, he believes, is not affected by the moot point of distribution of divine
names in both Hebrew and Greek texts.

[58] PG 81.

[59] By H. N. Sprenger, *Theodori Mopsuesteni commentarius in XII Prophetas*. Theodoret's
text is found in PG 81, as is his Commentary on the Song of Songs.

process of identification, book by book, which will benefit from a growing number of critical editions of the Antioch Fathers' commentaries.[60] Yet already it can be said that this recension had as its aim to fill in the gaps in the LXX in respect of the Hebrew text, to improve on mere transliteration of obscure terms by a puzzled LXX, to supply clarifying items, and in short to come up with "a full text with no omissions."[61] We await the further clarification—as, of course, we await further research into Hebrew texts more ancient than the Masoretic, and a wider acceptance by today's biblical scholars that LXX is not a univocal term and that access to editions of the LXX like those from Göttingen and to critical editions of Antiochene patristic commentaries like those from Paris and Madrid is essential if modern commentary is not to be as jejune as some in the past.[62] We should turn now to examine the degree to which the Antioch Fathers in our period possessed the necessary skills to read and mediate to their flock the text they had inherited.

---

[60] Notice has been given of inclusion in the Sources Chrétiennes series of critical editions of Theodoret's commentaries on the Song of Songs and the Twelve Prophets. A critical edition has been prepared by G. Bady of a commentary on Proverbs attributed to Chrysostom; the biblical text contains some distinctive readings.

[61] Fernández Marcos, *The Septuagint in Context*, 230.

[62] See Hill, "*Orientale lumen*: western biblical scholarship's unacknowledged debt." It is perhaps worthwhile also making the plea that miscellanies of patristic comments on the biblical text, like the *Ancient Christian Commentary on Scripture* and *The Church's Bible*, may also intimate to readers that the Fathers cited may be reading diverse forms of that text, giving rise to diverse interpretations.

CHAPTER FIVE

EXEGETICAL SKILLS AND RESOURCES IN ANTIOCH

Modern biblical textbooks that trace the history of Christian understanding of the Bible not infrequently draw comparisons between
"schools of exegesis" in the early centuries. In so doing they can be
guilty of imprecision in their use of these terms, implying overall
differences in interpretation of the text. The preference here, as noted
in the preface, has been both to avoid comparisons of Antioch with
other ancient centers and approaches and to achieve the *akribeia*,
precision, so admired in the biblical text and its readers by the
Antiochene commentators. For one thing, by the term "school" we
may properly refer in the case of Antioch or any other ancient center to a fellowship of like-minded scholars joined by birth, geography and scholarly principles.[1] And the term "exegesis" could helpfully
be confined to stages in a process of explication that involves establishing and critiquing the text to be read and commented on, dependent upon the commentator's ability to read it, and making judgements
on the authorship of the text, whether single or multiple, real or
pseudonymous, and on the history of that text. In speaking of "schools
of *exegesis*," textbooks often have in mind rather interpretation by a
group of scholars of texts already established and read[2]—a focus we
shall adopt in Chapter Eight on Antiochene hermeneutics.

Here instead the focus is not on the meaning given to texts,
whether superficial or more profound, but on the skills and resources
of Antiochene commentators in the fourth and fifth centuries to conduct exegesis in that more precise, if limited, sense. Once such skills
are identified, the commentaries nominated in the following chapter

---

[1] Quasten, *Patrology* 2, 121–23, goes beyond that sense in referring to the "school
of Caesarea," Origen's refuge after his exile from Egypt. B. Drewery, "Antiochien,"
104, admits of Antioch "keine Schule im formalen Sinn des Wortes."

[2] Likewise when Wallace-Hadrill remarks, *Christian Antioch*, 39, "Exegesis at Antioch
was not monolithic," he is referring rather to hermeneutics. Olivier in speaking frequently of Antioch's "méthode exégètique" has all aspects of the explanatory process
in mind, as does Schäublin, *Untersuchungen*, 173, in reaching his conclusion, "Die
antiochenische Exegese von der paganen Grammatik herkommt."

can be examined for the degree to which they exemplify them. We observed in Chapter Four, for instance, that none of the Antioch Fathers—or those elsewhere in the east, either, with the possible exception of Origen—had a good grounding in Hebrew, an obvious handicap in reading and interpreting Old Testament material. We also observed that the Antiochenes had as a *textus receptus* their own distinctive Greek version for reading and commentary, whose distinguishing features varied in degree from other forms of the LXX in different parts of the Bible—the latter books of the Octateuch, for instance, found to be more distinctive than the former. Modern commentators, we noted, would do well to note this distinctiveness and to concede that "Septuagint" is not a univocal term; and it should also not be presumed that the Hebrew *Vorlage* of (any form of) the LXX is identical with that of the Masoretic text commonly in use in exegesis classes today.

A. Establishing and critiquing a text

To what degree of criticism did Diodore, founder of the Antiochene school of exegesis,[3] submit the biblical text of Psalms when lecturing on them in his *askêtêrion*? The opening verse of Ps 41 gives us a clue; in the LXX it reads, "Blessed is the one who understands the poor and needy," but Theodoret will later observe, "The phrase *and needy* I found in some manuscripts (ἀντίγραφα), but it is not in the Hebrew or the Syriac or the other translators."[4] Industrious as he always is, Theodoret had checked his local text against the Peshitta and that great resource of Origen's, the Hexapla.[5] He found the discrepancy both in the former and in the columns of the latter providing him with the Hebrew and its transliteration (accessed more easily by reference to the Syriac) and with the alternative versions, whereas the LXX form in the Hexapla showed no such discrepancy.

---

[3] Though this title has been accorded also to Lucian, Bardy says without qualification, "Le vrai fondateur de l'école d'Antioche est Diodore de Tarse" ("Interprétation chez les pères," 580). Diodore's editor Olivier, *Commentarii*, ciii, though conceding to Lucian the title "initiateur" of Antioch's historical method, classes Diodore as "le véritable fondateur."

[4] PG 80.1161. No commentary of Chrysostom on this psalm is extant.

[5] Guinot, *L'Exégèse*, 182, though conceding Theodoret's (uneven) reference to the Hexapla, doubts that he possessed a copy.

The young Theodore, also typically, had not bothered to check anything beyond his local copy of the Psalter,[6] despite his mentor's taking some little trouble: Diodore had observed, "Symmachus says, 'The one who has a thought for the poor,'" and then simply applied the verse historically to Hezekiah.[7] Throughout commentary on the entire Psalter Diodore checks his LXX text against the alternative versions only at nine places,[8] generally that of Symmachus and then mainly to confirm the LXX rather than gain clarification from an alternative rendering. His editor Olivier is led to the conclusion that Diodore possibly did not have access to a copy of the Hexapla;[9] certainly his textual resources seem quite limited, as is his interest in employing them.

Since Diodore had shown so little concern for establishing the text on which he was commenting, we are not surprised to find pupil Theodore also little interested in such matters (though we have to concede that our text of the commentaries does not always come to us directly from the commentators). In his Psalms Commentary, where admittedly we are considerably dependent upon the catenae, his interest in textual matters is at best sporadic. While the relevance of v.14 to the movement of thought of Ps 10 in the LXX puzzles both Chrysostom and Theodoret, leading them to check with the alternative versions, Theodore simply observes, "This results from a bad translation from the Hebrew," without checking other versions, let alone the Hebrew itself. Ps 17:14 likewise proves obscure, even to modern commentators, who turn to Ugaritic and Akkadian for assistance,[10] and to Theodoret, who looks to the alternative versions; but the youthful Theodore magisterially condemns his LXX version, and has recourse only to rationalizing.

---

[6] *Le commentaire*, 254.

[7] A modern commentator like Dahood, *Psalms* 1, 249, will find the verse out of keeping with the psalm's movement of thought and amend it—not an option open to an Antiochene, even Theodoret.

[8] Olivier lists eight of these (*Commentarii*, xcix); a ninth could be added, of Aquila on Ps 3:4.

[9] *Commentarii*, c: "Peut-être l'auteur ne disposait-il pas des *Hexaples* et a-t-il simplement utilisé les lecons citées dans un commentaire qu'il avait sous le main." In comment on Ps 7:13b Diodore claims to have found a different reading in "some of the Psalters" which does not affect the meaning (*Commentarii*, 41), there probably being a number of available copies of the Psalter.

[10] Cf. Dahood, *Psalms* 1, 99.

The difficulty and obscurity in this place arise from the Greek translation, which we shall resolve by proceeding with God's help to the
interpretation. Now, it is Hebrew peculiarities in particular that made
this place difficult for us, since they can hardly be explained through
the Greek translation.[11]

He will frequently and gratuitously rule on what he styles "Hebrew
idiom," despite not having a good grasp of Hebrew. He fails to
detect the alphabetic structure of the Ps 9 in the LXX which appears
as two in the Hebrew:

> This ninth psalm, which is divided into two in the Hebrew and Syriac,
> has been combined into one with us for reasons I am unaware of.

He will occasionally cite both Hebrew and Syriac, perhaps from predecessors, of whom he can be typically disparaging. In Ps 16 the
reference in v.3 to "holy ones" is obscure, Theodoret opting for the
apostles, Dahood for Canaanite and Phoenician deities. It is not a
problem to Theodore.

> *You have shown your wonders to the holy ones who are in the land, because all*
> *my wishes are in them.* By the meaning which at first flush seems to arise
> from the Greek text, you could easily get the impression that the phrase
> *the holy ones who are in the land* was said of the Israelites; in fact, some
> commentators have taken that sense as being readily accessible, and
> have thus missed the truth and the force of the words. That is not
> the meaning in Syriac and Hebrew, however, where it reads this way:
> To the proud and mighty, to the powerful and strong—that is, the
> nations, who do not cease to surround us and cause us trouble—you
> have made yourself so much an object of wonder that *all my wishes*
> *were in them* when they perish under your attack and are consigned to
> ruin and the sword. This, in fact, was the wish of the people of Israel,
> for divine vengeance to scatter their assailants. According to this mean-
> ing everything said by him comes together with complete consistency.[12]

When he does cite Aquila or Symmachus, it can be a mere gesture,
contributing nothing to clarity of thought; to the LXX version of Ps
9:14, "I shall exult in salvation," Theodore mechanically adds, "Aquila,
'Delighted in your salvation,'" which hardly represents a refinement.
Though reference to these alternative versions in the Psalms Commentary is infrequent, at one place he feels competent to generalize

---

[11] *Le commentaire*, 108.
[12] *Le commentaire*, 92 (Latin version alone extant).

on the respective merits of Symmachus and the LXX. The opening clause of Ps 56:6 contains an apparent contradiction, which a modern Hebraist will solve by emendation,[13] but in regard to which Theodore's lack of Hebrew leaves him unsure which language is the source of the problem:

> We found this idiom in blessed David in many other places in the psalms as well, either arising from a Hebrew idiom or occurring this way in the translation, namely, the frequent contradiction where it seems he is saying two different things.

He proceeds to make a (rare) appeal to Symmachus, the alternative translator proverbial for his clarity, and balances this asset against the merits of his local text.

> We also compared Symmachus's version of each expression in the divine Scripture with the version of the Seventy, and showed how Symmachus seems to have been using a version of his own. We commented on it for this purpose, to clarify the meaning and to demonstrate that they were not speaking in discord, but actually have a close resemblance in meaning. Now, the difference is between one speaking more clearly by attending to the meaning, on the one hand, and the other in a less verbatim manner wanting to bring out the sense of the Hebrew by more striking expressions, on the other hand, as you can also find in many and almost the majority of places elsewhere as well. Hence, while the Seventy for their part were more anxious indiscriminately to preserve the emphasis in the Hebrew, Symmachus for his part gave signs of attending to clarity, though not in every place reading the text in a manner worthy of his own aspirations, in many places being found at variance with clarity and putting himself in opposition to the meaning.
>
> Hence some commentators, lacking an eye to sequence, believed Symmachus's version superior on the basis of the clarity in what was before them. But if you have an eye to sequence and composition of the sense of the text, you would never prefer another version to that of the Seventy. Not that everything is translated better by them: there are places, in fact, where they offer the weaker version, and sometimes they fall short of the others, who said things more clearly and logically. But in general by comparison with the others they are found far superior even if saying many things less competently. For the student there are many signs of the greater attention to effect by the Seventy and the care for greater clarity by Symmachus.[14]

---

[13] Dahood, *Psalms* 2, 43.
[14] *Le commentaire*, 364–65. Cf. Theodore's comment on Ps 68:33.

It is a comprehensive estimate on the part of one who has shown little deference to the alternative Greek versions. In his next work, furthermore, on the Twelve Prophets, Theodore will forfeit completely the option of consulting them, thus being left to his local text and unable to detect its solecisms, like the LXX's reading *ʽibdi,* "I am a servant (of the Lord)," for *ʽibri,* "I am a Hebrew," in Jonah 1:9. Nor is he prepared in this later work to accept the evidence of the Syriac, his argument this time being an *a priori* one, the uncertain pedigree of the Peshitta relative to the LXX:

> They ought to realise this before everything else, that whereas the contents of the divine Scripture are composed in Hebrew, they were translated into Syriac by somebody or other (his identity is unknown to this day). The translation into Greek, on the other hand, was done by seventy men, elders of the people, possessing a precise knowledge of their own language and a knowledge of the divine Scriptures.[15]

Though clearly aware of the legendary *Letter of Aristeas* (if not its reference to the task of the Seventy as translation of the Torah only), Theodore—typically—does not give his preference to the LXX on the basis of its divine inspiration, as will Theodoret.[16] In short, on the basis of his interest in textual criticism we would hardly be able to support the claim made for Theodore of the title "a forerunner of the modern biblical scholarship."[17]

A similar criterion of the degree of interest in textual resources can hardly be applied to a preacher in estimating his exegetical rigor, a pulpit allowing limited recourse to these, at least off the cuff. In this, Chrysostom is no exception when he delivers homilies on Genesis: in both the short series of eight in 386 and the longer series of sixty seven some years later he makes but one appeal to alternative versions, and at the same point, on the creation of woman. To bring

---

[15] *Theodori Mopsuesteni commentarius,* 283–84. For the *Letter of Aristeas* see Chapter Four.

[16] PG 80.864. Theodore was credited by his critics with a reluctance to concede divine inspiration even to authors of some canonical books; cf. Leontius, *Contra Nestor. et Eutych.* 13–16 (PG 86.1366).

[17] Zaharapoulos, *Theodore of Mopsuestia on the Bible,* 50. Greer, *Theodore of Mopsuestia. Exegete and Theologian,* 99–100, gives Theodore credit as a textual critic, invoking alternative versions including Syriac but preferring LXX as more faithful to the Heb. The Commentary on The Twelve is not cited by these scholars in much detail.

out the unique manner in which the woman is made here, in his sixth sermon he seizes upon a variant version of Gen 2:23.

> *This is now bone of my bones and flesh of my flesh.* Now, some commentators claim that he is suggesting not simply that fact but also the manner of creation, and that by saying *This is now* he suggests that such a genesis would not apply also to a woman—the meaning given by another translator as well in rendering it more precisely "This once," as if to say, Only now is a woman made from a man alone, whereas later it will not be in this manner but from both.[18]

The alternative rendering, highlighting the manner in which this particular woman (only) was formed, is that of Symmachus and Theodotion; and in almost identical terms it is cited in Homily 15 of the longer series. Similarity of passages in both these series is not infrequent, we shall note in Chapter Five, and it may be that the formation of womankind was a matter or particular interest (though it is not among the ζητήματα that Theodoret's "questioner" raises with him in the Questions on the Octateuch, unlike the creation of the angels, a matter of deep interest).

While we are not surprised, then, that a preacher like Chrysostom does not find it appropriate (or convenient) to cite a range of textual resources for the benefit of his congregations on the challenging book of Κτίσις, what does strike a reader of his homilies on the Psalms (if indeed they are homilies), by contrast, is the degree to which he treats his listeners in the διδασκαλεῖρον (classroom—or church?) to a great array of alternative readings, never by name and rarely evaluated. Would the listeners to vv.7–10 of Ps 10 be grateful for all the textual embellishment they were offered by the preacher on these verses, especially as he had earlier made some typically pejorative remarks about "the scholars"?

> *Whose mouth is full of cursing, bitterness and treachery, under their tongue suffering and trouble* (another version, "useless"). *They lie in wait with the rich in ambush so as to slay the innocent* (another, "lying in ambush by the halls"). *Their eyes watch for the needy, they lie in ambush like a lion in his lair* (another, "as in his den"), *they lie in wait to rob the poor, to rob the poor in the act of releasing them* (another, "in release of them"); *in their snare they will humiliate them* (another, "in the net"). *They will stoop and fall down in their act of dominating the poor* (another, "But they will be bruised and bent as

---

[18] SC 433.290–92.2.

they join forces with the strong against the weak"). Do you see them turned into a wild beast?[19]

And on the same psalm, though in haste to complete commentary on what is to him only the second half of a long Ps 9 in the LXX, he insists (sometimes needlessly—and erroneously) on offering the Hebrew; again in haste to get through Ps 46, he still insists on offering textual variants. He will also include "the Septuagint" among the variant readings, as on Ps 7:9–10, evidently referring to that different form of it found in the Hexapla. Are we to imagine the youthful preacher (we offered some indications above of Chrysostom's youth in this work) standing before his audience with an array of material about him as he tries to impress them with his erudition? Or should we accept the suggestion of G. Mercati (relayed to us in Gilles Dorival's similar proposal in reference to Theodoret's Psalm Commentary) that a copyist has later inserted such variant readings?[20] Chrysostom will come to acknowledge his (and his congregations') linguistic limitations, and defer to "those who know Hebrew." And in his homilies on the obscurity of the Old Testament he will impress on his listeners that they are reading only a version of the original, and hence while appreciating that the LXX is a gift from divine providence, they (and himself) must expect some difficulty: "It is not possible to transfer the clarity naturally contained in the words when moving to another language."[21]

Theodoret in the next century brought several exegetical advantages to the task of commentary on the Old Testament. He was already a bishop, not feeling a youthful need to impress with a display of (false) erudition; he was a native Syriac speaker; he was by nature painstaking yet concise; he had an openness to achievements of scholars of another school. Though convinced of the divine inspiration of the LXX, he could fault it, if not always correctly; in his first work, on the Song of Songs, he is wrong to criticize as "a servile rendering of the Hebrew" the phrase in 3:6, "like *a wisp of smoke* exuding myrrh and frankincense," preferring the version of the verse

---

[19] PG 55.137.10. For other examples, see Hill, *St John Chrysostom. Commentary on the Psalms* I, 6–8.

[20] G. Dorival, "L'apport des chaînes exégétiques grecques à une réédition des *Hexaples* d'Origène (à propos du Psaume 118)," 62.

[21] *Omelie*, 116.

by Aquila and Symamchus, who seem to have omitted the phrase. Reference to these alternative versions, which he cites a dozen times in the work, shows his access to a copy of the Hexapla,[22] in which he found also that form of the LXX alternative to his Lucianic text, citing it on 8:6, and also (in connection with 5:11 and 6:12) that further column of Origen referred to as "the fifth edition," another version that Eusebius and Epiphanius claimed he had discovered in Palestine.[23]

Likewise in the Psalms Commentary he will make ample use of the textual resources offered in a copy of the Hexapla. In upholding a singular form he finds in the LXX of Ps 74:3 he says, "Neither the Hebrew, nor the other translators, nor the Septuagint in the Hexapla used the plural 'in the holy places.'" The rogue phrase "of one of the sabbaths" in the title to Ps 24 he seems to attribute to a still further form of the LXX, remarking that he found it in "some copies (ἀντίγραφα), but it does not appear in the Hexapla." Theodoret's use of the versions of The Three has been taken both as an index of his zeal as a textual critic[24] and as so mechanical as to suggest (in the view cited above from Dorival) the later addition of a copyist. In the preface to the Psalms Commentary he examines the interpretation "always" given by Aquila to the puzzling rubric διάψαλμα found in some psalms before declining to accept it on the grounds that "I consider it unjustified to dismiss so many people of such caliber (the Seventy) and rely on the opinion of one single person," yet sometimes his citation of The Three seems mechanical and pointless. If one ignores his failure, like Chrysostom's, to detect the solecisms of the LXX in psalm titles, one might get the impression he had some knowledge of Hebrew from his invoking it frequently enough; but it would take little grasp of that language to enable him to notice phrases in those titles missing from the original (as with Pss 31; 65; 66; 70; 71), as elsewhere it is to Hebrew and Syriac together this Syriac speaker makes reference (cf. Pss 41:1; 68:2; 113:1; 116:9). Theodore would have done well not to cast scorn on that

---

[22] Or to texts citing the alternative versions; cf. note 5 above.

[23] Barthélemy, *Les devanciers*, 266–70, identifies it as a Palestinian revision of some books. Guinot, *L'Exégèse*, 215, attributes mention of it as an index of the degree of Origen's influence on Theodoret, though he shows little effect of Origen's textual criticism (637). It is also cited by Theodoret in connection with Ps 75:6.

[24] So Guinot, *L'Exégèse*, 177–80.

dialect of Aramaic, as Theodoret shows by capitalizing on it often to the benefit of his textual criticism.

This degree of interest in textual issues emerges similarly in Theodoret's other commentaries. His local form of the LXX enjoys his esteem, of necessity and out of his conviction of the divine inspiration of the Seventy; the alternative versions of The Three are frequently cited, but in disputed cases cannot compare, as in a case where their Jewishness makes them suspect. For example, in the Isaiah Commentary he defends the LXX's rendering *'almah* in 7:14 as "virgin."

> Now, I am amazed at the effrontery of Jews in not accepting the prophecy about the virgin; Aquila, Symmachus and Theodotion, they claim, rendered it not *virgin* but "young woman." They ought to have understood, first, that the testimony of the Seventy men is more reliable than that given by three, especially when it enjoys agreement in such a great number. They also have the advantage of trustworthiness from the point of view of time: before the Incarnation of our Savior they transposed the divine Scripture into the Greek tongue without any reason for distortion; in addition to this, there is also the fact that divine grace worked with them to arrive at a consensus. Theodotion, Aquila and Symmachus, on the other hand, translated the divine Scripture after the Lord's coming, and adopting the Jewish mentality they distorted the prophecies about the Lord.[25]

His local form of the LXX can present him with particular problems, as in the case of Ezekiel, where it often capitulates before obscure terms and settles for a transliteration, or makes two attempts at the one phrase (as in 21:30), Theodoret failing to recognize the doublet and commenting on both phrases. In Daniel, on the other hand, it is the text of Theodotion he is commenting on, though seeming to be aware of the LXX text as well; when at 8:2 he finds Theodotion retaining a transliterated Hebrew form (for "river") in its version, "I was at the Ουβαλ," he offers as a paraphrase, "I seemed to be standing at the gate (some translators rendering it this way)," thus revealing he is aware of the LXX's πύλη—but unaware that it is rather Heb. *'abul*, "gate," that the Seventy are (mistakenly) reading. Even his knowledge of Syriac does not allow him to advert to the book's survival partly in Aramaic; and his tight focus on its

---

[25] SC 276.286–88.

puzzling "historical" references discourages him from further interest in textual matters, the alternative versions rarely cited. Their
being omitted also in our text of the Jeremiah Commentary may be
attributable to its peculiar process of transmission, as outlined in
Chapter Five.

Although the Questions are a work of his declining years, Theodoret
retains his interest in textual detail and his willingness to deal with
it. If in the Questions on the Octateuch he invokes Syriac only once,
the alternative Greek versions are cited often, sometimes to excess.
In Q.1 on Leviticus dealing with the burnt offering of birds in 1:17
in the course of a long account of Jewish sacrifices, he goes to the
trouble of explaining,

> Now, for 'crop' Theodotion put 'gullet' and Aquila 'oesophagus;' it
> receives the food and conveys it to the rest of the body—hence the
> Septuagint's calling it 'crop' in being a receptacle for food.[26]

Readers could have felt the anatomical detail itself to be otiose, let
alone a range of translations. Even an obscure translator, by name
Josephus (not the historian), is cited on 2 Sam 13:18 in connection
with the robe worn by Tamar, the aim always being "to make clear
to readers what requires clarification." To this end Theodoret even
accesses a lexicon of Hebrew terms; in the incident in 1 Sam 20:20
when Jonathan conveys information to David by shooting arrows at
a "target," Theodoret finds the term transliterated in his text, but
refers to other resources:

> The term αματαραν I found occurring in that form in the lexicon of
> Hebrew words, as τάφρος (trench) in Greek, as *fossatum* in Latin, and
> as *skopos* in Syriac, for what those practicing archery normally aim at.[27]

It is an impressive array of textual resources, including (beyond the
Antiochene text) the form of the LXX in the Hexapla, the Peshitta
and even the (Old) Latin (or Vulgate?), consulted by a commentator lacking but one critical asset in treating of the text of the Old
Testament, namely, a knowledge of Hebrew.

---

[26] *Theodoreti Cyrensis Quaestiones in Octateuchum*, 156.
[27] *Theodoreti Cyrensis Quaestiones in Reges et Paralipomena*, 44.

B. Authorship and text history

In pursuit of the exegetical goal formulated by Theodoret, and most assiduously striven for by him in textual matters, as "making clear to readers what requires clarification" in Old Testament material, biblical commentators have examined as well the history of the text and its author(s). Centuries of investigation have led modern exegetes to suspect that the superficial impression of the final form of a biblical work being the original work of a single author belies the facts of a history of development involving many anonymous hands. They have thus been encouraged to examine a biblical (or any ancient) text for signs of multiple authorship, also searching behind the purported or pseudonymous author for clues to the identity of the real author(s). As well, the text in its final form may bear indications of later editing or assembling of diverse elements by a compiler, such that layers are detectable in the material, sometimes giving rise to discrepancies in detail. Those who approach a biblical text, however, with a deep conviction of the involvement also of a divine author are naturally loath to peer beyond the surface for all these clues to human tampering.[28] Though exegesis and interpretation at Antioch were conspicuous for an attachment to the text, its author and its roots in history, by comparison with commentators of another school who stayed at this level only as long as necessary before moving to a level removed from history, the Antiochene commentators in our period differed in their degree of readiness to take account of the history of the text itself.

In his extant work, the Commentary on the Psalms, Diodore admits he is to some extent transmitting what "I also in my own case had received from others."[29] Among these predecessors in Antioch would have figured the bishop Eustathius whom we saw taking Origen to task for attending to terms, ὀνόματα, rather than facts, πράγματα, that is, for an approach that used the text and its history only as a

---

[28] Ecclesiastical authorities, e.g., can resist such findings; cf. the response of Rome's Pontifical Biblical Commission in 1908 to a question about the possibility of recognizing multiple authorship in the book of Isaiah: "In the negative" (*Rome and the Study of Scripture*, St Meinrad: Grail Publications, 121). This conservative attitude contrasts with the more informed and positive approach of the same body's (1964 Instruction on the Historical Truth of the Gospels and) 2001 statement bearing on the Old Testament, *The Jewish People and their Sacred Scriptures in the Christian Bible*, Vatican City: Libreria Editrice Vaticana.

[29] *Commentarii*, 4.

springboard to move to senses beyond the factual. Whether rationalist, or simply "raisonnable" as Bardy prefers,[30] Diodore combines a belief in the Psalms' composition solely by the divinely-inspired David with a denial of authenticity to their titles, as we note in Chapter four. When the title of Ps 39 makes mention of Jeduthun, he dismisses the possibility that this attribution may involve authorship:

> It is likely that it was given by David to Jeduthun, a Temple singer, for singing—though the composition of the psalms was by David and no one else.

On the other hand, he wants to allow for reference in certain psalms to historical events up to the time of the Maccabees; while he gratuitously sees Ps 14 referring to the eighth century events involving Sennacherib and the Rabshakeh, far from letting the possibility arise that this could suggest multiple authors of the Psalms at various times, he simply observes,

> Now, it is worth marveling at the grace given to David of foretelling so many years before not only the events but also people's ways of thinking at that time.

The actual compilation of his Psalter, however, he does allow to have taken place in the course of history; the present order of the psalms, he says in accord with 2 Esdras 14, arises

> from the book's being lost in the Babylonian captivity and found later in the time of Ezra, not however as a whole book but scattered in ones and twos and perhaps also threes, and being assembled as they were found, not as originally recited.[31]

Further, the psalm titles lack any authenticity—an opinion most patristic commentators did not share.[32]

In his own work on the Psalter, Diodore's dutiful student Theodore predictably relays the positions he had received from his mentor. David was in receipt of divine inspiration in composing all the psalms, he insists, developing even further the traditional analogy of such a charism based on the opening verses of Ps 45, as we saw in Chapter Three. Yet the titles are not worth taking seriously, and are consistently ignored by him; on Ps 51 he remarks,

---

[30] "Diodore," 991.
[31] Commentarii, 6.
[32] Cf. R. E. Heine, Gregory of Nyssa's Treatise on the Inscriptions of the Psalms, 3–5.

At no stage have we given the impression of being dictated to by the titles, accepting only those we found to be true; and we said as much about this as was necessary in the preface before commentary on the text.[33]

While on his principles he would not admit interpolations in the text, the youthful Theodore is happy on the basis merely of sequence, ἀκολουθία, to re-arrange the psalmist's text; in his view the movement of thought in Ps 75:3 is interrupted because

the phrase *The earth was wasted* is inserted in the middle, the prophet making the insertion with a view to the metre[34]

—a rash claim in view of his ignorance of the language of the original.

There is a similar dissonance in his next work, on the Twelve Prophets, between an elevated notion of prophetic inspiration, on the one hand, and a readiness to make his own adjustment to the text of a prophet if it disappoints his expectations, on the other. In Chapter Three we saw Theodore, on meeting the word for prophetic oracle, λῆμμα, in his text of Nahum 1:1, and doubtless under the influence of his contemporary Didymus in Alexandria, briefly accepting a notion of ecstatic possession of biblical authors not generally acceptable to Antioch thinking. When he comes to Jonah, by contrast, his failure to grasp the author's satirical purpose compels him to embellish the text of 3:4 about the reluctant prophet's call for repentance in Nineveh (the LXX exacerbating his unease by reading "Three days more" instead of "Forty" under the influence of the previous verse). So he rewrites the text (as Theodoret will do when he similarly finds unacceptable Paul's teaching on the gratuity of divine mercy).

The verse, *The men of Nineveh believed in God*, also brings out that he did not carelessly say only, *Three days more, and Nineveh will be destroyed*: they could never have believed in God on the basis of this remark alone, from a completely unknown foreigner threatening them with destruction and adding nothing further, not even letting the listeners know by whom he was sent. Rather, it is obvious he also mentioned God, the Lord of all, and said he had been sent by him; and he delivered the message of destruction, calling them to repentance.[35]

---

[33] *Le commentaire*, 334. That preface is not extant.
[34] *Le commentaire*, 502.
[35] *Theodori Mopsuesteni commentarius*, 186. Cf. Hill, "Theodoret wrestling with Romans."

There are limits to respect for the biblical text; defects—and consequent emendation—are not entirely out of the question.

Though one does not expect a preacher on biblical texts to spend time in his pulpit discussing exegetical detail with his generally unlettered congregation (it was conceded above), he may be expected to have formed an opinion, which occasionally escapes him, especially if he has been schooled at the feet of a biblical critic. On the Psalms, Chrysostom did more than betray his views on the inspiration of biblical authors, taking occasion from commentary on that invitation in the opening of Ps 45, "My heart belched a good word, I tell of my works to the king, my tongue the pen of a rapid scribe." While at first toying with the notion of ecstatic possession, we saw in Chapter Three, he rejected it as akin to Plato's description of the pagan seers, μάντεις, and moved to an almost extremely opposite position of authorial composition as a journeyman job, "like a shipwright building a ship"—a notion that might allow for an author's assemblage of materials from various quarters, though Chrysostom does not proceed to follow that line. On the other hand, he does not evince any spirit of rationalist criticism imbibed from master Diodore: he not only accepts the psalm titles, but spends time treating them (not as mere liturgical rubrics, but) as relevant components that need—despite his inability to detect LXX solecisms—explicating. So his congregation is treated at the opening to Ps 5 to a lengthy disquisition on inheritances under (the LXX's and) his own mistaken impression that the term in the title derives, not from Heb. *nehiloth*, "flutes," but from *nahal*, "inherit." It is noteworthy, however, that after the block of Pss 120–34 classed as "Songs of the Steps (or Ascent)" that are attributed to the people in exile, though the name David continues to appear in later psalms, Chrysostom ceases mentioning him or commenting on the titles, perhaps having had his conviction of their Davidic authorship weakened. In the sermons on Genesis, on the other hand, perhaps harking from the same period, Moses is unquestionably the inspired author of that text, as he states in a striking simile in the first of them.

> At the beginning, then, God communicates directly with human beings as far as it is possible for human beings to hear. This is the way he came to Adam, this the way he rebuked Cain, this the way he spoke with Noah, this the way he was entertained by Abraham. But since our nature took a turn for evil, and separated itself by a lengthy exile, as it were, at long last he sent us letters as though we were absent for a long time and he intended to re-establish the former friendship

through an epistle. While it was God who sent the letters, it was Moses
who brought them.[36]

He will repeat the figure to the same effect in the eighth sermon
(the letter now an imperial edict) and in Homily 2 on this book.
Letters and edicts, of course, are accepted without question.

Although his preaching role in the tradition of the faith in Antioch
encouraged him to apply the Bible to the lives of his congregation—
a feature we find missing in the commentaries coming from the desks
of his fellow Antiochenes, as will be noted in Chapter Ten—this
moral dimension has been seen as militating against a critical spirit.[37]
Beryl Smalley cites Julian of Eclanum's summation a generation later
that Chrysosom proceeds "rather by exhortation than by exposition;"
and it has become customary to agree with her that though "he was
by far the best known representative of Antiochene principles in the
West," he was "at the same time the author who could teach his
readers least about Antiochene exegesis."[38] We saw him passing off
different creation stories in his Genesis homilies as mere repetition
on the Spirit's part, and his attempts to reconcile Cainite and Sethite
genealogies in Gen 4 & 5 (which modern commentators, resting
upon a document hypothesis, would distinguish as Yahwist and
Priestly, respectively). In Homily 20 he takes seriously the listeners'
presumed difficulty about the unnamed wives of Cain and his descendants in Gen 4, a text that is concerned simply with "tracing the
generations between Noah and Adam,"[39] not supplying personal his-
tories. While in his homily on Jer 10:23 and its (and other verses')
frequent misapplication he insists on the need to give attention to
"the whole context, to whom it refers, by whom, in connection with
whom, for what reason, when and how,"[40] he cannot be quoted for

---

[36] SC 433.143–50.1.

[37] Cf. the estimate of Photius in the ninth century: "Now, it is not surprising if
his attention to some of the expressions or interpretation or depth of insight was
careless; after all, he never at any stage neglected what the ability of the listeners
dictated and had relevance to their benefit and welfare" (*Bibliotheca* 174).

[38] *The Study of the Bible in the Middle Ages*, 18. Extant OT works of the respective
commentators do not completely support the verdict of Maurice Wiles, "Theodore
of Mopsuestia as a representative of the Antiochene school," 490: "Where Chrysostom
is essentially the preacher who makes use of the work of biblical interpretation,
Theodore is first and foremost biblical scholar and commentator." A less pastoral
manner at one's desk does not necessarily ensure a more critical approach.

[39] E. A. Speiser, *Genesis*, 36. Theodoret finds the issue still a burning one in Q.43
of his Questions on the Octateuch, and treats it at the same level.

[40] PG 56.156.2.

looking at the history *of* the text itself. A letter sent by God through nominated emissaries has not been subject to tampering in the course of delivery.[41] Just such an analysis as he recommends in the case of the Jeremiah text, however, Chrysostom's (eventual) listeners to his commentary/notes on Proverbs would have appreciated. He struggles to find meaning, let alone a sequence, in the series of disjointed items in "The proverbs of Solomon" (Prv 10–22), rendered more obscure by the faulty LXX translation; some remarks on the manner in which this collections of collections was compiled may have allowed his listeners (and the commentator himself) to desist from looking for a pattern—but no such guidance on the history of the text is forthcoming.

It is perhaps an index of Origen's influence in his Commentary on the Song of Songs at the beginning of his career that Theodoret shows an interest in the history of the text of that work and the Old Testament generally. Defending the Song against charges of factuality, on the one hand, and of unbridled eroticism, on the other, Theodoret in his preface traces its composition from Solomon through a rewriting by Ezra ("filled with the divine Spirit") following loss of the book at the hands of Manasseh. In this he is following an account found in 2 Esdras 14, which in Theodoret's view is a canonical work, "ranked by the blessed Fathers with the divine Scriptures."[42] His historical criticism, however, is fitful: though in that same preface he speaks of "psalmists" in the plural, he accepts the order of the sapiential books in the order in which they occur in the LXX to indicate order of composition (as well as parting company with Origen to accept Pauline authorship of Hebrews). Never one to shirk an exegetical challenge, Theodoret finds another in his next work on Daniel. He accepts it as a single, continuous, original work by one author; collection of previously existing haggadic tales is not an admissible view, nor is editorial insertion. The most he is prepared to admit is the difference in style after chapter 6 between those tales and the revelations, ἀποκαλύψεις, of the remainder; he comments at that halfway point,

---

[41] Kelly, *Golden Mouth*, 95, overstates the effect of Chrysostom's (and the Fathers' generally) conviction of inspiration of the biblical authors: "This assumption effectively blocked any open-minded examination of the bible."

[42] PG 81.29–32.

> Having recounted those things as a historian (συγγραφεύς), as it were, he now begins to convey the predictions he learnt about through the revelations.[43]

The anomaly of the author also being the central character he generally bypasses, forced to address it only when the text immediately presents Daniel and the young men in a favorable light:

> He mentions their self-control and sound values, not indulging in self-glorification but proposing a beneficial lesson to those prepared to accept benefit

—so there is no problem.[44]

While in the preface to his work on the Song Theodoret had been able to speak in passing of psalmists in the plural, the question of authorship naturally arises in addressing the Psalter. Some psalm titles suggest authorship by others like Jeduthun, Ethan or the Sons of Korah, he notes, which some predecessors had accepted;

> but I for my part have no strong view on these points: what does it matter to me whether all come from (David) or some come from them, as long as it is clear that they all composed under the influence of the divine Spirit.

While with typical flexibility allowing for alternative views, he applies a conservative (and uncritical) criterion: "Let the judgement of the majority prevail: most historians say the Psalms are David's." He is strangely less flexible about the psalm titles—"I consider it rash and quite foolhardy to brand them as spurious"—but prepared to admit that "people of a later age fixed the order" of the psalms.[45]

Prophetic material in the Old Testament poses several critical judgements for a commentator. As Theodoret had admitted lack of an original order of psalms in the Psalter, so he was prepared to concede it also in the case of the oracles in Ezekiel.[46] In comment on Jeremiah 31:34 he recognizes the work of compilers of prophetic oracles to be distinct from their authors: "It is customary with the divine Scripture to mix the prophecies together."[47] Though he could

---

[43] PG 81.1412.
[44] On Dan 1:5–6 (PG 81.1276).
[45] PG 80.861–64. Theodoret is equally flexible (and undiscriminating) on the authorship of Ps 73, "A psalm for Asaph," when he comes to comment on it.
[46] On Ezek 30:20 (PG 81.1116).
[47] PG 81.668.

not acknowledge multiplicity of authorship in the book of Isaiah, he does allow (in commenting on 51:9) for an editor's final collection of material composed at different periods:

> It must be understood, of course, that former and latter prophecies were not made at the one time; rather, some were made at one time, others at another, and later they were put together to form one book.[48]

The book of Jeremiah presents commentators with many texts whose history is complicated and debated, but where Theodoret cannot allow himself to become distracted. On 16:1–9 bearing on Jeremiah's prophetic celibacy, for instance, a modern commentaror like W. McKane summarises possible approaches thus:

> It is doubtful whether the right way of approaching 16.1–9 is to distinguish between a Jeremianic core and a Deuteronomistic elaboration of that core (Rudolph, Thiel, Nicholson), or to suppose that these verses are entirely Jeremianic (Weiser, Weippert) and give us direct access to a stance of the historical prophet Jeremiah.[49]

Theodoret, by contrast (at least in the text we have), is content to reduce the passage to a precis.

Questions about τὰ ἄπορα of the Octateuch often focused on textual discrepancies arising from a complicated process of composition and editing that left loose ends and suggested different layers. In his replies Theodoret generally does not read the clues to that effect: the title Deuteronomy means not a second law, he explains,[50] but suggests that the book "contains a summary of the legislation and the doings in Exodus, Leviticus and Numbers" for those who had grown up in the wilderness and did not hear the first one; there are more curses than blessings in Deut 27–28, not because of an interpolation or the impact of the exile on a Deuteronomistic editor, but because "promises of freedom do not benefit wicked servants to the same extent as threats of chastisement;" Balaam's changes of heart in Num 22–24 are not due to any difference in authorship. It is true that Moses as author of those books is presented here in various literary roles (beyond lawgiver, νομοθέτης)—as inspired author,

---

[48] SC 315.122.

[49] Jeremiah 1–25, 362, 367.

[50] Cf. A. Siquans, Der Deuteronomiumkommentar des Theodoret von Kyros, 98–101, for a range of patristic comments on the nature of the book.

προφήτης, like the psalmist and (latter) prophets, as simple composer
(not necessarily uninspired), συγγραφεύς, as historian/chronicler/annal-
ist, ἱστοριογραφός—which might be taken as a code for a reserved
admission of multiple authorship. At times, on the other hand, he
has no choice but to concede the point: citation from a book of
Jashar by the author of Josh 10:13 leads him to conclude rightly,
"It is clear from this that somebody else of a later age had written
this book, taking the material from another book." Judg 1:8 speaks
of the people taking Jerusalem, whereas 2 Sam 5:6–9 attributes to
David the capture of Jebus, later re-named Jerusalem; profiting from
this further exercise in tradition criticism, Theodoret again concludes,

> I believe this book was written later, my evidence being that the nar-
> rative refers to this city as Jerusalem, a name it had later after being
> called Jebus.[51]

The concession comes more easily to him in the case of Chronicles
because he is no longer dealing with προφῆται, original authors, but
with the compilers, συγγεγραφότες, who felt free to incorporate the
formers' work simply as leftovers, παραλειπόμενα—hence the title of
the work in the LXX.

While we possess only fragments of Diodore's Questions on the
Octateuch, we have grounds enough in the work of his followers for
discouraging any wish to "heroicize"[52] the school of Antioch as exegetical in the strict sense; in Chapter Eight we shall examine whether
their interpretative skills—probably the true focus of that general-
ization—measure up to such a claim. As founder of the school,
Diodore could not match Origen's interest in the text of the Old
Testament, only Theodoret in a later age profiting from it (principally through Eusebius).[53] Attention by the Antiochenes to textual

---

[51] *Theodoreti Cyrensis Quaestiones in Octateuchum*, 280, 289–90.

[52] Cf. R. E. Brown, "Hermeneutics," *NJBC*, 1154: "The exegetical school of
Antioch has been too naively heroicized as the champion of critical exegesis." It
might alternatively be claimed that Antiochene exegesis/hermeneutics has been
undervalued on the basis of theological prejudice. Edwin Hatch, *The Influence of Greek
Ideas on Christianity*, 82, claims of our period that "the question of exegesis became
entangled with the question of orthodoxy."

[53] The role played by Eusebius in mediating Origen's thought has been thought
most influential in the case of the Antiochenes, as Viciano maintains (citing Manlio
Simonetti), "Das formale Verfahren," 399: "Der Einfluß des Eusebius von Cäsarea
auf die Antiochener is so gros daß man von einem 'eusebianischen Kriterium' in
ihrer exegetischen Technik reden kann."

details of the works they were reading was generally fitful, even unin-
formed, especially considering their linguistic limitations; again they
were indebted to Origen for any use of the resources offered in the
Hexapla. A ministry of the spoken Word, as in the case of Chrysostom
in his pulpit, also discouraged textual analysis. Their deep conviction of the divine inspiration of the authors of Old Testament books,
προφῆται, was also generally (if not a "blockage," in Kelly's term) a
deterrent from scrutiny into diversity of authorship and layers of
composition of these letters sent by God and delivered by Moses or
David; the history *in* a text was of greater relevance than the history *of* that text. While Theodoret will admit that prophetic oracles
may have been assembled after a prophet's ministry, he is less ready
to recognize from textual discrepancies in Octateuch or Kingdoms
layers in a text deriving from redactional or editorial work. We
should now take stock of the degree to which these Antiochene commentators did present to their flock the principal bodies of Old
Testament composition.

CHAPTER SIX

OLD TESTAMENT COMMENTARY IN ANTIOCH

For all its Jewish character, its inevitable or intentional obscurity, the Old Testament was introduced to the Christian community in Antioch in the process of tradition of the faith. In the view of the commentators, such an introduction to these Jewish scriptures was essential for a grasp of Antioch's worldview. It was read aloud in a liturgy of the Word in church according to a lectionary no longer known to us; it was read privately to the family in the intimacy of the Christian home; it formed the subject of homiletics and catechesis at various stages of Christian formation. This ready acceptance of Jewish scriptures was due to the recognition of "a kinship of the Law with grace," and of a consensus and harmony between the testaments Old and New. In both, God communicated his revelation through a process of ὁμιλία in which could be seen a gracious gesture of συγκατάβασις akin to that visible in the Incarnation of the Word in the person of Jesus. For all its obscurity, the faithful felt at ease with the Old Testament, and resisted attempts by Marcionites and other dualists to have it expunged from the scriptures sacred to the community. "All scripture is inspired by God and useful for teaching," Diodore quoted from 2 Tim 3:16 in beginning his Commentary on the Psalter;[1] and the author of the Pastorals in that text meant primarily, if not exclusively, the scriptures inherited from and shared with the Jewish community—even if "the interpretation is ours."[2]

We should now, therefore, examine the extent of commentary on these texts bequeathed to us by the Antiochenes that has survived the ravages of time, leaving to Chapter Seven an analysis of their characteristic approach to the task of commentary. We should begin,

---

[1] *Commentarii*, 3.

[2] Cf. Chrysostom's second sermon on Genesis (SC 433.188.1): "While the books are from them, the treasure of the books now belongs to us; if the text is from them, both text and meaning belong to us."

as they did, with the Psalms, on which we fortunately have commentary by all four major commentators: Diodore, Theodore,
Chrysostom and Theodoret. Commentary on the prophets, if less
complete, is still substantial. Even less complete is attention to the
Octateuch and the historical books, while we only have individual
commentaries (by Theodoret or Chrysostom) on the Song of Songs,
Job and Proverbs.

A. PSALMS

Of all the Old scriptures it was the Psalter that was felt to have a
claim to pride of place in a pastoral—and exegetical[3]—scale of priorities. The liturgy regularly included (verses from) a psalm for recitation, if not for singing, by lector and congregation. We know from
Chrysostom that the opening verse of Ps 42 was customarily sung
as a responsorium, ὑπακοή, and that while in the case of Ps 118 he
felt free to nominate v.6 for singing, he admits that at Easter time
"the Fathers prescribed the singing" of v.24, "This is the day the
Lord has made, let us rejoice and be glad."[4] Even in their private
lives, Theodoret tells us,

> you can find most people making little or no reference to the other
> divine Scriptures, whereas the spiritual harmonies of the divinely-
> inspired David many people frequently call to mind, whether at home,
> in public places or while traveling, gain serenity for themselves from
> the harmony of the poetry, and reap benefit for themselves through
> this enjoyment.[5]

The consequence of this pride of place was that budding exegetes
of the time considered it incumbent on them early in their career

---

[3] The Psalter even in the original language is conceded to offer an extraordinary degree of difficulty to exegetes; further, in the view of a commentator on its
linguistic features, M. Dahood, *Psalms* 1, xxiv–xxvi, versions like the LXX "are not
always reliable witnesses to what the biblical poets intended." Dahood himself finds
it necessary to have recourse to Ugaritic to decipher some of the linguistic chal-
lenges of the Psalter—a resource not available to commentators in Antioch in our
period.

[4] PG 55.328.1. On Ps 145 he speaks of initiates (probably in the course of a
eucharistic liturgy) singing as an antiphon v.15, "You give them food in due sea-
son," whereas his listeners in the classroom, διδασκαλεῖον, are said to "read" the
psalm (PG 55.464.1).

[5] *Praef.* (PG 80.860).

to offer their flock some explication of these ancient, and often obscure, poems. We are the beneficiaries of this patristic estimation of the importance of the Psalter (surpassed only by the Gospels); Marie-Josèphe Rondeau lists eighteen Greek commentaries from the third to the fifth centuries.[6] Included among them are the works— oral and written—of all four Antiochenes in our period, all happily extant (if only partly in Greek in the case of Theodore, and not all critically edited).

Even if but the merest fragments survive of commentary by Eustathius,[7] we are particularly fortunate to have the Psalms Commentary of Diodore, as it is his sole fully extant work in Greek from an output that embraced all the Old Testament, and because his influence is patent in his pupils' commentaries.[8] Whether it was his first work is uncertain; it bears the marks of his period as director of the asketerion in Antioch before his becoming bishop of Tarsus in 378, the readers being the "brethren," ἀδελφοί, and the tone and stance magisterial. Mention is apparently made of the persecution during Julian's time in Antioch in 362–63 during which Diodore distinguished himself by his vigorous opposition, for which he was banished by Julian's successor Valens in 372.[9] Diodore is familiar with alternate recitation of psalm verses in monastic style, perhaps in vogue in the *askêtêrion*; in comment on Ps 24 (still similarly recited as an invitatory psalm in modern breviaries) he remarks,

> Since such verses had to be recited antiphonally, he gives the other response in the form of a question, *Who is this king of glory?* (v.8) They then utter their part in response, *A Lord mighty and powerful, a Lord powerful in war.*[10]

---

[6] *Les commentaires patristiques du Psautier (IIIe–Ve siècles)*, 1 *Les travaux des pères grecs et latin sur le Psautier. Recherches et bilan.* Rondeau lists also eight major Latin commentaries and eight minor.

[7] Cf. Quasten, *Patrology* 3, 304.

[8] Cf. Hill, "His Master's Voice: Theodore of Mopsuestia on the Psalms."

[9] In comment on Ps 19:12–13 Diodore remarks (*Commentarii*, 116), "By *hidden sins* he refers to the situation with lust in which we are overcome, and by *external influences* to what befalls us unexpectedly from without, normally called accidental by externs—or rather, to put it more plainly, what befalls us by way of temptation and an onset of the devil, as for example what happened in the case of the martyrs. When all of a sudden persecution came upon them in a time of tranquillity, then they fell under the power of the authorities, then they were subjected to torture and often, though having good intentions, they succumbed to the great number of tortures and fell into the indeliberate sin of denial."

[10] *Commentarii*, 142. J.-M. Olivier, editor of the first fifty one psalms (CCG 6), is

The preface also lays out prescriptively in textbook fashion the principles of interpretation to be followed in the case of any such biblical text, which we shall consider in detail in Chapter Eight.

Though Diodore is familiar with the singing of the Psalms, he speaks of them primarily as a text, not as songs. They have an instructive and moral value (hence his citation of 2 Tim 3:16–17), to a lesser degree doctrinal or ascetical: there may be people who recite them in times of joy, but for life's inevitable sorrows the Psalms are "a most helpful remedy." As we shall see in Chapter Ten, mystical rapture by those who read and pray the Psalms is not envisaged by Antiochene pastors, nor do they feel called to act as spiritual gurus.[11] While authorship of the Psalms is not up for debate (he is no rationalist, Bardy warned us above),[12] he is quite dismissive of the psalm titles:

> The psalms' titles, on the other hand, are quite ridiculous, and you would be unable to control yourself if you considered the superficiality of the titles.[13]

This is due, he says, to the way the "book of Psalms" (Diodore and other Antiochenes are unaware of a five-fold division) was compiled, haphazardly.

> The psalms have incurred this problem from the book's being lost in the Babylonian captivity and found later in the time of Ezra, not however as a whole book but scattered in ones and twos and perhaps also threes, and being assembled as they were found, not as originally recited. Hence the titles, too, are in most cases faulty, the compilers of the psalms mostly guessing at their connection and not placing them by meaning.[14]

---

not expected to complete the critical edition of Diodore's work. Much of Olivier's introduction is devoted to establishing Diodore's authorship of this work that appears in the best manuscript (for political reasons) under the name of Anastasius III, metropolitan of Nicea. Only Devreesse remains unconvinced; Olivier will return the compliment by voicing reservations about the transmission of the Psalms Commentary of Theodore edited by Devreesse.

[11] Cf. Hill, "Diodore of Tarsus as spiritual director."

[12] Diodore, 991.

[13] *Commentarii*, 170.

[14] *Commentarii*, 6. Such a role for Ezra is mentioned by Origen and Eusebius. Theodoret in introducing his commentary on the Song of Songs will expand it to involve actual composition of the lost Scriptures (on the basis of 2 Esdras 14; cf. Chapter Two).

The further significance of this and other aspects of the work will be explored in the following chapters on Antiochene, commentary and hermeneutics.

It may have been from Diodore that his most dutiful pupil Theodore took the lead to make a commentary on the Psalter his first work, too; in the absence of the preface he wrote we have the word of Facundus of Hermianae on its pride of place,[15] and a less objective statement as to the author's age from Leontius of Byzantium, "The fellow was no more than eighteen years of age when he took to subjecting the divine Scriptures to drunken abuse."[16] Certainly his next work, on The Twelve, contains documentation almost exclusively from the Psalter; and certainly also the Psalms Commentary shows signs of immaturity. He adopts a somewhat superior attitude: false claims of semitic science are made, chasing up textual details to background his text—a strength of Theodoret's—is beneath him, and (admittedly with Diodore's encouragement) the psalm titles are ignored ("at no stage have we given the impression of being dictated to by the titles, accepting only those we found to be true," he remarks on Ps 51). Predecessors' views are curtly dismissed, as in the case of the title to Ps 8 containing the intriguing Heb. term *Gittith* in which the LXX saw the word *Gat* for "winepress," eliciting some earlier comments which Theodore bypasses with some hauteur,

> Be this true or false, however, there seems no particular need for us to settle this, because we are interested rather in arriving at the psalm's meaning.

He had still to learn that dependence solely on one's mentor does not make for sound commentary: hard work and a little humility are also necessary if one is to earn the title The Interpreter. Still, we regret that we do not have more of the Commentary extant: Devreesse assembles from the catenae Pss 1–31 in a fifth century Latin version, then in Greek Pss 33–61—"une série d'extraits équivalents à une tradition directe, ou même une exégèse continue"[17]— and Pss 62–81 also in Greek.

---

[15] *Pro defensione trium capitulorum* 3, 6 (PL 67.602).

[16] *Contra Nestor. et Eutych.* 8 (PG 86.1364.8)—though Rondeau finds this "une exagération malveillante" (*Les commentaires* I, 103–104).

[17] *Le commentaire de Théodore de Mopsueste sur les psaumes*, xv.

There is internal evidence that the Psalms Commentary of Diodore's
other pupil Chrysostom, too, was a work of his (relative) youth. He
is given to that youthful display of false erudition we see in Theodore's
Commentary, somewhat pointlessly citing alternative versions and
even venturing to quote the Hebrew—sometimes erroneously, as we
saw above—whereas in his Homily Four on Genesis he will be content with a simple admission of ignorance, "Those who know that
language say . . ." But, as did Photius in the ninth century, we have
to admit that "we are not yet in a position to know anything about
the historical circumstances of the commentaries on the Psalms,"[18]
apart from making a case that they were in fact delivered as homilies to a group in a classroom in Antioch, perhaps after 386 and
before Chrysostom's appointment to Constantinople in 397.[19] His
biographer Dom Baur disputes the oral character of the homilies on
the grounds that we do not have both speaker's text and stenogra-
pher's copy, and that they lack "an appearance of actuality."[20] These
are stringent requirements to establish orality; spontaneity, which can
after all be manufactured, is an unreliable index of orality of texts.
From the knowledge we have of ancient stenographic resources, as
has been cited above in the case or Origen's homilies, I have argued
that the fifty eight pieces show Chrysostom at his youthful best as
an orator, rising at times to the heights, even if they do not qualify as "by far the best of his homilies on the books of the Old
Testament."[21] Why it is that not all psalms are included in the present collection (beginning at Ps 4) is unclear; homilists generally leave
no preface. The liturgy offered the preacher in Antioch other oppor-
tunities to treat of (verses from) individual psalms, his preaching giving him the liberty of greater expansiveness than written commentaries
and of applying the psalmists' sentiments to listeners' lives (a feature
conspicuously missing from the other Antiochenes).[22]

---

[18] *Bibliotheca* 174. Photius attributes the (youthful?) expansiveness rather to
Chrysostom's composing the homilies "while at leisure rather than involved in public affairs."

[19] The date is that of Rondeau, *Les commentaires* I, 130. (Is it possible Chrysostom's
διδασκαλεῖον is in fact a church? The occasion is clearly non-eucharistic.)

[20] C. Baur, *John Chrysostom and His Times* I, 222. A reader of Theodoret's
Commentary on Ezekiel (of ch. 28, e.g.) occasionally gets the impression of orality.

[21] Quasten, *Patrology* 3, 435. Cf. Hill, "Chrysostom, interpreter of the Psalms;"
"Chrysostom's Commentary on the Psalms: homilies or tracts?"; *St John Chrysostom.
Commentary on the Psalms* 1, 1–41.

[22] Cf. Hill, "Ps 41(42), a classic text for Antiochene spirituality;" *St John Chrysostom.
Old Testament Homilies* 3.

In the next generation Theodoret, too, acknowledged a sense of obligation to begin his exegetical career with a Psalms Commentary, pleading (in a possibly conventional justification) popular demand as the reason for allowing other books to receive prior attention.

> It would have been a pleasure for me to do a commentary on the inspired composition of the mighty David prior to the other divine sayings, especially since the students of religion, both city dwellers and in the country, have all given their attention to this work in particular . . . I wanted to do a commentary on this piece of inspired composition first of all, and offer to discerning investors the profit lying hidden in its depths, so that they might sing its melodies and at the same time recognize the sense of the words they sing, thus reaping a double dividend. But we were prevented from putting this desire into effect by those who requested from us commentaries on the other divine Scriptures.[23]

And so the bishop of Cyrus had already commented on the Song of Songs, Daniel, Ezekiel and the Twelve Prophets before coming to the Psalms in the 440s. There is thus no sign of the immaturity of a Theodore or a Chrysostom in his approach, nor does he feel constrained to adopt the narrowly historical approach of the *Ioudaiophrôn* in confining a Christological character to only four of the Psalms; instead, like his Isaiah Commentary, this work bears the mark of predecessors beyond Antioch, such as Eusebius.[24] Like Chrysostom, on the other hand, he will ignore the sage advice of Diodore against taking the psalm titles seriously, thus falling foul of the LXX's misreading of Hebrew musical directions found there. Despite Rondeau's claim that Theodore "peut aisément recourir à l'original sémitique,"[25] the only linguistic advantage he displays over his fellow Antiochenes is his native Syriac, which occasionally allows him to divine more closely the sense of the original, as in the case of Ps 68, "widely admitted as textually and exegetically the most difficult and obscure

---

[23] *Praef.* (PG 80.857).

[24] Cf. J.-N. Guinot, "La cristallisation d'un différend: Zorobabel dans l'exégèse de Théodore de Mopsueste et de Théodoret de Cyr," 546: "Theodore paraît appliquer sans grande souplesse les principes d'herméneutique hérités de Diodore de Tarse et donne, de manière un peu systématique, à son exégèse, une orientation vetéro-testamentaire. Théodoret, à l'inverse, tout en restant fidèle aux principes antiochiens, ouvre sans hésiter son exégèse sur le temps de l'Incarnation et la période néo-testamentaire; il rejoint ainsi l'ensemble de la tradition patristique dont il se veut l'héritier."

[25] *Les commentateurs* 1, 136.

of all the psalms."[26] As a commentator, on the other hand, Theodoret excels for his conciseness (where Theodore can be prolix) and his flexibility in respect of views of predecessors or even studious readers,[27] as we shall see.

B. Prophets

While no other part of the Old or New Testament provides us with such a substantial corpus of comment from Antioch as the Psalter, we are told that "the Antiochenes were fascinated with prophecy."[28] Perhaps, rather, prophecy represented a challenge to Antioch's historicism. The pity is that only two of the major figures have left us with any complete commentary on these Latter Prophets, in the terminology of the Hebrew Bible. Despite Diodore's reputation (relayed to us by Theodorus Lector in the sixth century) for having commented on the whole of the Old Testament, nothing of his survived on the prophets. Chrysostom has been rather more fortunate: while questions of authenticity remain about a commentary on Isaiah attributed to him,[29] no such doubts affect his six homilies on Isaiah 6[30] and one on Isaiah 45:6–7.[31] Henry Savile, we noted above,[32] was shown a commentary attributed to Chrysostom on Jeremiah in Munich but found it worthless, which leaves us with the single homily on Jer 10:23.[33] If he did compose a work on The Twelve, as Rufinus and Ephrem of Antioch report,[34] we do not have it. The picture of prophets and prophecy that emerges from these still meagre remains

---

[26] Dahood, *Psalms* 2, 133.

[27] "Modéré" is the appropriate term used of Theodoret by Bardy, "Interprétation chez les pères," 582. Cf. Hill, "Theodoret, commentator in the Psalms;" *Theodoret of Cyrus. Commentary on the Psalms* 1, 1–36.

[28] Young, *Biblical Exegesis*, 168.

[29] The Commentary is fully extant only in an Armenian version. The Greek text of 1:1–8:10 (CPG 4416) has been edited by J. Dumortier, *Jean Chrysostome. Commentaire sur Isaie* (SC 304), who entertains no such doubts; but cf. Quasten, *Patrology* 3, 436.

[30] J. Dumortier, *Jean Chrysostome. Homélies sur Ozias* (SC 277). Dumortier does question the authenticity of Homily 4 in this collection; but his objections have been magisterially countered by P. Augustin, "La perennité de l'Eglise selon Jean Chrysostom et l'authenticité de la IVe Homélie *Sur Ozias.*"

[31] PG 56.141–52.

[32] Cf. note 1 to Chapter 4.

[33] PG 56.153–62.

[34] So A. Mai in introducing Theodore's Commentary (PG 66.121–22.1).

is a mixed one; as we saw, the Jeremiah verse is taken in that homily as but one of many that people in Antioch were in the habit of misquoting to relieve themselves of moral responsibility, allowing the preacher to lecture on an adequate approach to reading scriptural pericopes if they are not to "mangle the limbs of the body of the divinely-inspired Scriptures."[35] While the homily on Isa 45:6–7 is not grist to our mill here, being delivered when Chrysostom was bishop in Constantinople (and apparently finding him unprepared as second speaker on the day's reading), we have seen above the richness of his thinking in the six Antioch homilies on Isa 6 on the Scriptures as God's ὁμιλία with his people, a gift that may be withdrawn (though the focus moves from Isaiah—"the most articulate of all the prophets"—to the King Uzziah of 2 Ch 26 as an exemplar of Anomean temerity). It is an elevated vision of the role of the prophets (and other Old Testament authors) in the divine scheme of things, without the accent on historical fulfilment we find in Diodore's more dutiful pupil that encourages a more pedestrian approach.[36]

What might be thought, then, to be the more typically Antiochene approach to prophecy we find in Theodore, though we have only his early Commentary on The Twelve as evidence. Claims in the Syriac catalogues of his having worked also on the "four" major prophets (Daniel included) have been contested on the grounds of silence on the part of the Greek historians and council statements.[37] Its being an early work, following directly on the Commentary on the Psalms, is suggested by his documenting his text principally from them ("as was pointed out on many occasions in blessed David's usage") and not the other Latter Prophets, and from the still youthful

---

[35] Cf. Hill, "'Norms, definitions and unalterable doctrines:' Chrysostom on Jeremiah." When Theodoret at the end of his career comes to bring his work on the prophetic corpus to a close with a full commentary on Jeremiah, he notes this same tendency to misquote the verse.

[36] In the second homily, on the other hand, Chrysostom does launch into a rebuttal of views of the irrelevance of factual data in Scripture, like chronology (SC 277.96): "It is, in fact, what proves prophecies to be prophecy: prophecy is nothing else than the prediction of future events. How, then, will the person ignorant of the mention of events and outcomes be able to prove to the adversary the worth of the prophecy?" But it is not a preoccupation of his throughout.

[37] Cf. J. M. Vosté, "La chronologie de l'activité littéraire de Théodore de Mopsueste," 69–70. The manuscript Vat.gr.2304 forms the basis of the Mai edition of The Twelve Commentary appearing in PG 66 and also of the modern critical edition by H. N. Sprenger, *Theodori Mopsuesteni commentarius in XII prophetas*.

smugness, as appears in his introduction of the work as "an indict-ment of those who presume to apply themselves to the prophetic utterances without due preparation."[38] The survival of the work, the only one of Theodore's that is extant fully in Greek, has been thought to be due to its containing "almost nothing of Christological import," a facile comment oft repeated that perhaps disguises an unwilling-ness to delve into the text.[39] We shall see in Chapter Eight, in fact, that though the author, drilled in the principles of Aristarchus, wants to see prophecies realized within the bounds of the Old Testament, and will prefer to bring Zerubbabel into focus rather than Jesus, he recognizes the fate of the people to be, under the supervision of God, set within a context culminating in the Incarnation:

> Its occurrence had been told and foreseen well in advance by God, who understood these people's wickedness and clearly realized how he needed to conduct affairs in their regard by way of preparation for the manifestation and coming of Christ the Lord.[40]

Within that overall οἰκονομία, admittedly, Theodore sets about iden-tifying the historical situation of each prophet. Finding them in his Antioch text in the order of the Hebrew Bible (not the LXX gen-erally), he envisages four as eighth century prophets (Hosea, Joel, Amos, Micah), three prior to the fall of Samaria in 722 (Obadiah, Jonah, Nahum), two prior to the fall of Jerusalem (Habakkuk and Zephaniah), with Haggai and Zechariah assigned to the restoration, and Malachi to the period after the rebuilding of the Temple.

In his attempts to determine, as he says, the prophecy by The Twelve of "what would shortly happen," Theodore is handicapped by his imperfect formation in literary genres. Two prophets in par-ticular impede his following this goal: Jonah and "the novel and extraordinary things" he finds there, and Zechariah and the "full-

---

[38] Cf. Leontius, *Contra Nestor. et Eutych.* 11 (PG 86.1364.11): "In his misinterpre-tation of the divine Scriptures that coarse fellow never ceased mocking and jeering at the efforts of the holy teachers who have worked on them."

[39] The remark occurs first, apparently, in F. A Sullivan, *The Theology of Theodore of Mopsuestia*, 1, and then in Quasten, *Patrology* 3, 405, and later in D. Z. Zaharopoulos, *Theodore of Mopsuestia on the Bible. A Study of Old Testament Exegesis*, 32. It needs nuanc-ing, such as by a reading of the text of the Commentary, now available in English translation.

[40] Sprenger, *Theodori Mopsuesteni commentarius*, 2.

blown apocalyptic"[41] in the book's second half in particular. He resists the biblical author's intention of portraying the former prophet as an object of ridicule, defending him almost to the last and rewriting the text where necessary to preserve his credibility. The apocalyptic visions in the latter test his instinctive resolve to take texts "at first flush," κατὰ πρῶτον λόγον; Didymus in Alexandria,[42] open before him, cannot help him remedy this deficiency, opting instead to adopt Origen's solution of taking the text at another level. Apocalyptic motifs such as the Day of the Lord (in Joel, for instance), also go without comment.[43] Theodore's commentaries on The Twelve and the Psalms show him anxious to find history there, a history he reads in the light of "his strong theological conviction of the radical nature of the break between the two ages or dispensations before and after Christ,"[44] of which only the former is the constant focus of Old Testament authors.

It was an Antiochene extreme that Theodoret in the next generation preferred to avoid, a resolve that perhaps accounts for the survival of his full coverage of the prophetic corpus of the Old Testament. Even Daniel was included, a commentary on this book being composed second after the Song of Songs in response to requests (so he tells us) by those "anxious to have a close knowledge of the Man of Passion"[45] (the term for Daniel in the Theodotion version of 9:23). It may be, too, that in giving attention to a book classed by today's commentators as rather a mixture of haggadic tales and apocalyptic visions, and relegated from the prophetic corpus—much to Theodoret's chagrin—by the Jews of his day, he burnt his hermeneutical fingers as he struggled to uphold its prophetic credentials.

> For us to establish their brazen behavior convincingly, let us pose this question to them: what do you claim is typical of a prophet? Perhaps

---

[41] P. D. Hanson, *The Dawn of Apocalyptic*, 369.

[42] The Commentary on Zechariah (CPG 2549) is the only complete work in Greek by Didymus on a biblical book whose authenticity is established, which comes by direct transmission and of which a critical edition exists (SC 83). The text, long lost, was discovered in 1948 at Tura outside Cairo.

[43] Cf. Hill, "Theodore of Mopsuestia, interpreter of the prophets;" "Jonah in Antioch."

[44] M. F. Wiles, "Theodore of Mopsuestia as representative of the Antiochene school," 503.

[45] *Praef. in Pss* (PG 80.860). The text of the Daniel Commentary is found in PG 81; there is no modern critical edition.

your reply would be, Foreseeing and foretelling the future. Let us see, therefore, whether blessed Daniel had a foreknowledge of it and foretold it.[46]

He had thus set himself an impossible task, as he realizes in trying to establish the historical status of "Darius the Mede" of Chapter 6 and the book's characters and events generally, including the sweeping scenario of epochs and rulers and empires in the apocalyptic second half of the book. A commentator naturally inclined to background the text for the benefit of his readers with a view to "making clear to those in ignorance the inspired composition of the most divine Daniel" thus made a rod for his own back. Try as he may, numbers employed in a spiritual sense and periods devoid of historical foundation resist his attempts at elucidation. Though he is typically open to influence from predecessors of another school,[47] their different approach to biblical eschatology only compounds the problem; and the initial misjudgement of genre proves an insuperable obstacle. A similar misjudgement is made in Theodoret's next work, on Ezekiel,[48] a book which to a more limited extent employs the genre of apocalyptic, as in the case of the Gog of Chapters 38 & 39. Though previously he had—unusually for an Antiochene—warmed to the extended allegories of the book in persuading his readers of the Song of Songs of the figurative character of Scripture, and though he also finds the liturgical themes in Ezekiel to his liking, he still has to confront the objection of the book's obscurity, which he denies:

> Let no one, especially devotees of the true religion, adopt such a presumptuous attitude to the divine Spirit as to accuse his words of obscurity.[49]

---

[46] PG 81.1260.

[47] He admits his indebtedness to them in accepting the interpretation of the fourth beast enumerated in chapter 2 as the Roman empire, which had been espoused by Hippolytus, Irenaeus, Origen, Eusebius and Jerome; cf. Guinot, L'Exégèse de Théodoret de Cyr, 715.

[48] The text of the Commentary appears in PG 81; there is no modern critical edition. The biblical text it incorporates is of interest both for the difficulty the LXX finds in rendering obscure terms to do with Temple structure (where it often settles for transliteration), and for the doublets occurring in the Antioch text. Cf. L. McGregor, The Greek Text of Ezekiel.

[49] PG 81.809.

It is, he claims, another case of prophecy confirmed by the facts, πράγματα; as an Antiochene he proceeds to work at this level, unconcerned that others saw it is a treatise on mystical theology.

It may be an argument in favor of Theodore's not having commented on the four major prophets that Theodoret does not raise an objection to the historicism of predecessors in their regard after having earlier done so in his work on the Song and later repeating the point on the Psalms. In coming to compose a Commentary on the Twelve (minor)[50] Prophets, by contrast, he is aware of previous Antiochene comment in which the hermeneutical perspective in particular is foreshortened, too Jewish and not inclusive of a Christological dimension.[51] He has also had the opportunity to see the way these composers could be interpreted by a moderate Alexandrian like Cyril. While *suo more* he can be tolerant of alternative views on matters such as the true nature of the locust plague in Joel, allowing for a figurative reference to Assyrians and Babylonians such as Theodore had adopted, he is atypically irritated at the latter's unwillingness to entertain an eschatological reading of the prayer that is Chapter 3 of Habakkuk:

> I thought it absurd, however, now that the reality is in force and the shadow has been blotted out by the body, to apply the prophecy to other things when it definitely does not relate to them.[52]

And he gets equally indignant at other offerings of a Jewish interpretation by people who should know better—"teachers of religion"—which is a long-hand way of referring to his *Ioudaiophrôn* predecessor. One such irritating interpretation is the latter's repeated nomination of Zerubbabel as the referent where Jesus is thought by Theodoret to be more properly in focus, as we shall see in Chapter Eight.[53] He himself, on the other hand, is not immune from the effects of failing to recognize the genre of apocalyptic in the case of Joel and Zechariah.

---

[50] The qualification, unknown to Antioch and Alexandria at the time, is Augustine's, and is not meant pejoratively, referring only to relative length: "Quia sermones eorum sunt breves" (*De civ. Dei* 29; CCL 48.619).

[51] The text of the Commentary is found in PG 81. There is no modern critical edition. The endorsement of the *Pax Romana* in the text suggests a date in the late 430s for its composition.

[52] PG 81.1836.

[53] Cf. Guinot, "La cristallisation d'un différend;" Hill, "*Sartor resartus*: Theodore under review by Theodoret."

Theodore, of course, suffered a limitation not affecting Theodoret, that though he may have been exposed to the works of predecessors with which the latter was also familiar, his sense of superiority seems not to have permitted him to profit from them to the same extent.[54] Hence his dismissive remarks about them and implicit claims to a sounder approach (as at the opening of The Twelve Commentary and as early as Psalm 2), and his insistence on adhering to an Antiochene historical approach even when aware of alternative views, as in the case of commentary on Zechariah with Didymus's work available to him. Theodoret, on the contrary, will generally begin by admitting that he is small fry by comparison with his predecessors (as in the case of commentaries on the Song and—though not relevant here—Paul), and will present their views—including Theodore's—fairly. Guinot points out that of all his works it is only in the prefaces to Ezekiel, Isaiah and Jeremiah that he makes no mention of his predecessors.[55] In moving to Isaiah late in the 440s, nevertheless, Theodoret implicitly acknowledges his indebtedness, assuring his readers that "I too am making an effort to overcome the limits of poverty and share with my fellow believers the crumbs I have received" from "the affluent."[56] Acknowledgement is due, in fact, the work showing a pervasive influence of Eusebius of Caesarea and Cyril of Alexandria in particular in the way the Song Commentary betrays the influence of Origen (via Eusebius) throughout; Antiochene attention to the historical situation is relatively limited. Yet Theodoret's aim and characteristic features here are, he feels, the same as ever:

> With the exception of the remarkable Jeremiah, the other prophets' thought we have with God's help explicated as far as is possible, giving particular care to conciseness and clarity.[57]

---

[54] Cf. Guinot, L'Exégèse, 799, "Le caractère propre de l'exégèse de Théodoret tient surtout au fait qu'il a su s'ouvrir largement, à l'inverse de Théodore et même de Diodore, à d'autres formes d'interprétation."

[55] L'Exégèse, 632. Guinot has performed a major service by identifying all explicit and implicit references to predecessors in Theodoret's works (631–799).

[56] The long-lost text of the Commentary has been edited by Guinot, Théodoret de Cyr. Commentaire sur Isaïe (SC 276, 295, 315). The manuscript discovered in Constantinople (no. 17 of the Metochion of the Holy Sepulchre, containing also a text of the Jeremiah Commentary), is now in Athens in a "mauvais état de conservation," in Guinot's words, to such an extent as to be illegible.

[57] SC 276.140.

That exception he dealt with shortly before claiming in a letter to Eusebius of Ancyra in 448 that he had commented on "all the prophets, the psalter and the apostle."[58] It was perhaps a reluctant completion of the prophetic corpus, if we can judge from the extreme conciseness, συντομία, of the Jeremiah Commentary (which includes Lamentations and Baruch, but not the Epistle of Jeremiah) in the form we have it.[59] The biblical text cited (not always fully) in the work is especially valuable for today's exegetes comparing Greek with (our) Hebrew in the case of a book where the former is much briefer. The Antiochene text, in fact, incorporates elements declared "missing from the LXX" by modern commentators insensitive to its local forms, as we noted in Chapter Four. While the conciseness of treatment (or process of transmission) results in omission of the usual citation of alternative versions, Theodoret does exploit the advantage of his knowledge of Syriac and acquaintance with the Peshitta. He shows none of his recent indebtedness to predecessors of another school; instead of the eschatological dimension he gave to Isaiah, here his approach is consistently historical, and his characteristic attention to textual items of history, geography, topography and the natural sciences unremitting (which, admittedly, he often found in Eusebius's *Onomasticon*).[60] In his Questions on Chronicles, his final exegetical work, Theodoret in failing health felt with some satisfaction that he had previously done justice to Jeremiah: "That book in its entirety we commented on as well, thanks to divine grace."[61] We,

---

[58] SC 98.202.

[59] In regard to the authenticity of the text of the Commentary in PG 81, M. Geerard, CPG 6205, cites the doubts of M. Faulhaber, *Die Propheten-Catenen nach Römischen Handschriften*, 113sq. J. Paramelle also in a survey article on "Christianisme Byzantin" in *Annuaire de l'Ecole Pratique des Hautes Etudes* 88 (1979–80) 379–86 makes a passing reference to "l'inauthenticité du Commentaire de Jérémie" (380), but without elaboration. For his part Guinot nevertheless feels we are confident in claiming "l'on est désormais en possession de tous les commentaires de Théodoret sur les prophètes" (SC 277.15), not being prepared to dismiss the claim to authenticity of the Migne text of Jeremiah, even if it may have to be conceded to be "composite et lacunaire." The Athens manuscript containing the text of the Isaiah Commentary also contains a text of the Jeremiah Commentary whose opening words differ from the PG text; but its completely corrupt condition allows for no full comparison. A reader of the PG text is struck by the resemblance to Theodoret's normal style, if exceptionally concise.

[60] Cf. Guinot, *L'Exégèse*, 798.

[61] *Theodoreti Cyrensis Quaestiones in Reges et Paralipomena*, 299.

too, are gratified by his thus leaving us a complete sample—if not
always typical—of Antiochene commentary on the Latter Prophets
of the Old Testament, whose exegetical, hermeneutical and other
accents we shall examine in the following chapters.

C. Octateuch, historical books, Song of Songs

If Antiochene pastors were not as "fascinated" with some other parts
of the Old Testament as they were with prophecy, tradition obliged
them to introduce their flock also to the mysteries of the book of
Genesis, as they had to the Psalms for different reasons. In fact, the
difficulties, τὰ ἄπορα, of the whole Octateuch called for attention,[62]
and Diodore responded in the Questions genre that had been in service, even to deal with the text of Homer,[63] since Aristotle and Philo
in the east (but not including Origen), and would be employed in
the west by Augustine, Jerome and medievals like Abelard. Diodore's
work, of which we have only fragments,[64] would prove invaluable to
Theodoret as a source of predecessors' views when he adopted this
genre. Theodore had not emulated Diodore by adopting this genre;
while the Syriac catalogues refer to a commentary of his on Genesis,
of which fragments alone remain, there is no mention of one on
Exodus.[65]

It was probably because of his role as preacher in Antioch that
Chrysostom delivered a number of series of homilies on Genesis in
the period of (an eight-week) Lent, a customary text used also for
catechesis of candidates preparing for baptism at Easter. We have
three such series from him, all devoted to at least a part of the book
(known also as Κτίσις or Κοσμοποιΐα, "Creation"), but for various

---

[62] The term Octateuch was known in the early Church (so O. Eissfeldt, *The Old
Testament*, 156). We do not find Antioch commentators speaking of Pentateuch or
Torah.

[63] For Bardy, "La littérature patristique patristique des '*Quaestiones et Responsiones*' sur
l'écriture sainte," *RB* 41 (1932) 211, Homer was "la source inépuisable d'apories."

[64] These have been edited by J. Deconinck, *Quaestiones in Octateuchum et Reges*;
R. Devreesse, *Les anciens commentateurs grecs de l'Octateuch et des Rois*.

[65] Devreese assembles the Genesis fragments in his *Essai sur Théodore de Mopsueste*,
5–25; comments by Theodore bearing on liturgical details Devreesse believes belong
to a commentary on Hebrews rather than Exodus.

reasons differing considerably. The series of eight "sermons" (so called to distinguish them from the long series),[66] getting no further than the first three chapters, seems to have been delivered at a late stage in Lent of 386, in Quadragesima (western Lent's forty days); from those days only eight sermons are extant. The second series became celebrated rather as the Homilies on the Statues (or Homilies to the people of Antioch)[67] because interrupted after the first homily on February 21, 387, by what ensued after the vandalizing of the images of the imperial family, the emperor's harsh response and Bishop Flavian's hasty journey to Constantinople to seek clemency for the city. Only the third series, given in the next year or two, treated of the whole book in the course of sixty seven homilies,[68] not surprisingly repeating some passages given earlier.[69]

Though the bishop and perhaps other clergy are present during the series of eight sermons, Chrysostom obviously feels under no obligation to move systematically through Genesis. He selects only certain verses for examination of particular items, like the sense of "dominion" found in the word *image* in Gen 1:26, and moves onto such topics as the need to give alms to the poor and whether the robber on the cross was actually admitted to heaven or only to paradise. There is also a typically positive (if literalist) presentation of the Fall, and a moving treatment of the domestic church to which the participants return to read and pray, as well as some jousting with a range of heresies. Even the congregation's distraction provokes a memorable rebuke in Sermon Four.

> Wake up there, and dispel indifference. Why do I say this? Because while we are discoursing to you on the Scriptures, you instead are averting your eyes from us and fixing them on the lamps and the man lighting the lamps. What extreme indifference is this, to ignore us and attend to him! Here am I, lighting the fire that comes from the Scriptures, and the light of its teaching is burning on our tongue. This light is brighter and better than that light: we are not kindling a wick

---

[66] Edited by L. Brottier, *Jean Chrysostome. Sermons sur la Genèse* (SC 433).
[67] PG 49. There is no critical edition; but cf. the study by F. van de Paverd, *St John Chrysostom: The Homilies on the Statues.*
[68] PG 53, 54.
[69] Cf. W. A. Markowicz, "Chrysostom's sermons on Genesis: a problem," 664: "Partial repetitions triggered by similarity of circumstance are no surprise to any teacher-preacher of many years."

saturated in oil, like him: souls bedewed with piety we set alight with
the desire for listening.[70]

There are more pressing distractions in the Statues homilies, try
though the preacher may in Homilies 7–9 to stay with his text; with
amusements and factories shut down and rumors rife, the church
was the place to hear the latest developments in the bishop's mis-
sion.[71] Attention is also given to moral topics like the needless taking of oaths and abuse of alcohol; perhaps these homilies qualify
only loosely as biblical commentary. It is in the long series of sixty
seven homilies delivered in 388 or 389 that we find systematic coverage of Genesis, but at such a slow rate initially that only twelve
chapters have been covered in thirty two homilies by the end of
Lent, the series then interrupted to resume at Pentecost. The treatment of the preacher's text is as literalist as in the sermons.[72] He is
not ready to admit diversity of contributions to a composite narrative, explaining the appearance of a second creation story in Gen 2
as the Spirit's wish to be insistent about the true origins of things
and "prevent anyone's being able to engage in controversy later on."
Likewise, the two overlapping attempts to develop a genealogy of
Adam's descendants in Gen 4 and 5 are seen as deliberate exercises
by the one author. On the positive side, we have seen above in
Chapter Three Chrysostom's theology being developed in these homilies of the biblical word as parallel to the Incarnation of the Word
through a divine gesture of συγκατάβασις. If apora in Genesis remained
for Theodoret to clarify later in a more focused manner, Chrysostom's
listeners had been treated by the recently ordained preacher to a
profound theology of the inspired word.

Theodoret, by contrast, was at the end of his exegetical career
when despite poor health he succumbed to requests by his coadju-
tor Hypatius in the decade after the council of Chalcedon to deal

---

[70] SC 433.238–40.3.
[71] Cf. Kelly, *Golden Mouth*, 72–81.
[72] Cf. Hill, *St John Chrysostom. Homilies on Genesis 1–17*, 1–19. The term "literalist" has been thought extreme when applied to Chrysostom's commentary on such
heavily figurative narratives as Gen 3; cf. F. Asensio, "El Crisóstomo y su visión
de la escritura en la exposición homilética del Génesis," 334: "Exégesis innegablemente literal, pero no literalista." While the figures may properly be taken literally
(i.e., in the sense intended by the author), however, it is surely a literalist reading
to take them as factual statement, as does Chrysostom. See below in Chapter Eight.

under the genre of Questions with the problems or questions, τὰ ἄπορα or τὰ ζητήματα, of the Octateuch (including Ruth, on which we have no other patristic commentary)[73] and also of Kingdoms (1 Sam–2 Kgs) and Chronicles (also a unique Greek commentary).[74] Not only are readers of these Old Testament books often at a loss; there are some commentators on them, Theodoret maintains, who "inquire irreverently, believing they find the divine Scripture wanting, in some cases for not teaching right doctrine, in other cases for giving conflicting instructions." While the "questioner" thus frequently pinpoints an item in the text that is obscure (perhaps already selected by a predecessor),[75] the commentator exploits the genre to give himself a cue to discourse on subjects of interest to him, like the details of liturgical practice or Temple structure and furnishings (in Leviticus and Chronicles, for instance). Clarity and conciseness are again Theodoret's priority, as well as an eye for detail in the interests of precision, ἀκρίβεια. As well, thanks to Diodore's previous Questions (at least on the Octateuch) he has access to predecessors' views, to which he typically gives consideration, thus admitting eschatological, Christological, spiritual and/or sacramental interpretations. Predictably, his approach to his vast corpus generally does not reflect the critical spirit of modern commentators: he is slow to acknowledge layers in a composite text, the many textual discrepancies are not seen to reflect diversity of authorship, individual theologies of a Deuteronomist or Chronicler are not identified. Nevertheless, Photius (who himself later adopted this genre of questions and answers, ζητήματα καὶ λύσεις) was justified in acknowledging Theodoret's relatively competent use of it, "It would not be easy to find anyone better at elucidating obscure points."[76]

---

[73] The critical edition is by Fernández Marcos and Sáenz-Badillos, *Theodoreti Cyrensis Quaestiones in Octateuchum*. Theodoret's opening "question" on Ruth implies commonly held doubts as to its relevance, "Why on earth was the story of Ruth composed?" After summarizing it, he supplies the reason, "This narrative is sufficient of itself to offer great benefit to those who realize the kind of benefit accruing from it."

[74] The critical edition is by Fernández Marcos and Busto Saiz, *Theodoreti Cyrensis Quaestiones in Reges et Paralipomena*.

[75] The view of Bardy, "La littérature patristique," *RB* 42 (1933) 351–52.

[76] *Bibliotheca* 203 ed. Henry, III, 103. Photius proceeds to declare Theodoret's Questions a "book which is, on the whole, helpful (χρήσιμον)." Cf. Hill, "Old Testament *Questions* of Theodoret of Cyrus."

If in the course of his late use of the Questions genre Theodoret has left us with unique Antiochene and in fact Greek patristic coverage of Ruth and Chronicles, he was not the first to show an interest in Former Prophets and Chronicler. Not to mention Eustathius's study of 1 Sam 28 preceding our period, Chrysostom had found value in the figure of the presumptuous King Uzziah in 2 Chr 26 in the course of his fourth homily on Isa 6 to develop his notion of the Scriptures as God's ὁμιλία with humankind, cited above in Chapter Four. And in the context of the political crisis in Antioch in 387 after the Statues incident, the young preacher had ventured to comment on developments and even suggest obliquely to the emperor how clemency was the appropriate response by detailing in three homilies, known as homilies on David and Saul, the stormy relationship of these two Old Testament figures and especially David's admirable gentleness, πραότης, in declining to react to injustice with force.[77] Again, shortly after the emperor accepted this advice and showed the city clemency, Chrysostom delivered five further homilies, now known as homilies on Hannah, which touch on the recent crisis. The attention to the mother of Samuel, however, extends no further than the beginning of her prayer in 1 Sam 2:1–2 after she has served her purpose for the preacher's themes of formation of the young, prayer and divine providence.[78]

To complete our survey of commentary on the Old Testament composed in Antioch in the fourth and fifth centuries, mention should finally be made of Chrysostom's Commentary on Job and Proverbs and Theodoret's work on the Song of Songs. It was to the Song that Theodoret devoted his first commentary,[79] composed around the time of the council of Ephesus in 431. In acknowledging predecessors within and beyond Antioch, he refers to similar works (no longer extant) by Diodore, Chrysostom and—possibly—Theodore,[80] none of which are extant.

---

[77] The text of the David and Saul homilies appears in PG 54; cf. Hill, "Chrysostom's homilies on David and Saul." Van de Paverd, regrettably, does not find them of value in dating the critical events of 387.

[78] The text of the Hannah homilies appears in PG 54; cf. Hill, "St John Chrysostom's Homilies on Hannah."

[79] The text of the commentary appears in PG 81. A critical edition is in course of preparation in the *Sources Chrétiennes* series.

[80] Despite claims by Leontius and in some documents from the fifth ecumenical council in 553 that condemned his works, the Syriac catalogues do not list such a

Many of the ancients also commented on it; those afterwards who did
not do so have adorned their own compositions with passages from
it—not only Eusebius of Palestine, Origen of Egypt, Cyprian of Carthage,
who also wore the crown of martyrdom, and men more ancient than
they and closer to the apostles, but also those after them who gained
distinction in the churches. They knew the book to be spiritual—Basil
the Great, who commented on the beginning of Proverbs, both Gregories,
one boasting kinship with him, the other friendship, Diodore, the noble
champion of piety, John, bedewing the whole world with the streams
of his teaching to this very day, and—to put it in a nutshell and avoid
length of discourse—all those after them.[81]

This initial work represents a significant declaration of intent by this
bishop with pastoral experience, displaying both an awareness of his
Antiochene heritage and also an openness to other predecessors like
Origen (accessed through Eusebius),[82] to the effect that his flock
required commentary more urgently on Old Testament material than
on the Gospels and Paul. His aim, as always, is "to bring obscurity
to clarity"[83] in the case of a work in danger of rejection for its sex-
ual explicitness, which by application of a hermeneutic not generally favored by Antioch could be shown to have spiritual and even
Christological meaning. He claims in his preface,

> It teaches us the major forms of God's goodness and reveals to us the
> innermost recesses and the holiest of holy mysteries of divine loving-
> kindness (the latter phrase deriving from the rabbis via Origen).

It comes almost as a codicil to mention what we have of Chrysostom's
works on the sapiential books, Job, Proverbs and Ecclesiastes, partly
because a question of authenticity hangs over the latter two, and
partly because they come to us not as homilies preserved by the
processes of stenographic transmission to which we are indebted for

---

work by Theodore. He would thus not be the predecessor (though generally taken
to be) whom Theodoret pillories in his preface for his historicism: "Some commentators misrepresent the Song of Songs, believe it to be not a spiritual book,
come up instead with some fanciful stories inferior even to babbling old wives' tales,
and dare to claim that Solomon the sage wrote it as a factual account of himself
and the Pharaoh's daughter."

[81] PG 81.32. An omission from this list is the early commentary of Hippolytus,
which survives in a Georgian version; otherwise surviving are only those of Origen
(a commentary and homilies, partly, and in Latin) and of Gregory of Nyssa.

[82] Cf. Guinot, "Théodoret a-t-il lue les homélies d'Origène sur l'Ancien Testament?";
Hill, *Theodoret of Cyrus. Commentary on the Song of Songs*, 3–18.

[83] PG 81.212.

the major commentaries but in note form for the preacher's later
use, as the Job editor concedes.[84] The works on Proverbs and Ecclesiastes, which are found in the same single manuscript on Patmos,
where they have been accessed by French scholars Marcel Richard[85]
and Guillaume Bady, are in the process of being critically edited;
these scholars themselves, while agreeing on Chrysostom's authorship of the former work, disgree on the latter. A reader of the
Proverbs Commentary can see both why for the Antioch Fathers the
authors rate only as sages, σοφοί, not as προφῆται, the term normally applied to those Old Testament authors enjoying divine inspiration, and (if only because of partial coverage of the biblical text)
why the work has come to us in only one manuscript (though abun-
dantly represented in the catenae). It is significant that, though
Hippolytus, Origen, Didymus, Evagrius and others wrote on Proverbs,
Chrysostom's is the only patristic commentary to survive; it and the
other sapiential commentaries deserve editing and further study.

In the period under discussion in this volume which closes with
Theodoret's death around 460, an imposing amount of commentary
in word and writing on the Old Testament was produced by the
leading Antiochene figures—on Psalms and Prophets, on Octateuch
and historical books, on the sapiential books, the Song of Songs and
The Chronicler. Clearly, the biblical tradition of Christianity received
ample attention in the formation of the faithful in Antioch at the
hands of these pastors, and the Jewish scriptures loomed no less large
in discharge of this pastoral duty, these books being felt to illustrate
key tenets of Antiochene theology. It is ironic and perhaps unfortunate that it is the works of Theodoret, and less so Chrysostom, that
(arguably for reasons of *odium theologicum*) have survived more completely than commentaries adopting more inflexibly the principles of
Diodore, the founder of Antioch's exegetical method. We should now
turn to examining in more detail all these pastors' approach to the
task of commentary and Antioch's distinctive hermeneutic.

---

[84] H. Sorlin, *Commentaire sur Job* 1, SC 346, 35, n. 1: "Ne serions-nous pas en
présence d'un texte incomplètement élaboré, de notes de lecture dans lesquelles
Chrysostome se proposait de puiser ultérieurement, en vue d'éventuelles homélies
sur le livre de Job?" While the notes on Proverbs can be almost telegraphic in their
brevity, however, the Job work is full of rhetorical verve, if uneven in its development.

[85] Cf. Richard, "Le commentaire de Saint Jean Chrysostome sur les *Proverbes de
Salomon*." Bady is preparing the Proverbs Commentary for publication in the SC series.

CHAPTER SEVEN

ANTIOCHENE APPROACH TO THE
TASK OF COMMENTARY

For the principal figures of the school of Antioch in the fourth and fifth centuries, "reading the Old Testament" meant also commenting on it for the congregations for which they had pastoral responsibility. These lay people, even if affluent and lettered enough to read it at home, found it obscure for reasons Chrysostom had detailed in his homilies on the subject, and the commentators felt obliged (in the words of Theodoret in his first work, on the Song of Songs) to "bring obscurity to clarity."[1] The great volume, even of their extant works, highlights the pastors' degree of commitment to the task of discharging this responsibility within the overall compass of *cura pastoralis* in the church of Antioch (in the wide sense outlined in Chapter One) among the various forms of tradition of the faith. While later ages neglect to their peril this vast corpus of biblical comment, especially students of the text of the Old Testament and the history of exegesis, the term "exegesis" in the strict sense examined in the previous chapter should not be freely used of these commentators' work. J. N. D. Kelly in his study of Chrysostom remarks,

> Neither John, nor any Christian teacher for centuries to come, was properly equipped to carry out exegesis as we have come to understand it.[2]

a caveat we have seen validated. It was therefore biblical commentary that they embarked on as a necessary task to be performed.

Kelly proceeds to add to his timely caveat about his subject the further caution,

> He could not be expected to understand the nature of the Old Testament writings, still less the complex issues raised by the study of the gospels.

One could arguably claim that the antiquity and diversity of Old Testament material raise more difficult critical questions for a com-

---

[1] On 8:12 (PG 81.212).
[2] *Golden Mouth*, 94.

mentator than the New Testament, including the Gospels, and that
Chrysostom rises to the challenge of Matthew and John, and Theodoret
to Paul, better than they do to the book of Genesis with its complicated history of composition. That is not a question to be debated
in these pages, however; it is rather the former assertion that should
be examined, these commentators' (in)ability to grapple with ancient
semitic works, oral and written, composed in a range of literary genres not all familiar to the readers, arising from a variety of historical periods and life situations, betraying signs of differing cultures,
religious and political systems, and theological mindsets, and representing different purposes of different composers. Even if they willy-
nilly fell short of dealing adequately with textual questions of Old
Testament works, the commentators would need to touch on those
other matters if their readers were to appreciate fully the content of
the letters sent by God and delivered by Moses, David and the other
προφῆται. We should now study their approach to this task, leaving
to the next chapter a study of the rather different challenge of interpreting this variegated material.

A. Diodore

In as far as the commentators in Antioch can be said to be members of a school, two having sat at the feet of master Diodore, and
Theodoret (to judge from his preface to the Song of Songs and from
works like his Commentary on the Twelve Prophets and his Questions)
familiar with his local predecessors' work and method, we may presume that to some extent they approached the task of commentary
in similar fashion. Though this fashion of commentary owed little
to any philosophical system, we noted in Chapter One, it has been
recognized as bearing hallmarks of the approach of the rhetoricians.[3]

---

[3] Young, *Biblical Exegesis*, 169–76, makes the point repeatedly: "The principal
Antiochene exegetes (sic) could have been expected to practice exegesis (sic) according to rhetorical conventions . . . The principal Antiochene exegetes (sic) undoubt-
edly had a rhetorical education . . . Antiochene exegesis (sic), then, is grounded in
the exegetical (sic) activities of the rhetorical schools . . . (Eustathius's) interpretation
is rooted in the traditional *paideia* of the rhetorical schools." It is the basic drift of
Schäublin's work, *Untersuchungen*, that Diodore and Theodore show the marked
influence of pagan rhetoricians. For Olivier, *Commentarii*, xciv, Diodore's style of
commentary has nothing original about it: "Elle est celle de tout exégète (sic)
d'Alexandrie, d'Antioche et d'ailleurs." The same, surely, could not be said of the
commentators' hermeneutics.

That these features did not derive only from Libanius's tutelage is indicated by their presence in Diodore's extant Commentary on the Psalter. The Psalms in Diodore's view are primarily a text, not songs (deriving from and) to be sung in a liturgical context; he opens his preface by referring to "the book of the divine Psalms," showing none of the interest in *Sitz im Leben* evident in some modern commentaries[4] (which is not to say he will not try to identify author and historical incidents associated—credibly or not—with each psalm, as we shall see). The Psalter as a whole has a ὑπόθεσις, as does each psalm—that is, a theme and/or (in the case of individual psalms) a narrative setting. As a whole the Psalms are moral or doctrinal in their theme, Diodore tells us in the preface, whereas he can find the one narrative setting in the case of groups of psalms:

> The twenty seventh, twenty eighth, twenty ninth and thirtieth psalms have the same ὑπόθεσις, composed from the viewpoint (πρόσωπον) of blessed Hezekiah and directed against the Assyrians.[5]

Point of view is important for a commentator who wants both to see David as author and yet to relate psalms to a range of historical periods and personages, in whose person, πρόσωπον, the psalmist speaks, including in four cases (alone) Jesus—the term thus taking on particular theological overtones.[6] In addition, there is a particular purpose, σκοπός, detectable in (at least) some psalms:

> The fortieth psalm has a Babylonian setting (ὑπόθεσις). Blessed David's purpose (σκοπός) is to show the Israelites benefiting greatly from the prolonged hardship, and the actual text makes the psalm clearer.

Such distinctions are the rhetoricans'.

Accepting the analysis of Diodore's commentary by L. Mariès, editor Olivier sees in his procedure traditional methods of a teacher in antiquity when dealing with texts.[7] He does, indeed, impress us a methodical teacher; in the preface he systematically categorizes psalms on the basis of content, ὑπόθεσις, and in introducing Ps 19 he schematically lays out different positions on divine providence.

---

[4] Cf. S. Mowinckel, *The Psalms in Israel's Worship*; A. Weiser, *The Psalms*.

[5] *Commentarii*, 152. For convenience, psalm numbers have been transposed in accord with the Hebrew and modern versions.

[6] Cf. Greer, *Early Biblical Interpretation*, 188, on Theodore's (and thus Diodore's) intentions in using the term.

[7] *Commentarii*, xciii–xciv.

This nineteenth psalm is doctrinal: just as the fourth, also being doctrinal, censures those claiming that existing things do not benefit from providence, so too the present psalm levels an accusation against those who claim that things exist of themselves. The latter are worse than those saying they do not benefit from providence: those saying they do not benefit from providence do not go so far as to claim also that they exist of themselves, only that they were made by someone yet are not shown providence. Likewise of those denying providence there are many different kinds: some absolutely deny providence, others confine it to heaven, still others to the things of earth and the common lot of humankind, not actually to each person individually altogether. Amongst the latter there emerges a variety of differences. . . .[8]

Old Testament material originally composed in Hebrew, however, does not always yield to the application of general rhetorical principles from pagan antiquity, even by a methodical teacher. Diodore's linguistic limitations do not allow him to detect the alphabetic structure underlying Ps 25 that could account for his unease about its movement of thought, or to vindicate the LXX's combining Hebrew Pss 9 & 10 into one psalm, or to acknowledge the diversity in numbering of Pss 114–116 and 147 in Hebrew and Greek. While he spends time in the preface systematically distinguishing different genres represented in the psalms, an exception is that of apocalyptic, a serious omission that will undermine his pupils' treatment of prophetic literature in particular. When for example the opening verses of Ps 46 (a psalm which he has predetermined is dealing with conflict between Ahaz and the northern kingdom) depict "the cosmic upheaval . . . of the great final catastrophe,"[9] he resists any recognition of the wider horizons. It is not until Ps 40:10 that he takes note of one of Hebrew prosody's stock devices: "*I did not conceal your mercy and your truth from a numerous congregation.* He repeated the same thought in parallelism."

The rhetoricians had taught Diodore to attend primarily to a literary work's meaning, διάνοια (certainly not their sentiment, as we shall observe in Chapter Ten), and thus to conduct commentary in line with the movement of thought, ἀκολουθία (subjectively arrived at by the commentator), with which individual difficulties should be reconciled. The dangers of eisegesis in such a procedure are patent.

---

[8] *Commentarii*, 108–109.
[9] Dahood, *Psalms* 1, 279.

Diodore's LXX version had experienced consistent difficulty with Heb. verb forms indicating tense and mood, and had often altered them. Presuming the discrepancy to be attributable to the author, Diodore feels free to adjust these instances of ἐναλλαγὴ χρόνου in the light of his judgement of the proper movement of thought, ἀκολουθία, doing so over a hundred times.[10] Ps 40 in the Heb. suggests combination of two different pieces, vv.13–17 in fact appearing again in the Psalter as Ps 70. Not noting this latter fact, and unable to check the Hebrew, Diodore takes it upon himself on the basis of presumed ἐναλλαγὴ χρόνου rather to change mood and tense of ten verbs in these verses in accord with his judgement of the psalmist's intended ἀκολουθία. Theodore will be encouraged to adopt this licence in his own Psalms Commentary.

A feature of the commentary of other Antiochenes, intertextuality, does not appear in Diodore's work here. Perhaps he feels he can rule on the meaning of the psalmist's phrasing, even when it calls for documentation from elsewhere in the Bible, without further recourse. On Ps 17:10, which in his text reads, "My foes surrounded my soul; they hemmed in their fatness," Diodore simply comments, "*Fatness* means the joy and prosperity of life, giving the sense, They abused their own prosperity (the meaning of *They hemmed in*)." Theodoret will consider Diodore's offering for "fatness" and differ from it;[11] a modern commentator like Dahood will see rather arrogance as the sense, citing in support Deut 32:15; Jer 5:28; Ps 73:7–8.[12] Chrysostom, who generally regaled his listeners with such scriptural documentation, is not extant here. The result in Diodore's case, one finds, is a rather bare commentary.

To the extent that many of the features of Diodore's style of commentary reappear in the works of his pupils Theodore and Chrysostom, and later in their intellectual protegé Theodoret, thus constituting a considerable group of like-minded scholars we may refer to as a "school," it is he and not Lucian who may fairly claim to be its

---

[10] Olivier, *Commentarii*, ci, reports that Mariès identified 117 cases of such adjustments. Cf. Schäublin, *Untersuchungen*, 131–32, who again sees the influence of the rhetoricians in this habit.

[11] PG 80.969: "Some commentators gave the name 'fatness' to prosperity and good health, but I prefer to speak thus of kindliness and good health."

[12] *Psalms* 1, 97.

leader and theirs. Olivier and not Downey,[13] therefore, would seem
to have right on his side, the former claiming for Diodore the title
"le véritable fondateur," allowing Lucian only "l'initiateur."[14]

B. Theodore

We would expect the young Theodore's style of commenting on the
Psalter to resemble his mentor's, and we are not disappointed. He
shows little interest in the cultic context of the Psalms' composition
and recital, or (though we no longer have the preface he wrote) in
different genres.[15] His procedure is to identify a psalm's ὑπόθεσις and
focus on its sense, or διάνοια (a psalm's spiritual appeal again going
unnoticed), as with the first psalm, which he takes to be moral rather
than historical.

> This, then, is the theme of the present psalm. Our task now is, with
> God's help, to proceed to plumb its meaning. If it should prove nec-
> essary to explain some things at greater length in the light of matters
> that arise, we shall nevertheless not be unmindful of the conciseness
> we promised in the preface.[16]

Most of the psalms, however, are given a narrative setting and a
πρόσωπον for whom David speaks, as determined by Diodore—the
people captured by Nebuchadnezzar in Ps 5, David lamenting his
own sin in Ps 6, and in the case of Ps 51, the principal penitential

---

[13] *The History of Antioch*, 337–42.

[14] *Commentarii*, ciii. Bardy's similar term for Diodore, "Interprétation chez les
pères," 580, is "le vrai fondateur de l'école d'Antioche." Drewery, "Antiochien,"
106, traces back to Lucian the contrast betweeen Alexandrian and Antiochene
hermeneutics.

[15] Theodore likes to find synecdoche in his text of the Psalms, convinced it is a
specifically biblical figure, as he says on Ps 16:9, "By *my flesh* he means I myself,
naming the whole from the part, the divine Scripture normally referring to the
whole person by flesh, soul and the like" (*Le commentaire*, 98).

[16] *Le commentaire*, 3. That promise of conciseness we find Theodore generally
infringing; Photius (perhaps a biased judge) had good grounds for faulting his pro-
lixity. Simonetti must be unfamiliar with the OT commentaries of Theodore to
claim, *Biblical Interpretation*, 71, "The tendency towards conciseness is such that, on
occasion, parts of his commentaries are nothing more than paraphrases of the scriptural text itself." Paraphrase, unlike precis, of course, can run to considerable length.
Simonetti is correct, at least, in pointing to Theodore's tendency to avoid explanatory comment for paraphrase.

psalm of the early Church, not David but the people asking for-giveness on return from captivity.

Theodore feels the freedom Diodore enjoyed of detecting ἐναλλαγὴ χρόνου in verb forms. In these cases he will find the author respon-sible, or the LXX; in comment on Ps 35, where he sees David speak-ing in the πρόσωπον of Jeremiah under assault from his foes, he comes to v.8: "*He will fall*, that is, Let them fall . . . there is a change in tense as often happens from the translation." The basis for his judgement in these cases, since he lacks a knowledge of Hebrew, is ἀκολουθία, as was also Diodore's criterion; yet he can presume that his determination of that movement of thought arises from the Heb. itself, as he does in disputing an alternative opinion on Ps 36:1:

> It is in fact actually opposed to the sequence of the interpretation as a whole, what follows not being in accord with such an interpreta-tion, as a more precise reader of what follows can find from our expla-nation. This form of interpretation happens to be at variance with the Hebrew, and interpreting from that is more authoritative than all.[17]

"The sequence of the interpretation as a whole" is to Theodore more influential and significant than individual textual items, and for a reader's benefit that view is arguably true. It is a pity, however, that frequently he invokes that principle to discharge himself as com-mentator from the need to background his text (in the way Theodoret will excel) by explicating such items.

> Now, this practice we shall particularly observe both in the present psalm and in all the others, to make a summary of the overall mean-ing and thus unfold precisely what has to be said. The task set us, you see, is not to follow up every matter in detail but succinctly to touch on the sense of each statement so as to make possible some illumination of the obvious sense of the text, leaving those of greater intelligence to add other things if they wish, though not departing from the interpretation already given. A true understanding, in fact, results in such an insight that we should maintain a sequence of explanation

---

[17] *Le commentaire*, 195. Cf. Schäublin, *Untersuchungen*, 131–32. Devreesse, *Essai sur Théodore de Mopsueste*, 59–60, lists the instances of ἐναλλαγὴ χρόνου in the com-mentaries on Psalms and The Twelve. Theodore's rulings on Hebrew usage, prob-ably prompted by some source, lead Devreesse to change his earlier opinion about Theodore's knowledge of Hebrew, *Essai*, 56, n. 3: "Tout démontre, en effet, qu'il n'entendait pas l'hébreu et qu'il ne le voyait qu'à travers des intermédiaires."

in faithful accord with history, and accordingly should propose what ought be said.[18]

He chides those who want to apply Ps 72 to both Solomon and Christ for failing to follow correct priorities:

> The cause of this problem is the fact of some people's commenting on the words by slavishly keeping to the text (λέξις) of the psalm and not having an overall view of the meaning (διάνοια)

an interpretative stance we would class rather as eisegesis. As a result the reader at times gets the impression of what might be styled creative commentary when the effort proves too much. Verses 4–5 of Ps 74 in the Heb. Dahood classes as "among the most difficult of the entire Psalter,"[19] yet Theodore simply blames the LXX—"the verse involves great difficulty resulting from the translation"—and despairing of relating the verses to the Maccabees (Diodore's choice before him), he clutches at the straw Symmachus's version offers to develop an ingenious paraphrase. Theodoret will work harder on several such difficulties in that psalm; he also provides a wider range of scriptural documentation for his readers throughout, intertextuality not being a feature of Theodore's Commentary, either, as it was not of Diodore's.[20]

While Theodore has likewise left us no comprehensive preface to his Commentary on the Twelve Prophets, evidently his next work after the Psalter,[21] in introducing Haggai he does state his overall purpose, "by the grace of God to bring clarity" to the prophet's work. He does this by first relating each of The Twelve to his historical situation in the order in which they occur in his local text, which is the order of the Hebrew, not of the LXX; and on coming to Haggai he again surveys their placement from the eighth century to the return from exile. Having thus established a narrative setting, ὑπόθεσις, as on the Psalms Theodore is little disposed (at least by comparison with Theodoret) to depth the background of his text by supplying details of an historical, cultural, geographic or topographical nature, despite his rather superior attitude in introducing

---

[18] *Le commentaire*, 3.
[19] *Psalms* 2, 202.
[20] Cf. Hill, "His Master's Voice: Theodore of Mopsuestia on the Psalms."
[21] The basis of this conclusion is outlined in Chapter Six.

his work "as an indictment of those who presume to apply themselves to the prophetic utterances without due preparation, and also
by way of education of those coming after."[22] His readers might have
cared to have the commentator locate for them the home towns of
prophets, like Micah's Moresheth and Nahum's Elkosh, or investigate why it is that Malachi is to transmit a word of the Lord to
"Israel" long after the fall of that kingdom, but he declined. If in
the interests of precision, ἀκρίβεια, a virtue of Antiochene commentators, they expected him to pinpoint the location of the Tarshish
to which Jonah initially headed, and for which some commentators
had suggested also Tarsus or Rhodes, Theodore dismisses the item
as a mere exercise in ἀκριβολογία:

> For my part, however, I consider this entire chase after detail to be
> irrelevant to the subject in hand in so far as the account by the prophet
> is just as equally beyond question, no matter which city you think it
> to be.[23]

His predecessors often met with that fate from the young commentator, who for all his "due preparation" could himself be astray in
those historical details he did offer, as in introducing Hosea and
Haggai.

We shall in Chapter Ten observe Theodore responding to the
stirring passages on social justice themes to be found in Amos 8,
Micah 3 and Zechariah 7 for the benefit of his readers no more
sensitively than he had risen to the pathos of some psalms. By contrast, he does in this work unpack images employed by the prophets
(e.g., by Hosea 4:19; 5:13–14; Amos 4:12–13) and recognize some
of the literary genres to be found in The Twelve, with the exception
of apocalyptic—a serious flaw in commenting on Joel and Zechariah—
and the satire intended by the author of Jonah. When Nahum
indulges in what modern commentators refer to as a taunt song in
2:11–13, Theodore empathises with the prophet's satiric purpose and
imagery:

> *Where has the lion gone to gain entrance?* A very mocking remark: whereas
> they were ever doing battle and always making an assault on some
> one somewhere as though on prey of some kind, he asks, Where now

---

[22] *Theodori Mopsuesteni commentarius*, 1.
[23] *Theodori Mopsuesteni commentarius*, 178. Theodoret will venture to demur (PG
81.1724); cf. Hill, "*Sartor resartus*: Theodore under review by Theodoret."

has your leader gone? after what prey has he gone? He means, There
is an end to your fighting, your former power and might is finished.[24]

And while he succumbs in this work, too, to the temptation to detect
and adjust instances of ἐναλλαγὴ χρόνου in the text to suit ἀκολουθία
as he sees it (as at Joel 2:19–20), he has an eye to this movement
in thought by an author. When Mic 4:1–4 speaks in terms identical to Isa 2:2–5, a resemblance he does not acknowledge (not having composed, at least by that stage, a commentary on Isaiah), he
does note the vacillation between gloom and optimism in the prophet,
and finds biblical precedent for it.

> After mentioning the disasters being inflicted on them to this point,
> however, he then mentions also what will happen to them after its
> capture, and the degree of change for the better that will ensue. This
> custom of the other prophets and blessed David we have often demon-
> strated, namely, the disclosure of pleasant things after the experience
> of harsh things and in turn mentioning baleful events in order that
> through both they might instruct them by the frequency of the dis-
> closure, bringing them to their senses by the mention of baleful things
> and encouraging them by the brighter to hold fast to hope in God.[25]

Reference to "blessed David" here is typical of the limited intertextuality of this work of Theodore's as well, the Psalms Commentary
providing him with the bulk of his limited scriptural documentation.

It is the book of Jonah with its "novel and extraordinary things,"[26]
however, that finds the Achilles' heel in his approach to prophetic
material. Theodore disputes the statement in the text that Jonah fled
from God ("he had gone off to some other place far removed"),
went below (not on boarding ship, but) only when the hubbub began,
and enjoyed success in Nineveh after a brief call to repentance; as
we saw in Chapter Five, he feels he must rewrite the text. Jonah
had every right to be distressed (in 4:1) at Nineveh's reprieve: he
ran the risk of "gaining the reputation for being a sham and a char-
latan." An inherited accent on τὸ ἱστορικόν prevents Theodore's real-
izing that "all attempts to defend the prophet's reputation . . . miss
the purpose of the book within the canon. Such apologetics serve

---

[24] *Theodori Mopsuesteni commentarius*, 249–50.
[25] *Theodori Mopsuesteni commentarius*, 206.
[26] *Theodori Mopsuesteni commentarius*, 173. Cf. Hill, "Jonah in Antioch."

to weaken rather than enhance the truth of the book."[27] On the basis of these two extant Old Testament commentaries, then, one would therefore have to nuance the extravagant claims that have been made for Theodore as a literary critic.[28]

C. JOHN CHRYSOSTOM

Though Chrysostom also sat at Diodore's feet, and was even Libanius's preferred candidate to succeed him as Antioch's official rhetorician, we do not gain the impression from his homilies of a dutiful alumnus echoing the accents of his masters. To an extent, admittedly, the difference in style of commentary from, say, Diodore's and Theodore's on the Psalms is due to the difference in genre between works composed at the desk and homilies delivered to a congregation in a church or διδασκαλεῖον (and recorded, presumably faithfully, by stenographers). But there is also a sense of independence in departing from the structured approach to a text recommended in the schools, and in arriving at a different position on critical matters. Chrysostom does not abide by Diodore's ruling on the inauthenticity of psalm titles, a ruling duly accepted by Theodore, and he pays the penalty for the extra risk to which this independence exposes him. In Chapter Five we saw him embarking on a lengthy and irrelevant disquisition on inheritances at the opening of commentary on Ps 5 under the mistaken impression that the musical direction about "flutes" in the Heb. title derived instead from the verb "inherit." And though the text of his commentary on Ps 45 begins by distinguishing the reference in the Heb. title to a melody, "For the lilies," *shoshanim*, it also registers the faulty LXX version of the term, "On those to be changed," as though from *shanah*, leading Chrysostom to begin,

> This psalm, you see, was composed with Christ in mind; hence it bears the title 'for the beloved' and 'those to be changed.' He worked a

---

[27] B. S. Childs, *Introduction to the Old Testament as Scripture*, 426.

[28] Cf. Devreessee, *Essai*, 58: "Théodore, le premier et vraisemblablement le seul des anciens commentateurs, fait intervenir la critique littéraire;" Quasten, *Patrology* 3, 402: "He wrote commentaries to nearly all the books of the Bible which are remarkable for their free and critical investigations into questions of authorship and date and for their highly scientific, philological and historical approach. He was the first to apply literary criticism to the solution of textual problems."

great change in us, remember, both transformation and alteration in
circumstances. Paul, too, suggests this change in the words, 'So that
if anyone is in Christ, there is a new creation' (2 Cor 5:17).[29]

Chrysostom generally feels under no obligation to subject particular
psalms to historical categorization according to ὑπόθεσις (theme, or
narrative setting), σκοπός (purpose, thrust) and πρόσωπον (person,
point of view) in the style religiously adopted by Diodore and
Theodore, relating psalm and individual verses to the narrative setting and central character thus determined.[30] Ps 47, for example,
Diodore and his servile pupil decide relates to a Maccabees' victory
in the time of Antiochus and is uttered in their person, including
the call in the opening verses to praise the Most High God, which
they curtly bypass. Chrysostom, by contrast, after citing a number
of alternative versions of these verses—a further departure from his
fellows' practice—simply launches into one of his finest oratorical
crescendos that must have vastly impressed the congregation.

> Hence the psalmist says, *Most High, fearsome*. Rather, on the contrary,
> what could anyone adequately say in describing that day,
> when he sends his angels everywhere throughout the world,
> when all things tremble,
> when the earth is confused to be surrendering the dead in its keeping,
> when the myriad bodies rise,
> when the sky shrinks like a shrunken veil,
> when that fearful tribunal is established,
> when the rivers of fire are made to flow,
> when the books are opened,
> when he makes public each one's deeds done in darkness,
> when retribution and punishment are unbearable,
> when powers are menacing,
> when swords are drawn,
> when the way leads down to hell,
> when all rank counts for naught—kings, generals, supremos, viceroys,
> when a host of angels appears,
> when ranks of martyrs, prophets, apostles, priests, monks,

---

[29] PG 55.183.1. For other instances, see Hill, *St John Chrysostom. Commentary on the
Psalms* I, 10, 26.

[30] When a psalm title refers to an historical incident, like that of Ps 7 mentioning the encounter between David and Hushai, Chrysostom can go to great lengths
to turn the incident into a moral lesson. He is also aware that Ps 44 was generally taken to refer to the Maccabees, and gives a succinct account of that chapter
in Israel's history.

> when rewards are past telling, trophies and wreaths,
> when the good things surpass all understanding?[31]

There is here not simply a difference in hermeneutical perspective; the opportunity is taken to exploit the sentiments of the psalmist for the benefit of appreciative listeners, as we shall see in Chapter Ten being adopted by Chrysostom though neglected by his fellow Antiochenes of that century. Diodore and Theodore never moralize; in that regard they do not intrude into the preacher's domain, and thus escape the criticism we have seen Chrysostom incurring for a moral slant.

The apocalyptic character of that crescendo also alerts us to Chrysostom's awareness of the psalm genre and liturgical *Sitz im Leben*, that psalms are for singing, and are not just a text, as far as church practice in Antioch required. The congregation was expected to sing at least a responsorial verse, ὑπακοή, like the opening verse of Ps 42. Because there was the danger that "those singing it daily and uttering the words by mouth do not enquire about the force of the ideas underlying the words," he says at the opening of commentary on Ps 141, his responsibility lies in the direction of comprehension (which does not center on a psalm's supposed historical background): of Ps 44:12 he remarks, "The verse seems to be extremely unclear; yet pay attention so that your singing (ψάλλειν) may be done with understanding." He cannot allow himself the luxury of explaining only the responsorium, even if this be a particularly significant one like v.24 of Ps 118, which at Easter (as today) "the Fathers prescribed for singing (ὑπηκεῖυ) by the congregation; . . . we must address ourselves to the whole psalm."

Before the difficult verses with which the Psalter teems, Chrysostom like his fellows can fall to rationalizing when their modern counterparts have recourse to linguistic data. Ps 48:2 may have light shed on it from Ugaritic by a commentator like Dahood,[32] but for Chrysostom it is

> a cause of great bewilderment in the person who reads it casually, whereas the one approaching it with precision will see the sense and precise sequence of the ideas.

---

[31] PG 55.211.2.
[32] *Psalms* I, 289–90.

Precision, ἀκρίβεια, he esteems like Antiochene and other commentators, in his case seeing it as an effect of the divine considerateness, συγκατάβασις, manifest both in sacred history and in the inspired text, where the normal language of human intercourse is employed to convey a divine message. On Ps 47:4 he comments,

> He calls the nation *his inheritance*, not as though disregarding the others, but to give evidence of the extent of his love, his affinity for them, and the added gift of his providence. For you to learn the inspired precision, see how he employs the expression of common people, which they adopt in matters of commerce.[33]

No detail of the text is without significance; an apparently superfluous phrase in the opening verse of Ps 44 is shown to be relevant:

> Why did he not say simply (ἁπλῶς) 'We have heard' but *We have heard with our ears*? With what other part of the body does one hear? Surely the words are superfluous? Far from it: it is a common practice with human beings . . .[34]

A feature we noted missing from the treatment of the Psalter by Diodore and Theodore was documentation from other parts of Scripture, rendering their commentary bare. Chrysostom's commentary could never be called bare on this score; intertextuality can be so generously adopted as to submerge the verse under comment, as on the psalm that begins the series, Ps 4.

> *Be angry, and do not sin; what you say in your heart, repent of at bedtime* (v.4). What I said before I repeat now. That is to say, since his intention is to lead them to knowledge of God, he rids their spirit of ailments. He knows, you see, that a corrupt life proves an obstacle to elevated thinking. So that is what Paul too was suggesting in saying, "I could not speak to you as spiritual persons but as carnal persons;" and again, "As though to infants in Christ I fed you milk, not solid food" (1 Cor 3:1–2), and again, "On this matter we have much to say that is hard to explain, since you are slow to understand" (Heb 5:11). Isaiah as well, "This people seek me, and desire to know my ways, like a people that have practised righteousness and not forsaken my ordinance" (Isa 58:2). And Hosea: "Sow seeds of righteousness for yourselves, light the light of knowledge" (Hos 10:12 Grk). Christ in his teaching said, "Whoever does shoddy things hates the light and does not move to

---

[33] PG 55.213.4. Cf. Hill, *"Akribeia, a principle of Chrysostom's exegesis."*
[34] PG 55.168.1.

the light" (John 3:20); and again, "How can you have faith when you accept praise from one another and do not seek praise from the one who alone is God?" (John 5:44), and again, "His parents said this because they were afraid of the Jews, fearing they would be put out of the synagogue" (John 9:22), and again, "Many came to believe in him, and on account of the Pharisees did not confess their faith" (John 12:42). In all these cases you could see a corrupt life proving an impediment to committed belief.[35]

While it is a rich scriptural fare offered to his congregation, the abundance of citation may be a mark of immaturity (if not of editorial embellishment). It can lead to disproportion in treatment of psalms, so that the consequent haste by the preacher to reach a conclusion can by contrast result in the complete omission of scriptural reference, as in the case of Pss 44; 45; 49.

It is therefore perhaps not surprising that Chrysostom's homilies and sermons on Genesis, in which Photius noticed what Baur would later call a higher degree of an "appearance of actuality,"[36] are to a correspondingly less extent characterised by intertextuality as also by reference to alternative versions of the biblical text—features that may be thought by some (such as Mercati)[37] to suggest later editing of the Psalms homilies, or perhaps a difference in venue and purpose. It is clear that in both the Genesis series (as in the homilies on the Statues) the preacher engages more closely with his congregation(s); we saw him upbraiding them in one series for allowing a lamplighter to distract them from his words, while in the other he devotes much of Homily 6 to chastising absentees for abandoning him for a day at the races.[38] These two series also differ from each other in purpose: in the short series in 386 Chrysostom clearly has no intention of following closely the text, even of Gen 1–3, whereas in the longer series of sixty seven homilies it is the whole book that has to be covered systematically, even if it takes all of Lent to treat of twelve chapters and—after a break on the book of Acts—then resume at Pentecost.

---

[35] PG 55.50.7. Cf. Young, *Biblical Exegesis*, 115, on Chrysostom's manner of allusion to Scripture.

[36] Baur, *John Chrysostom* 1, 223. Photius, we noted, reported that engagement with the listeners was such during the Gen homilies that in his view they should be called not λόγοι but ὁμιλίαι (*Bibliotheca* 172).

[37] As conveyed by Dorival, "L'apport des chaînes," 62.

[38] Cf. Hill, "On giving up the horses for Lent."

As with many a preacher, he proceeds at a more leisurely pace early in the long series, thus having to gallop towards the end; and as also with many a preacher, it is possibly his longwinded treatment, μακρολογία, and departure from his text in the short series that makes the lamplighter's activity more interesting to a bored congregation. Still, even while himself digressing in Sermon 7 to examine the fate of the repentant brigand on the cross, he can entrance his listeners with his golden mouth.

> Let us see, however, whether the brigand gave evidence of effort and upright deeds and a good yield. Far from his being able to claim even this, he made his way into paradise before the apostles with a mere word, on the basis of faith alone, the intention being for you to learn that it was not so much a case of his sound values prevailing as the Lord's lovingkindness being completely responsible. What, in fact, did the brigand say? what did he do? did he fast? did he weep? did he tear his garments? did he display repentance in good time? Not at all: on the cross itself after his utterance he won salvation. Note the rapidity: from cross to heaven, from condemnation to salvation. What were those wonderful words, then? what great power did they have that they brought him such marvelous good things? "Remember me in your kingdom" (Luke 23:42).[39]

In the little time he addresses the Gen text in the short series, Chrysostom is still alert to details he finds significant, like the provision of a helpmate for the man in 2:18 who is not (he insists) the same as the animals:

> Lest you say so, he accordingly makes a precise distinction: he did not say simply, No helpmate was found for him, but *No helpmate like him was found for him.* Likewise here, too, he did not say simply, Let us make him a helpmate, but *Let us make him a helpmate like him.*[40]

The precision of the text requires precision in the commentator. Chrysostom labors the point in the corresponding passage in Homily 15 in the longer series:

> *God caused drowsiness to come upon him,* the text says, *and he slept* (2:21). Notice the precision of the teaching. This blessed author had stipulated both things—or, rather, the Holy Spirit through his tongue, teaching us the sequence of what happened. *God caused drowsiness to come upon Adam,* the text says, *and he slept.* It wasn't simply drowsiness that came

---

[39] SC 433.328.4.
[40] SC 433.222.1.

upon him nor normal sleep; instead the wise and skilful Creator of
our nature was about to remove one of Adam's ribs . . .[41]

There would hardly be a homily of Chrysostom where this point is
not made, as a consequence of his concept of the nature of the
Scriptures. It is basic to his reprimand of those who were less than
precise in quoting Jer 10:23 (and snatches of other scriptural verses)
to their own ends:

> Hence the need to give precise attention to the text. From two points
> of view it is a hazard and a pitfall, unless we read the verse soberly.
> What, in fact, are we to say—that the prophet lied? But that is peri-
> lous: they are God's words he utters.[42]

This was not a conviction that Chrysostom learnt from pagan
rhetoricians.

D. Theodoret

Those rhetoricians were not the source of the same conviction in
Theodoret's case, either; he shares Chrysostom's view, if not always
expressing it so eloquently—or at such length, conciseness being his
rule of thumb.[43] He begins his first piece of commentary, on the
Song of Songs, by querying the apparent tautology in that title:
"After all, the fact that nothing that is the result of the divine Spirit's
action is said idly and to no purpose" (a phrase occurring endless
times in Chrysostom) "is clear to people of a sober and pious mind;"
and he begs the reader's forgiveness "should the commentary
not strike you as precise."[44] In Chapter Five we noted Theodoret
acknowledging not only the influence of Chrysostom but a long list
of other predecessors on the Song; and it is a feature of his biblical
commentary that he allows himself to be indebted to those from

---

[41] PG 53.120.2.

[42] PG 56.156.2. Cf. the second homily on Isa 6 (SC 277.92.2): "The mouths of
the inspired authors are the mouth of God; such a mouth would say nothing idle.
Accordingly, let there be nothing idle in our attention."

[43] In acknowledging Theodoret's conciseness, Photius makes a generous estimate
of his abilities as a commentator (*Bibliotheca* 203): "On the whole, he reached the
top level of commentators, and it would not be easy to find anyone better at elucidating obscure points."

[44] PG 81.48–49.

beyond Antioch. Yet he is also aware of the dictates of the gram-marians and rhetoricians to which his own school had been exposed; in the case of the Song and other works attention is given to ὑπόθεσις, σκοπός, διάνοια, and as well he supplies a foreword or synthesis, προθέωρία.[45] We observed above that Theodoret brought particular gifts to the task of commentary, not only an openness to a range of resources and critical opinions, but also an independent spirit; in the case of the Song he acknowledges the opinions of "the holy fathers" but is ready to admit that "I am inclined to the view . . ." He is also sensitive to literary genres, surveying a range of them before identifying the Song as an epithalamium: "Solomon the sage com-posed a song that was not for triumph in battle or for morning prayer but for a wedding."

The challenge of the Song, of course, if the Christian commen-tator is to rebut the accusation of its being erotic, is to prove that it accords with the Bible's use of allegory and other figurative devices. Theodoret begins with that general principle, "Even in the Old Testament the divine Scripture says many things in a figurative man-ner, using different names for different realities;" and he proceeds to develop at great length in his preface Ezekiel's allegory of Jerusalem as an abject waif, with its own explicit sexuality. He is responsive to the lavish imagery of the Song, and capable of improving on it; when he comes to 4:11, "Your lips distil a honeycomb, bride, honey and milk are under your tongue," he elaborates on the image.

> Here it refers to the teachers of the church, offering religious teach-ing and, as it were, carrying honeycomb of bees on its lips, and dis-tilling drops of honey, containing not only honey but also milk, and providing to each the appropriate nourishment, both suited to the infants and adapted to the mature. Now, honeycombs borne on the lips of the teachers are the divine Scriptures, which contain bees that make honeycombs and produce honey, the sacred prophets and apos-tles; these latter fly about the meadows of the Holy Spirit, as it were constructing the honeycombs of the divine scriptures, filling them with the honey of doctrine and dispatching them to us for our benefit. The letter resembles the honeycomb, while the sense hidden in it resembles the honey; the lips of pious teachers release the drops of this honey. Also, milk flowing from their tongue reaches those in need of milk.[46]

---

[45] Cf. Viciano, "'Ο σκοπὸς τῆς ἀληθείας: Théodoret de Cyr et ses principes her-méneutiques dans le prologue du Cantique des Cantiques."
[46] PG 81.141.

The poetry of Solomon does not suffer at the hands of this commentator, even if we shall have to examine in the next chapter whether or not Antioch's hermeneutical principles are being respected.

The poetry of the Psalms is also in good hands when Theodoret later comes to comment on them. He begins by acknowledging that the Psalter is the staple spiritual diet of "those who embrace religious life and recite it aloud at night and in the middle of the day," and that people generally "gain serenity for themselves from the harmony of the poetry." The bishop of Cyrus, however, even while frequently recognising a sacramental reference in a psalm (e.g., Ps 23:5), shows little interest in any liturgical *Sitz im Leben* of the psalms in the manner of a Mowinckel. His classification of them shows signs of influence of Diodore's preface, with an eye to an historical ὑπόθεσις, but evinces also from other predecessors a readiness—unlike Diodore—to adopt a Christological interpretation.

> (David) employs not only prophetic discourse but also parenetic and legal discourse as well; sometimes the teaching he offers is moral, sometimes dogmatic; in one place he laments the misfortunes of the Jews, in another he foretells the salvation of the nations. Frequently, however, it is the passion and the resurrection of Christ the Lord he is predicting, and to those ready to attend he offers great satisfaction from the variety of inspired composition.[47]

He characteristically unpacks the psalms' imagery without warming to those whose religious sentiments have moved generations of singers and readers, like Ps 42. This psalm is simply assigned an historical setting by Theodoret (like Diodore and Theodore before him) and recited in the person of the people in Babylon, but plumbed by Chrysostom for its personal intimacy in these terms:

> What, then, is the introduction? *As the deer longs for the springs of water, so my soul longs for you, O God.* This is the way with lovers, not to keep their love a secret but to communicate it to the neighbor and say they are in love, love by nature being an ardent thing, and the soul not managing to conceal it in silence. Hence also Paul's statement of his love to the Corinthians, "Our mouth was opened to you Corinthians" (2 Cor 6:11), that is, I am unable to keep to myself and be silent on my love; instead, always and everywhere I carry you about in my

---

[47] *Praef.* (PG 80.861). Cf. Rondeau's verdict on this commentary, *Les commentaires* I, 137, "l'*oeuvre classique* of a bishop who regales his people with the knowledge to which he himself has access."

mind and on my tongue. Likewise also this blessed man, loving God
and on fire with love, cannot bear to keep silent, but at one time says,
As the deer longs for springs of water, so my soul longs for you, O God, and
at another, "O God my God, for you I watch at break of day, my
soul thirsted for you like a trackless waste, waterless and desolate" (Ps
63:1), as another of the translators likewise said. In other words, since
he is incapable of demonstrating his love, he goes about searching for
an example so as to convey his feelings to us, if only in that manner,
and makes us sharers in the love. Let us take his word for it, then,
and learn to love in similar fashion.[48]

It is not that Theodoret does not invoke alternative versions, we
have seen, or lend depth to the text with an intertextual approach.
His readers, in fact, are generally offered a rich scriptural fare (exceptions being certain psalms with which he feels no affinity, like the
Pilgrim Songs Pss 120–34, which he leaves quite bare of reference
to other parts of the Bible). It is just that, as we shall see in Chapter
Ten, these Antiochene pastors at their desk (as distinct from a preacher
in his pulpit with congregation before him) saw it as their responsibility, not to expatiate on the Psalms' spiritual riches, but to offer
their readers "some benefit in concentrated form," such as by concise exposition of content and precise recognition of textual detail.[49]

Even if it is true that "the Antiochenes were fascinated by prophecy,"[50] and even if he is not one to shirk an exegetical challenge,
in turning from Old Testament lyrical material to Daniel and Ezekiel
in particular after work on the Song Theodoret as commentator has
to change gear. He does not accept the judgement of the Hebrew
Bible that the book of Daniel sits rather amongst the Writings as a
collection of haggadic tales and apocalyptic visions than among the
Latter Prophets. So he is immediately involved in controversy with
Jewish adversaries (or with a *Ioudaiophrôn* like Theodore) who "cor-
don off this author from the band of the prophets and strip him of
the prophetic title itself,"[51] and addresses to them the question, "What

---

[48] PG 55.159.3. This homily, devoted only to the opening two verses of the
psalm, does not belong to the longer series of fifty eight. Cf. Hill, "Psalm 41(42):
a classic text for Antiochene spirituality."

[49] In the interests of ἀκρίβεια, Theodoret notes, for instance, that Ps 1 is lacking a title, that there is a definite article missing in Ps 2:1, "For what purpose did
nations rage?" and that in Ps 37:20 the LXX reads "but" for the "and" of Aquila
and Symmachus.

[50] Young, *Biblical Exegesis*, 168.

[51] Guinot, *L'Exégèse*, 746–47, accepts that it must be Theodore's work on the

do you claim is typical of a prophet?" Having accepted without question the reply, "Foreseeing and foretelling the future,"[52] Theodoret is intent throughout the commentary on establishing that Daniel measures up to this prospective notion of prophecy by validating the chronology and *dramatis personae* of the whole book, an (impossible) task which we saw distracted him from a critical approach to the text. He begins like a good Antiochene: "Let us first make clear the ὑπόθεσις of the inspired work, and then in this fashion come to the textual (κατὰ λέξιν) commentary;" and so he sets the scene in sixth century Babylon, entertaining no thought (we noted in Chapter Five) of there being different parts of the book composed by different authors in a later age.

While his readers may have expected also some initial sketch of the book's structure, they could not complain that the commentator does not enter into the spirit of the haggadic tales in the book's first half. And when in the text of Dan 3 (Theodotion's version) he comes to the song of the three (young)[53] men, his relish for the lyrical section leads him to embellish it, as he had improved on Solomon's and David's imagery.

> We praise and highly exalt you for bringing us kindnesses through angels, for creating heaven for our sake, illuminating the day with the sun and blending the darkness of the night with the moon, and teaching us the periods of time.
> We praise you for causing the sky to produce stars for us like a meadow, feeding our eyes on unfading blooms, and through their course providing us with knowledge of the stages of the night. Who could adequately sing your praises on seeing the changes, the alterations in the seasons, . . .[54]

Within this "willing suspension of disbelief" Theodoret proceeds in customary fashion to commend the biblical author for his ἀκρίβεια as a guarantee of the work's being true prophecy:

---

major prophets, as well as that of his brother Polychronius of Apamea, that Theodoret is rebutting as promoting a Jewish point of view. We note in Chapter Six, however, that there is no certainty that Theodore did proceed beyond his work on The Twelve to compose such commentaries.

[52] PG 81.1260.

[53] Swept up in the haggadic tale, Theodoret chooses not to advert to the time reference in 3:1 (Theod.) to Nebuchadnezzar's eighteenth year, when the "youngsters in the very springtime of their lives," as he puts it, would have matured somewhat. So much for precision.

[54] PG 81.1340.

> Blessed Daniel, after saying the first captivity happened in the third
> year of the reign of Jehoiakim king of Judah, then went on, *In the sec-*
> *ond year of his reign Nebuchadnezzar had a dream* (2:1), adding this further
> detail not without purpose, but for us to get a precise grasp of the
> time as well. This is the reason the divine prophets in mentioning the
> kings also record the number of years.[55]

He goes to his usual trouble to background the text for his readers,
initially sketching the succession of kings of Judah at the fall of
Jerusalem and their alternative names—Jehoahaz/Shallum, Eliakim/
Jehoiakim, Jehoiachin/Jeconiah. Inevitably, this careful background-
ing and precision come to grief at the beginning of Dan 6 with that
figment of the author's imagination, "Darius the Mede," where the
commentator is desperate to get the names and dates and reigns to
add up—without success, taking issue with an equally partial Josephus:
"The word of Josephus is completely incredible. I for my part, on
the contrary, put my trust in the divine Scripture."[56] It is a pity that
such a painstaking commentator should have embarked on an impossible task; his Antiochene mentors did not equip him adequately to
distinguish prophecy from haggadah and apocalyptic.

In turning to Ezekiel, then, where the apocalyptic genre figures
again, Theodoret labors under a similar handicap. Again he begins
by relating the prophet to his historical situation by nominating the
work's ὑπόθεσις:

> Let us venture upon a commentary on the divinely-inspired Ezekiel,
> attempt to plumb the depths of the prophecy as far as is possible for
> us, and make available to all religious people the value drawn from
> it. So come now, before the commentary let us outline the narrative
> setting in summary form.

Refuting the claim that the book is "shrouded in obscurity," he further backgrounds his text, as in Daniel, by leading his readers at
the outset through the maze of late Judah's kings and their alternate names, wresting from Josephus the detail that Jehoiakim was
left unburied by Nebuchadnezzar.[57] He is equally anxious to get the

---

[55] PG 81.1285.
[56] PG 81.1396.
[57] *Jewish Antiquities* 10.6.3, probably accessed through Eusebius. In his thorough
survey of Theodoret's sources in chronological, geographical, topographical and religious details, Guinot, *L'Exégèse*, 631–799, recognizes the indebtedness to the *Onomasticon*
of Eusebius.

measurements of the Temple to compute that were conveyed in a vision in the final eight chapters of the book, which he like his modern counterparts senses is an addendum, but which unlike them he is unable to allow to be the work of others. Typically he worries about burdening his readers with length of treatment here:

> Lest, however, by length of discourse we wear out the readers of this book by commenting on every detail, we intend to give in summary form a kind of paraphrase of what was revealed in spiritual fashion to the divinely-inspired prophet.[58]

It is all standard Antiochene commentary, taking prophecy in a prospective sense, concerned for the maintenance of "narrative coherence" (in the words of Frances Young) and benefiting in this case from his knowledge of Old Testament Judaism.

It is the inability to recognize and respond to apocalyptic that again brings Theodoret undone, as it had Theodore on The Twelve. Though he can appreciate the author's imagery as well as ever,[59] and allow the vision of the New Temple described in the final chapters to be "a spiritual vision, not a bodily one," he cannot make a similar allowance for apocalyptic material. The Gog and Magog of chs 38–39 have to be supplied with "a local habitation and a name" like any other historical characters; they are identified at once with the Scythian nations, and Theodoret's Antiochene predecessors are cited with approval in support of an historical interpretation of these figures in refutation of a commentator like Apollinaris who would deny them historical status:

> After the return from Babylon (those who were lately teachers of the Church claim) these nations advanced on Israel, and their interpretation is in accord with the prophecy.[60]

---

[58] On 40:1 (PG 81.1220). His unease about these final chapters emerges in his brevity of treatment and the paucity of intertextuality.

[59] When in Ezek 33:32 the Lord describes the exiles listening idly to the prophet's advice "like the sound of a sweet and melodious harp," Theodoret paraphrases the image, "Like people listening to an instrument producing harmonious music, drawing pleasure from it but not the knowledge of the way to play it, so too your words, O prophet, only charm their ears, they do not entice the soul addicted to wickedness" (PG 81.1152). A modern commentator L. C. Allen does no better, *Ezekiel 20–48*, 154, "(Ezekiel's) hearers functioned as a concert audience rather than a congregation."

[60] On 38:7–8 (PG 81.1201).

Theodoret will hold to this view in his next two works, on Haggai in The Twelve and on the Psalms.

The flaws in this style of commentary on prophetic material predictably emerge again when the authors have recourse to apocalyptic. Theodoret's Commentary on the Twelve Prophets appeals to us by comparison with two of those to which he had access, by Didymus in Alexandria and by his fellow Antiochene Theodore, for its serious approach to the historical situation of the prophets, in the one case, and its willingness to adopt a longer hermeneutical perspective than the *Ioudaiophrōn*; in this he resembles and is indebted to Cyril. He will follow his habit of outlining a book's ὑπόθεσις and σκοπός, as in introducing Hosea and Habakkuk; his purpose as always is "to make clear for the readers the thinking of the Twelve Prophets," as he says in the preface, "using the divine word like a lamp." He is attentive to detail, appreciative of his predecessors, tolerant of Theodore's outburst against Syriac translators (of Zechariah) if impatient with his Jewishness at times, and responsive to the prophets' figurative language. But apocalyptic motifs like the Day of the Lord in Joel and the sweeping scenario of "full-blown apocalyptic"[61] in Zechariah 14:1–2 escape him; in the latter case he conflates the text of Luke 21:20 and Mark 13:14–15, looks to Eusebius for a "story" with encouragement from Didymus,[62] and (possibly influenced by Cyril) adopts a New Testament perspective which, if more extended than Theodore's finding a fulfilment in Zerubbabel and Maccabees, is more limited than usual.

> The story is that when Vespasian and Titus were on the point of attacking, the faithful by a revelation then left the city; Christ the Lord also gave that advice in the divine Gospels, "When you see Jerusalem surrounded by armies, know that its end is nigh; then let those in Judea flee to the mountains, and the one on the roof not go down to get something from the house." He forecast this also in blessed Zechariah.[63]

It would be otiose to continue documenting this pattern of commentary in Theodoret's final work on the prophetic corpus, on Isaiah and Jeremiah, only to find him in similar fashion beginning the for-

---

[61] Hanson, *The Dawn of Apocalyptic*, 369.
[62] *Historia Ecclesiastica* 3.5.3; cf. Didymus, *Sur Zacharie* (SC 85.1076–80).
[63] PG 81.1952.

mer (where he is heavily indebted to Cyril and other Alexandrian predecessors) with the commitment,

> Before everything else we shall enunciate the work's ὑπόθεσις; in this way the commentary on individual sections will be visible at a glance,

but failing to recognize apocalyptic elements in sections of the book like 2:12; 14:2 and the so-called Isaian Apocalypse 24–27. The bareness and extreme conciseness of the Jeremiah Commentary (including Baruch and Lamentations), while displaying the above typical features of Theodoret's approach to a biblical text (which in our view corroborate its claim to authenticity), are probably due to its process of transmission. In closing that work, Theodoret could justly feel content in "thus leaving not even a single piece of prophecy without comment, thanks to God's grace."[64] It had been a remarkable achievement in the cause of introducing Antiochene readers to the Latter Prophets.

The work of this pastor was not complete even in advanced years, however, without attention also to those puzzling sections of the Old Testament, the Octateuch especially and Kingdoms & Chronicles, where in some cases predecessors had not ventured before. It is clearly the same Antiochene commentator at work in these two sets of Questions, attentive to detail, tolerant of others' views, knowledgeable of Judaism. The creation of the angels, as was mentioned above, occupies several questions, obviously to satisfy readers' interest;[65] "yet I shall state what I believe is in keeping with the σκοπός of the divine Scripture," he informs them in reply to Q.3 on Genesis. Though it seems that in responding to "questions" Theodoret is following a series of items determined to some extent by previous users of this genre, particularly Diodore,[66] the "modéré" Theodoret does not dogmatize when the biblical author is not specific:

---

[64] PG 81.805.

[65] In his Commentary on Paul's letters and elsewhere Theodoret comments on the widespread cult of the angels. See Hill, *Theodoret of Cyrus. Commentary on the Letters of St Paul* I, 3.

[66] Bardy, "La littérature patristique," 42 (1933) 224–25. Cf. Guinot, *L'Exégèse*, 794: "Il a trouvé en Diodore de Tarse le modèle auquel il emprunte la plus grande partie de son information, et qui, si l'on excepte les *QG*, a vraisemblablement été sa source unique." The epithet "modéré" applied to Theodoret is also Bardy's, "Interprétation chez les pères," 582.

> I do not state this dogmatically, my view being that it is rash to speak dogmatically on what the divine Scripture is not clear in stating; rather, I have stated what I gathered is in keeping with religious thinking.[67]

Despite some such limitations on his freedom to deal with textual issues, it can be said that the coverage of the key difficulties, ἄπορα, of the Octateuch and of Kingdoms and Chronicles is comprehensive (with the reservations voiced in Chapter Five about Theodoret's stance on critical matters of exegesis); there is no attempt to sensationalize pericopes like the sun's standing still in Josh 10:12–13 or David's slaying of Goliath in 1 Sam 17, and Ruth for the first time comes in for comment. On the matter of Saul's vision of Samuel in the encounter with the witch of Endor in 1 Sam 28,[68] Theodoret differs both from Origen and from Eustathius in maintaining that the vision was real and the prophecy was real, and so *a priori* both were God's work. The bishop may be forgiven for waxing eloquent on liturgical matters, such as Temple construction, measurements and furnishings, with which he is well acquainted. After a unique Commentary in Greek on the books of Chronicles, having despite his age not stinted attention to all parts of a further huge portion of the Bible in this Questions genre, Theodoret concludes his contribution to the biblical tradition of the faith in Antioch shortly before his death around 460, thus bringing to a close our period under examination.

Reading of the Old Testament in the course of that tradition was extensive, as outlined in Chapter Six. And we have now identified features of the commentary on it conducted by Antiochene pastors orally and in writing. It is, in fact, commentary they are conducting on these books, not exegesis strictly speaking. At the outset we acknowledged Kelly's reminder of this, though leaving to this stage a decision on his further caveat about patristic commentators, that they "could not understand the nature of Old Testament writings." By their attention to ὑπόθεσις, σκοπός and διάνοια, and aiming at promoting the readers' comprehension in particular, the Antiochene commentators kept their focus on the thrust of the material, even if they differed in their readiness to supply background for items in

---

[67] The compliment "modéré" is paid to Theodoret by Bardy, "Interprétation chez les pères," 582.
[68] Q.63 on 1 Sam.

the biblical text and illuminate it from other parts of the Bible, and even if one particular literary genre, apocalyptic, consistently resisted their approach. We may conclude in general, however, that readers in Antioch thus stood to come to a deeper understanding of the Old Testament than those in churches where commentators were less inclined to take the text at face value. If the Antiochenes owed something of this methodical style to pagan rhetoricians, Hebrew prosody presented a different challenge that often escaped them; on the other hand, they brought to the task their own theology of the inspired Word. In short, it is possible to identify an Antiochene style of commentary on the Old Testament; there is a degree of adherence to principles expounded by Diodore in his Psalms preface, though in the fifth century Theodoret will prove more independent and eclectic, displaying an enriching openness to other influences. This enrichment emerges also in the levels of meaning that could be found in, or given to, the utterances of lawgivers and poets, prophets and historians. To the ways of interpreting the Old Testament in Antioch we should now turn.

CHAPTER EIGHT

INTERPRETING THE OLD TESTAMENT IN ANTIOCH

If admissions of the obscurity of the Old Testament come more readily to commentators in Antioch, it is probably due to the commitment they have to elucidating the obvious sense of the text and
bringing their readers to comprehend it. We have seen them, like
modern commentators, acknowledging the difficulty presented by the
Psalms, for example, and regretting that, while people are in the
habit of reciting and singing them, they do not always "recognize
the sense of the words they sing,"[1] as Theodoret laments in his time.
That would be to their detriment, all the Antiochenes agree: the
Jewish Scriptures are intended for the formation of Christians as
well. For all their resentment against Jews of their time, they never
question the gift represented by the literature and institutions of
ancient Judaism, though this can be adduced as a reproach to later
generations of Jews; as Theodoret paraphrases Ezek 16:51, "You had
Law, priests, prophets, the divine Temple and worship according to
the Law."[2] Diodore evinced his esteem for these compositions by
writing commentaries on them all, we are told, and Theodore may
have done likewise, even if little of their work has survived; and
though Chrysostom wrote formally on the topic of Old Testament
obscurity, and his homilies on the New Testament are more celebrated, we still have a hundred and fifty on Old Testament books.
Theodoret even reversed these priorities by his claim late in life to
have commented on "all the prophets, the psalms and the apostle,"[3]
proceeding to add Octateuch, Kingdoms and Chronicles to that
impressive corpus.

For all the obscurity of these Old Testament texts, then, and for
all the exegetical limitations of the commentators, the biblical tradition of the faith in Antioch gave ample place to interpreting the
works of the προφῆται. We need to examine the levels of meaning

---

[1] *Praef.* (PG 80.857).
[2] PG 81.592.
[3] Ep. 82 to Eusebius of Ancyra, written in Dec. 448 (SC 98.202).

they found in them, beginning—notoriously—with that obvious sense, but not staying at that level. The question arises as to whether their hermeneutic can be classed as literalist, even fundamentalist, or simply literal. Ultimately, the further question arises as to where the Antiochenes judged the "truth," ἀλήθεια, of the Scriptures to be found.

A. A DISTINCTIVELY ANTIOCHENE APPROACH

The deeper theological underpinning of the pastoral commitment to explication of the Old Testament was, of course, the pastors' conviction of the divine inspiration of the authors and their text: "The same Spirit gave voice through both the Old Testament and the New Testament tongue," Theodoret says in comment on Isaiah 8:13–14, and we saw in Chapter Three Chrysostom's many such statements of the common source of both testaments. The challenge lay, however, in determining what the Spirit was saying in those more ancient, more variegated, more oblique compositions; we disputed above Kelly's judgement that the Gospels proved more opaque to ancient commentators, a thesis Chrysostom also rejected in his homilies on the subject of obscurity.[4] As in its style of commentary on the Old Testament, so in its hermeneutics Antioch distinguished itself from other interpreters to such a degree that, as we noted, modern writers have this aspect of biblical commentary in mind when contrasting Antiochene "exegesis" with that of other schools.

That it was a distinctive and contrasting manner of interpreting the Old Testament is clear already from Eustathius's criticism of Origen and his followers (specifically in respect of the incident of Saul's consultation of the witch of Endor in 1 Sam 28) for "concentrating not on the facts (πράγματα), as they should, but on the words (ὑνόματα)."[5] The criticism has been rephrased by Wallace-Hadrill thus,

> that Origen, and the exegetical (sic) school of Alexandria with him,
> lack the specifically historical cast of mind without which an exegete
> (sic) is hardly fully-equipped to handle the Old Testament.[6]

---

[4] Cf. Kelly, *Golden Mouth*, 94; Hill, "Chrysostom on the obscurity of the Old Testament."

[5] *Origenes, Eustathius von Antiochien und Gregor von Nyssa über die Hexe von Endor*, 16.

[6] *Christian Antioch*, 32. We noted in Chapter Five that it is not uncommon to find

Though from an exegetical point of view we may chide Eustathius for not at some stage acknowledging Origen's attention to textual matters, and expressing gratitude for such a useful textual resource as the Hexapla, his criticism is leveled and the contrast drawn on the basis of interpretation of texts (or "reading strategies"),[7] whether meaning is to be found primarily in words or in what they denote— facts, events, reality, πράγματα, ἀλήθεια, ἱστορία. Theodore and Theodoret found Didymus in Alexandria too little interested in the historical situation of the prophet and the restored community in his Commentary on Zechariah; he spends much more time developing levels of meaning that "it is possible" to extrapolate from the text. While Theodoret is more prepared than Theodore to leave room for an eschatological interpretation of the text beyond its obvious sense, they both find Didymus's priorities flawed. For them the text is primarily a window onto the events Zechariah is alluding to, not a mirror in which the commentator may see himself and the life of his contemporaries reflected,[8] not to mention a series of further layers of meaning rising upwards from the text, such that one is reminded of Young's metaphor, "Origen's exegesis finds it apex in 'spiritual' meanings."[9]

Why did the hermeneutical accent fall so differently in these commentators' approach to the same text? It is not the place here to enter the debate as to whether the Antiochenes' theology influenced their approach to the biblical text, or vice versa;[10] it may be possible in Chapter Eleven to contribute to it from the evidence adduced here from the principal commentators of the period. Philosophical schools, for their part, it was noted in Chapter One, did not exercise the influence in Antioch they did elsewhere. In so far as Diodore influenced pupils in his asketerion in Antioch, however, it is possible

---

writers speaking in terms of exegesis/exegete when it is rather interpretation that they have in mind.

[7] For examples of the reading strategies found suitable for interpreting the OT's "texts of terror" by commentators like Origen and Augustine, see J. L. Thompson, *Writing the Wrongs*, 242–46.

[8] Cf. A. C. Thiselton, *New Horizons in Hermeneutics*, 171–72, who sees Antioch adopting an adequate historical, spatio-temporal understanding of texts, more text- and author-centered than reader-centered.

[9] *Biblical Exegesis*, 122.

[10] Cf. Viciano, "Das formale Verfahren der antiochenischen Schriftauslegung," 404, for the respective positions of Schäublin, Greer and Simonetti in this debate.

to observe several hermeneutical principles, or reading strategies, being formulated and applied in his sparsely extant Old Testament works. We have seen him, as himself the recipient of the tutelage of "others" (doubtless including Eustathius) and possibly also during his Athenian studies the beneficiary of formation by rhetoricians of the kind to which Libanius exposed those pupils, directing the "brethren" in commentary on biblical texts to focus primarily on the author and his text—the former for his σκοπός, and the latter for its ὑπόθεσις. This focus would ensure that the accent in reading and commentary would fall on the factuality, ἱστορία, of biblical discourse, whether narrative or prophetic or lyrical (not that all were to be regarded as historical in the modern sense of the word).[11] Such an accent would preserve the reader and commentator from following arbitrary and gratuitous directions in the search for meaning of the kind Theodore and Theodoret found Didymus following; ἱστορία provided a sound basis for that search, and should not be undermined in a legitimate quest for other senses than the obvious— a quest conducted by the process of discernment, θεωρία.

> The factual sense, in fact, is not in opposition to the more elevated sense; on the contrary, it proves to be the basis and foundation of the more elevated ideas. One thing alone is to be guarded against, however, never to let the discernment process be seen as an overthrow of the underlying sense, since this would no longer be discernment but allegory: what is arrived at in defiance of the content is not discernment but allegory.[12]

As Eustathius had faulted Origen for shifting the focus in biblical commentary from πράγματα to ὀνόματα, in similar fashion Diodore criticized such "self-opinionated innovators who in commenting on the divine Scripture undermine and do violence to the factual sense" by substituting ἀλληγορία for a legitimate θεωρία,[13] the former in his view eschewing any connection with factuality.[14] Consequently, he

---

[11] Young disputes "the assumption that Antiochene literalism meant something like modern historicism . . . Whatever they meant by 'literal,' it was not exactly 'historical' in the modern critical sense" (*Biblical Exegesis*, 166, 168).

[12] *Commentarii*, 7.

[13] Diodore at this place in the preface to his Psalms Commentary has therefore, on his principles, to deny that Paul is employing allegory in his contrast of the earthly and the heavenly Jerusalem in Gal 4 by reference to Hagar and Sarah in Gen 16:15; 21:2,9, despite the apostle's use of the word in 4:24.

[14] It remains to be seen whether Diodore was correctly representing ἀλληγορία as practiced in Alexandria.

says, in our hermeneutics "we far prefer to ἱστορικόν to τὸ ἀλλη-γορικόν."[15] On the other hand, Diodore resists any tendency to

> draw us to Judaism and suffocate us by forcing us to settle for the literal sense (λέξις) alone and attending only to it, instead of allowing us to proceed further to a more elevated understanding.[16]

The biblical text is not necessarily monovalent, in Antioch's view.

From this preface to Diodore's Commentary on the Psalms, his only extant work, one gets the same impression of a reaction to reading (or misreading) works of another person or group with which the reader disagrees as one gets from Eustathius, rather than the impartial and irenic development of principles on an independent basis.[17] Perhaps this observation is relevant to the question we declined to enter at this stage, whether Antiochene hermeneutics is a result of theological positions or vice versa; in Diodore's case personal animus leads to hermeneutical obduracy, even to the extent of calling black white in reading Galatians.[18] We shall notice this *a priori* hostility to hermeneutical positions of others declining as the period progresses. Initially at least, however, Diodore's stance prevails in Antioch when it comes to commentating on the Old Testament.

B. The primacy of the historical sense

There is no questioning in Antioch in the period under discussion the conviction that Old Testament authors speak primarily about

---

[15] From a fragment of Diodore's work on the Octateuch; cf. Schäublin, "Diodor," 765, who cites also a work of Diodore reported by Theodorus Lector on the topic, "What is the difference between θεωρία and ἀλληγορία?" Socrates and Sozomen, perhaps not impartially, both contrast Diodore's attention to the "mere letter of the divine Scriptures" or "surface meaning of the divine words" with his avoidance of their θεωρία (PG 67.668,1516).

[16] *Commentarii*, 8. On the other hand, C. Kannengiesser, "The Bible as read in the early church," 32, may need to allow for some Antiochene interpretation in denying that in patristic hermeneutics "the Old Testament was scrutinized independently from the New."

[17] Cf. K. Froehlich, *Biblical Interpretation in the Early Church*, Philadelphia: Fortress, 1984, 20: "There can be little doubt that the hermeneutical theories of the Antiochene school were aimed at the excesses of Alexandrian spiritualism."

[18] Not that Origen's motives in downplaying the literal sense of a text were above reproach, either, in the view of R. P. C. Hanson, *Allegory and Event. A Study of the Sources and Significance of Origen's Interpretation of Scripture*, 257, who maintains that his finding a threefold sense in Scripture "was largely a façade or a rationalization whereby he was able to read into the Bible what he wanted to find there."

πράγματα, and that to most if not all of their books there is a factual character, ἱστορία. The Psalms are no exception, and it seems
that even one Antiochene commentator, perhaps Theodore, had
adopted the same principle in the case of the Song of Songs, if to
Theodoret's later disdain:

> Some commentators misrepresent the Song of Songs, believe it to be
> not a spiritual book, come up instead with some fanciful stories infe-
> rior even to babbling old wives' tales, and dare to claim that Solomon
> the sage wrote it as a factual account of himself and the Pharaoh's
> daughter. Others of the same ilk, on the other hand, portrayed Abishag
> the Shunammite as the bride instead of the Pharaoh's daughter . . . We
> therefore thought it necessary in beginning the commentary to take
> issue with this former interpretation, which is falsified and harmful,
> and then thus to render the purpose of the writing clear.[19]

It would be interesting for us to have a copy of Diodore's own commentary on the Song along with Chrysostom's. Theodoret acknowledges them as his predecessors—"Diodore, the noble champion of
piety, John, bedewing the whole world with the streams of his teaching to this very day"—where significantly the compliment for teaching as distinct from heroism goes only to Chrysostom; yet one cannot
imagine Diodore writing "in accord with the norms of allegory" like
Theodoret.[20]

It would likewise be logical for Theodore to look in the Song for
ἱστορία, having been encouraged by Diodore to find it in such mov-
ingly lyrical pieces in the Psalter as those beginning, "Lord my God,
in you I hoped, save me," which Theodore puts into the mouth of
David on hearing of the death of Ahithophel, and "As the deer longs
for the springs of water," on which he baldly comments, "Here
blessed David prophesies the fortunes of the people in Babylon."[21]
It is not sufficient that an unnamed psalmist at an unspecified period
gave voice to sentiments of hope and despair, joy and grief, love
and loathing, which might fruitfully be sung and meditated on later
by believers in the commentator's own time. To their detriment, as
we shall see in Chapter Ten, the faithful in Antioch had rather to
imagine the sentiments to be uttered by David in his own person

---

[19] *Praef.* (PG 81.29).
[20] *Praef.* (PG 81.40).
[21] *Le commentaire*, 35, 260 (on Pss 7 and 42).

or in the πρόσωπον of an historical character at some particular period of Israel's history, whether Hezekiah, Jeremiah, the people in exile or on return from exile, or even the Maccabees (Ps 44).

Faithful to his own principles, Diodore found such a factual basis in the great bulk of the Psalms; even amongst the few that he allows to be moral or doctrinal in content it is the Jewish people who are in focus, so that perhaps only three (Pss 1; 37; 49) are allowed to speak for people in general and none for the individual worshiper.[22] "The Lord is my shepherd" (Ps 23) is a sentiment of the people returning from exile, "The Lord is my light and my salvation" (Ps 27) of Hezekiah, "As the deer pines for the springs of water" (Ps 42) of the people in Babylon. Only occasionally is the odd verse of a psalm referring to an historical character allowed a general reference, like 33:5, "The Lord loves mercy and judgement" ("At this point he develops his theme in more general fashion"), the psalm being referred as a whole to Hezekiah.

Theodore clearly took a leaf out of Diodore's book, as we have seen; an historical reference can be discerned even in psalms that seem to be of general import, like Ps 36:

> After all, even if such psalms of blessed David do not actually contain an historical account of what he suffered, nevertheless it is thus possible at least to find out from his words the kind of person he was through what he suffered.[23]

It is on historical grounds that he establishes the exception that Diodore allowed for Ps 1 to be one of the three psalms of general applicability:

> No credence is to be given, however, to these commentators, who try to derive false comparisons drawn from history with a view to eliminating the true interpretation of the psalms . . . Joash, by contrast, is not presented in the text of history as a person of the kind to be thought worthy of being pronounced blessed. It is thus a moral psalm.[24]

The tradition that Diodore had accepted from "others" that tied the bulk of the Psalms to an historical ὑπόθεσις and πρόσωπον, which

---

[22] Cf. Olivier, *Commentarii*, lxxxi: "Il n'en est aucun considéré comme touchant à la morale strictement individuelle."

[23] *Le commentaire*, 194.

[24] *Le commentaire*, 2.

Theodore in his youthful deference had also adopted, his other pupil
John largely ignored, despite his interest in psalm titles. He is aware
of the belief that Ps 44 is recited "in the person of the Maccabees,
describing and foretelling what would happen at that time," and he
adds the comment, "The inspired authors (προφῆται) are like that,
you see: they span all times, the past, the present, the future,"[25] proceeding to fill the listeners in on the Maccabees' struggle with
Antiochus Epiphanes before moving on to almsgiving, proper behavior in church and other moral topics. And we have seen him adding
considerable length to his commentary on Ps 7 by detailing the incident of David's befriending by Hushai touched on in the title. But
the class in the didaskaleion that year in Antioch were not treated
to a series of history lessons when Chrysostom commented on the
Psalter; it was in no sense used as a history book, as would have
been the case with Diodore or Theodore in charge.[26]

To judge not only from his treatment of the Song of Songs but
also from his complete commentary on the Psalter, Theodoret would
also not have lectured on history; in fact, in his preface he gives
salutary warning of those commentators

> who make the inspired composition resemble historical narratives of a
> certain type with the result that the commentary represents a case
> rather for Jews than for the household of the faith.[27]

While it would seem that he has Diodore and/or Theodore principally in focus here, however, judging from the frequency with which
he rejects their approach throughout the work,[28] Theodoret at his

---

[25] PG 55.167.1. Artur Weiser, *The Psalms*, 354, is wide of the mark in claiming,
"The early church fathers of the Antioch school held that the psalm was composed
at the time of the Maccabean wars during the second century BC, and have been
followed by Calvin and the great majority of recent commentators."

[26] To omit Chrysostom from the profile of Antiochene exegesis/interpretation,
therefore, as J. J. O'Keefe does ("'A letter that killeth': towards a reassessment of
Antiochene exegesis, or Diodore, Theodore, and Theodoret on the Psalms," an article taking Ps 28 as a typical locus, where Chrysostom is not extant), is to encourage unbalanced generalizations about "the failure of the larger Antiochene exegetical
project" (86). O'Keefe is on firmer ground when he warns that "we should take
care not to lump all the authors together" (104)—as we should take care to include
all Antioch's major figures, as could have been done by choosing a psalm on which
all four are extant, like Ps 42.

[27] PG 81.860, where he warns also of those commentators who "have recourse
to allegory with considerable relish."

[28] Guinot, *L'Exégèse*, 712–13, finds that of the more than two score occasions

desk—as compared with Chrysostom in his classroom—is predictably readier to detect historical allusions in the Psalms, showing a fascination for marginal figures, like the Rabshakeh and Jonathan's treasonous son Mephibosheth (in Pss 25; 27; 31; 52).

In respect of the Old Testament's lyrical material, therefore, we can accept that Antiochene commentators found a (greater or lesser) degree of attention by the authors to πράγματα and ἱστορία. While we should also concede that particularly in this part of the Bible "exegesis (sic) at Antioch was not monolithic,"[29] its accent on the historical character of the Psalms was characteristic. Characteristic, too, and likewise not monolithic, was its attention to history in the works of the (Latter) Prophets; Didymus's interpretation of Zechariah κατὰ ἀναγωγήν in Alexandria could never be taken as Antiochene, and yet the two commentators on that prophet from Antioch differed in their degree of attachment to ἱστορία, Theodoret having the advantage of reading Cyril.[30] Diodore has left us nothing on the prophetic corpus of the Bible, though we can see his hand at work in Theodore's writings. Chrysostom has not left us a complete commentary on any prophet, either, but again we can see in what is extant a pattern similar to what we found in his treatment of the Psalms, where historical elements occurred fitfully and became an occasion for moral development of a topic the preacher chose to emphasize.

The only authentic piece of his on Jeremiah, a single homily on 10:23, focuses on the verse because of its frequent citation by people using it and other texts to discharge themselves of moral accountability. Chrysostom accuses them of "mangling the limbs of Scripture" by taking out of context the single verse, "Lord, people's ways are not their own, nor will human beings make progress or direct their own going." He insists that, in quoting the Bible, they need to take account of the historical and literary context of individual verses. The former context in this case is not easy to determine, there being conflicting views, to which he refers.

---

when Theodoret rejects a previous opinion to reach his own on the Psalms, it is that of Diodore/Theodore he rejects twice as frequently as that of Eusebius, who gives him access to the interpretation of Origen.

[29] Wallace-Hadrill, *Christian Antioch*, 39.

[30] A. Kerrigan, *St Cyril of Alexandria, Interpreter of the Old Testament*, 110, notes the "really striking" affinities of Cyril with the Antiochenes.

Some say it refers to Nebuchadnezzar: since the savage intended to make war on them, destroy the city and take them off into captivity, he wanted to convince everybody that he would prevail over the city on the basis not of his might and main but of their sins, God commanding the army and leading it against his own city; so he says, "I know, Lord, that people's ways are not their own, nor will human beings make progress or direct their own going." Now, what he means is something like this: this way which the savage is treading in waging war against us is not of his own doing, nor was he responsible for this war and victory; rather, had you not given us into his hands, he would not have prevailed or succeeded. Hence, he says, I beg and implore, since you have decided this, that the punishment be inflicted moderately. "Correct us, but deliberately and not in anger" (Jer 10:24). Since, however, some take a contrary view to this, and claim that it does not refer to the savage but to ordinary human nature, it is necessary to take issue with them as well.[31]

While on the subject, he mentions other scriptural verses equally lightly bandied about, including Haggai 2:8, which begins, "The silver is mine, and the gold is mine," to which people often added, "And I shall give to whomever I wish," thus again arriving at a justification for irresponsible behavior in defiance of the text. He retorts, "Such is the devil's malice, to introduce harmful doctrines by addition or subtraction or distortion or alteration of the contents." The only way to detect the distortion is to trace the verse back to its historical context.

Now, the prophet Haggai did not say that. When in fact the Jews returned from the foreign land, and were bent on rebuilding the Temple and restoring it to its former magnificence, they lacked resources, with enemies surrounding them, a great need felt, no supplies evident anywhere. So with the aim of bringing them to firm hope and of persuading them to be confident of the outcome, he said on God's part, "The silver is mine, and the gold is mine, and the final glory of this house will exceed the former."[32]

Antioch cannot tolerate arbitrary interpretation of prophetic and other texts that have been disconnected from their historical roots. The text should be a window, not a warped mirror.

---

[31] PG 56.159.4.
[32] PG 56.158.3. Cf. Hill, " 'Norms, definitions, and unalterable doctrines': Chrysostom on Jeremiah."

A preacher like Chrysostom, however, ran the risk of developing a text, once rooted in history, in a direction perhaps not intended by the biblical author. In 387 he delivered a series of homilies (the number a matter of dispute)[33] on the vocation of the prophet Isaiah in the opening verses of Isa 6 beginning, "In the year of King Uzziah's death," and proceeding to the vision of the seraphim attending on the Lord. What distinguishes the commentary (we saw in Chapter Three) are some beautiful formulations of Antiochene appreciation of the inspired Scriptures as a means of revelation and as an example of divine considerateness (συγκατάβασις) for human limitations (ἀσθένεια). Chrysostom reviews the divine considerateness demonstrated in the privilege accorded the seraphim and still more in the eucharistic κοινωνία with Christian communicants—a development permissible in Antioch once the preacher has given it some basis in factuality, ἱστορία. But this preacher has also a further theme to develop, the temerity of the Anomeans in presuming to examine the un-examinable; and for them Uzziah would serve as an exact paradigm, and his punishment very condign. Chrysostom therefore embarks on a further historical account from 2 Chr 26 of this king's attempt at usurping the privileges of the high priest, only to be struck down with leprosy. "Such is the evil of not keeping to the limits of the gifts given us by God, whether this concerns office or knowledge," he adds, with a codicil of his own added to The Chronicler's text to contrast the Anomeans' temerity with the seraphim's deference.

> This is the reason, at any rate, why they turn aside their faces and use their wings as a barrier, unable to bear the rays streaming from that source. And yet, you say, the vision was an example of considerateness (συγκατάβασις); so how was it they could not bear it? You ask me this? Ask those who pry into the ineffable and blessed nature, who presume where presumption is illicit.[34]

And, with a loose recall (not unusual in a preacher) of an historical situation applying rather in the time of Eli in 1 Sam 3:1, he dwells on the interruption of scriptural ὁμιλία as a punishment for the king's temerity. Despite the intertextual approach to the theme, the connection with historical roots has been preserved.

---

[33] Cf. Hill, "St John Chrysostom as biblical commentator: Six homilies on Isaiah 6."
[34] SC 277.90.2.

The loose connection with πράγματα evidently satisfied Chrysostom's congregation, whereas at one point in Homily One he concedes that an allegorical reference to another part of Isaiah would upset them, and "those not happy to accept allegories will reject our testimony." It would probably have upset also his master Diodore and fellow alumnus Theodore, to judge from the latter's single extant essay into commentary on the prophets, his Commentary on The Twelve (a work we are told Chrysostom also composed, though we do not have it). Theodore had read the work of Didymus, who treats the text of Zechariah as a mirror reflecting the situation of his readers, especially people dedicated to the contemplative life, for whom he develops a number of "spiritual" (μυστικός, πνευματικός, νοητός) meanings of particular verses by a process of ἀναγωγή or ἀλληγορία (the words arguably used interchangeably)[35] after a brief reference to the historical situation of prophet and restored community. That approach is anathema to Theodore. Those meanings and that process are not what his readers should look for—rather, it is the historical context in which a prophet exercized his ministry.

From the outset, then, he draws attention to the factual basis provided by the first of the Twelve in Hos 1:1:

> This is a kind of title to the book summarizing its contents, indicating both the prophet to whom the words belong and the time he uttered them . . . As a more precise indication he cites also the fathers' names. He had to mention also the time he disclosed the future according to the revelation given him from God, saying it was at the time that Uzziah, Jotham, Ahaz and Hezekiah reigned.[36]

The ensuing marriage of Hosea to the "prostitute" (in the LXX) strikes Theodore like any reader as unusual, but by no means beyond belief, let alone merely allegorical; and he proceeds to vindicate its historicity.

> The fact that God had the prophets do a number of things that to the general run of people seemed unseemly, like ordering Isaiah to appear naked and barefoot in the midst of everyone (Isa 20:2–6),

---

[35] This is the view of L. Doutreleau, *Didymus L'Aveugle. Sur Zacharie* I, 55–64, and of Simonetti, "Lettera e allegoria nell'esegesi veterotestamentario di Didimo," *Vetera Christianorum* 20 (1983) 341–89, but contested by J. H. Tigcheler, *Didyme l'Aveugle et l'exégèse allégorique. Étude sémantique de quelques termes exégètiques importants de son Commentaire sur Zacharie*, Fr. trans., Nijmegen: Dekker & van de Vegt, 1977.

[36] *Theodori Mopsuesteni commentarius*, 2–3.

clearly has the following explanation. Since we general run of people normally listen to words idly, but are startled at the novelty of what happens and comes to our attention, especially if it is at variance with the normal behavior of the one doing it, it made sense for God with the Jews' disobedience in mind to have the prophets frequently perform such things so that the people might in some fashion be converted by the novelty of what happened, and come to learn the reason and be instructed in their duty. Accordingly, he bade the prophet marry a prostitute.[37]

And so on throughout The Twelve, the narrative's ἰστορία always defended and always the focus of comment, even when an author has in fact ventured into satirical fiction (as in Jonah) or an apocalyptic scenario (as in Zechariah). The primacy given to the historical sense of Scripture by Antioch is in those cases shown to have its limitations.

In the next generation Theodoret in his work on "the book of The Twelve" will admit those limitations, though not abjuring Antioch's attention to a prophet's historical context or capitulating before Didymus's preponderantly spiritual interpretation of prophecy. In Cyril he had found a commentator who avoided hermeneutical extremes. Theodoret's overall aim, he says in his general preface, is "to find an interpretation in keeping with the reality (ἀλήθεια)" of the text; and in justifying the historicity of Hosea's marriage he not only relays the argument of Theodore and Cyril[38] but seems to allude also to the contrast drawn by Eustathius between looking in the text for πράγματα and treating it as mere ὀνόματα.

> I am very surprised at those who presume to claim that these words have no fulfilment, and that while God gave the instruction, the prophet did not accept it; instead, though the words were uttered, their fulfilment did not occur. Those rash enough to make this claim should, on the contrary, realise that God frequently gave many such instructions: he bade Isaiah take off the sackcloth from his loins, go around naked and unshod, and deliver his prophecy in this state; he urged Jeremiah at one time to put on his neck a wooden collar, at another an iron one (Jer 27:2; 25:13); and he instructed Ezekiel to lie down on his left side

---

[37] *Theodori Mopsuesteni commentarius*, 4–5.

[38] P. E. Pusey, ed., *Sancti Patris Nostri Cyrilli Archiepiscopi Alexandrini in XII Prophetas* 1, 15–17. Cyril takes issue with those commentators who deny any factual basis to Hosea's marriage or declare it distasteful; a Florentine catena is cited by Pusey attributing the former view to Origen, the latter to Eusebius of Caesarea.

for a hundred and fifty days and on his right side for forty days (Ezek 4:4–6 LXX) . . .[39]

But though he is no better equipped by his Antiochene formation to deal with apocalyptic in Joel and Zechariah, he sees no value in resisting the author's satirical approach to Jonah, and will look beyond the historical situation of Hosea to find an eschatological dimension to the Lord's marriage with his people in Hos 2:19.

As we have observed before of Theodoret's commentary on Old Testament texts, he shows the benefit of being exposed to different approaches, as emerges from his treatment of the whole prophetic corpus. From his Antiochene heritage he derives his commitment to establishing the πράγματα of the prophet's ministry and the ἀλήθεια of his prophecy confirmed in its outcome (ἔκβασις, τέλος). We saw him in Chapter Seven struggling to verify the chronology and characters in the haggadic tales of Daniel, and to vindicate Daniel as a prophet by his foretelling future events (prospective prophecy for the Antiochenes being the only valid analogue of that charism).

> The divine writings show him to be a prophet,

he claims in the preface in rebuttal of Jews who would remove the book from the prophetic corpus,

> and the fulfilment of the prophecy confirms the foreknowledge: witnessing the events in our time, we understand those ancient prophecies, and with guidance from them we easily appreciate the occurrence of the events.[40]

And he proceeds to cite historical and prophetic books as of equal value in establishing chronology. Moving to Ezekiel, where he is indebted to predecessors of another vintage,[41] Theodoret will still

---

[39] On Hos 1:4 (PG 81.1556). Theodoret will, under Cyril's influence again, come to take another view of a text's ἀλήθεια in his Commentary on Isaiah later in his career.

[40] PG 81.1264. That this seemingly naïve approach has not been completely superseded is clear from its recurrence in recent works such as that of R. B. Chisholm, *Handbook of the Prophets*, Grand Rapids MI: Baker Academic, 2002, which on the word of Jesus and Josephus instals Daniel as a prophet, endeavors to vindicate the historicity of the book's details (including "Darius the Mede"), and similarly defends the historicity of Ezek 38–39 and Zech without recourse to apocalyptic.

[41] Guinot, *L'Exégèse*, 747, sees Theodoret in this work resisting a Jewish interpretation (perhaps of Polychronius and his brother Theodore) to align himself with that of Origen, even if not directly in touch with his work.

begin by relating the prophet to his historical situation and insist
that even in olden times "the readers of the prophetic books found
their interpretation in the outcome." Faced with the prophet's visions
and prophetic actions, however, he allows that these must be taken
as non-physical, and admits another level of interpretation, criticiz-
ing the reluctance of an Antiochene predecessor (perhaps Theodore's
brother Polychronius of Apamea) to adopt a spiritual interpretation
of the ruler of Tyre in Ezek 28. This impatience with a consistently
historical interpretation of prophetic material is heightened in
Theodoret's Commentary on Isaiah, where the influence of Eusebius
and Cyril is pronounced: "Of the prophetic composition some things
are clear and have an obvious sense," he says in the preface, "while
others are spoken figuratively and require explanation." It may partly
be because of the form in which the text of the final Jeremiah
Commentary comes to us that this movement towards a less historical interpretation of prophecy is not so observable there.

If Origen chose not to take the book of Joshua at face value lest
it encourage critics of the Scriptures for its crassness, commentators
in Antioch on the Octateuch, though conscious of such critics and
more particularly the Marcionites, did not forsake their commitment
to the text's ἱστορία.

Some readers inquire irreverently,

Theodoret concedes,

> believing they find the divine Scripture wanting, in some cases for not
> teaching right doctrine, in other cases for giving conflicting instruc-
> tions; others by contrast search in a spirit of learning, longing to find
> what is sought. Accordingly, we shall stop the blasphemous mouths of
> the former

by

> bringing to the fore the διάνοια (meaning) concealed in the text.[42]

That meaning is generally a factual one, including the sense to be
given to the Fall in Gen 3; the tree of life and the tree of the knowledge of good and evil in 2:9 "also were products of the soil," though
given a further significance as well because associated with Adam's
fateful choice, just as

---

[42] *Theodoreti Cyrensis Quaestiones in Octateuchum*, 3.

baptism is called living water, not because the water of baptism has a different nature but because through that water divine grace makes a gift of eternal life.[43]

It is a delicate balancing act by a commentator at the end of his career, aware of the richness of a text's meaning, yet counseled by his betters against the arbitrariness of those interested only in spiritual meanings. The influence of Diodore, apparently his only source of alternative views in these Questions, would have been decisive.[44] Theodore, of whose work on Genesis only fragments survive, had warned against such interpreters,

> When they turn to expounding divine Scripture 'spiritually'—spiritual interpretation is the name they would like their folly to be given— they claim Adam is not Adam, paradise is not paradise, the serpent is not the serpent. To these people I should say that if they distort *historia*, they will have no *historia* left.[45]

So Theodoret insists that "it is necessary to adhere to the facts (ἀλήθεια) of the divine Scripture" in replying to Q.25 on Exodus about the division of the Red Sea; yet he can also take much of the liturgical detail in the Octateuch eschatologically for the benefit of Christian readers. Need for that flexibility does not arise so much in interpreting the narrative in the Questions on Kingdoms and Chronicles.

C. "The letter killeth"

If as is clear, then, the Antiochenes gave pride of place to an historical sense of the Old Testament text in their commentary on it, does that mean it was unsophisticated and literalist commentary? Or were the commentators aware of the danger of developing funda-

---

[43] Q.26 on Gen (*Theodoreti Cyrensis Quaestiones in Octateuchum*, 29–30). Bishop Theodoret will frequently detect a sacramental meaning in texts.

[44] Cf. Guinot, *L'Exégèse*, 792, 794, believes that Diodore's Questions would have been Theodoret's only source—hence we find in the latter "un recueil fortement marqué par l'influence du maître antiochien de l'exégèse." Only fragments of Diodore's work are extant.

[45] In commentary on Gal 4:24 according to the fifth century Latin version edited by H. B. Swete, *Theodori Episcopi Mopsuesteni in epistolas B. Pauli Commentarii* I, Cambridge: CUP, 1880, 74–75. Severian of Gabala had spoken in quite similar and equally polemical terms in the last of his six homilies on the Hexameron (PG 56.492.7).

mentalist readers in the course of the biblical tradition of the faith? Wallace-Hadrill defends Antioch "against any charge of crude rigidity of mind," claiming to find instead "an elasticity of approach which is in some respects more sympathetic to twentieth-century minds than is the Alexandrian." He believes that literalism is a term that

> hardly fits the Antiochenes. There is nothing crudely literal-minded about insisting that an ancient text should be seen primarily in its own terms, a procedure involving an effort at historical understanding and presupposing what may be called a sacramental view of historical events.[46]

Perhaps as well as reminding him of his own caveat, that "exegesis at Antioch was not monolithic" (we recall the flat-earth approach to Gen 1 by Severian),[47] and that generalizations are unwise,[48] we need here again to decline an invitation to enter into a full-scale comparison between Antioch and Alexandria, as also between either of these schools and modern critical approaches—a pointless exercise.

As another commentator on Antiochene hermeneutics, Thiselton helps us distinguish a literalist commentator from one who is merely literal in approaching the text. For Chrysostom, he remarks,

> the 'literal' may include the use of metaphor or other figures of speech, if this is the meaning which the purpose of the author and the linguistic context suggest.[49]

In those terms all the Antiochenes approach the Old Testament literally, as hopefully we all do; of them all, Theodoret perhaps works hardest to engage with the literary artifice of the author, even gilding the lily at times, whereas Theodore is more often shown unwilling to take the trouble. Diodore, too, can be seen in places as perversely unwilling to recognize a figurative expression in a psalm; when in

---

[46] *Christian Antioch*, 33, 32. The editors of the *Ancient Christian Commentary on Scripture*, Downers Grove Ill: InterVarsity Press, 2001–, in its several volumes have appended the following "Biographical Sketch" (not to Diodore but) to Theodore: "founder of the Antiochene, or literalistic, school of exegesis."

[47] Homily 3 *In Cosmogoniam* (PG 56.447–56).

[48] B. Nassif, "'Spiritual exegesis' in the School of Antioch," 374, remarks that people have "overgeneralized the extent of hermeneutical unity among the Antiochenes... The Antiochene Fathers need separate monographs."

[49] *New Horizons in Hermeneutics*, 173. Cf. Asensio, "El Crisóstomo," 334, of Chrysostom, "exegésis innegablemente literal, pero no literalista."

reference to Jerusalem Ps 48:8 says, "God established it forever," the psalmist would have been amused to find the commentator correcting him for looseness of expression:

> *Forever* does not mean for the whole of time: how could it, when the city was later besieged both by Antiochus and by the Romans? Instead, it is customary with Scripture often to call temporary things eternal.[50]

It was possibly Theodore who took the Song of Songs at face value as Solomon's account of his relationship with Pharaoh's daughter, whereas Theodoret lectured such commentators on the need to

> understand that even in the Old Testament the divine Scripture says many things in a figurative manner: it uses different names for different realities."

And citing Paul's strictures in 2 Cor 3:6 (which refer rather to interpretation of the Torah), he assures lazy readers that

> we do not take (the Song) in the way that we read it, nor do we rely on the letter that killeth; instead, by getting within it, we search for the Spirit's meaning, and enlightened by him we take spiritually the Spirit's sayings.[51]

A literalist, on the other hand, is content to take a statement or work at face value without attempting or managing to divine the author's intention; Theodore of set purpose fails to acknowledge the intention of the author of the book of Jonah to satirize a brand of prophetism in Israel in the person of this reluctant, self-obsessed grouch who begrudges the Lord his willingness to forgive the repentant of any race or nation—just as today's creationists with their own agenda are not willing to respect the intentions of the authors of the Genesis creation stories, and thus may be classed literalists or fundamentalists. Depending on the degree to which their commentaries have survived, every Antiochene will at some stage fail on the score of simplistic interpretation; even the "modéré" Theodoret fails to recognize the purpose of the haggadic tales and apocalyptic visions of Daniel, and in his zeal to reinstate the book among the Latter Prophets he believes he sees a sixth century prophet uttering prospective prophecy that is validated in later history.

---

[50] *Commentarii*, 288.
[51] *Praef.* (PG 81.33,37).

To the extent, however, that all four Antiochenes in our period simply "insisted that an ancient text should be seen primarily in its own terms" (if they could recognize what this meant in every case), their procedure was generally not literalist or fundamentalist. Diodore was doing only that in allowing for "an elevated sense" in a psalm on the proviso that the underlying sense was not prejudiced; and he could not be called uncritical in subjecting psalm titles to scrutiny as the work of later interpolators. Chrysostom comes to Genesis aware that he will find levels of meaning in this sometimes obscure text: "There is a great treasure stored up in the Scriptures, concealed beneath the surface," he tells his congregation in Homily 45; "so there is need of study so that we can learn the force hidden beneath the surface."[52] Yet we would class him as unsophisticated in failing to see different hands at work in multiple creation stories in Genesis 1 and 2 and in multiple genealogies in 4 and 5. He is also at least naïve in his paraphrase of Gen 2:18, "The man gave names to all cattle," in Sermons 3 and 6: as an exercise of his government of all things, Adam gave all the animals names, God has never changed them, "and the names given by him have remained current." He likewise has no difficulty with a talking serpent, and though "in the narrator's mind it is scarcely an embodiment of a 'demonic' power and certainly not of Satan,"[53] Chrysostom readily makes that identification in the course of his moral treatment of the Fall. Many of the "questions" posed on the Octateuch were predictably of a fundamentalist nature, wanting the commentator to resolve apparent discrepancies of a factual kind (hence Origen's declining to adopt the genre). In his replies to such queries Theodoret does not always remind the reader of the priority of truth to fact in biblical discourse; when Q.20 on Exodus reads, "If all the water was changed into blood, how did the Egyptians' enchanters do likewise with their charms?" in reference to Exod 7:22, he simply replies to them on their own terms,

> The sea was near them, and only the river water had been changed into blood; so they were able to bring seawater into the palace and change it to the color of blood.[54]

---

[52] PG 54.414.1.
[53] G. Von Rad, *Genesis*, 83.
[54] *Theodoreti Cyrensis Quaestiones in Octateuchum*, 115.

More than once, however, he will remind them that recourse to the face value of the text, τὸ γυμνὸν γράμμα, is not an adequate hermeneutical principle; when the questioner sees injustice in Exod 20:5 in God's inflicting punishment on later generations, Theodoret cites Deut 24:16 and observes: "The fact that paying attention to the face value of the text is a mark of impiety God himself brings out by requiring the opposite."[55]

D. A LEGITIMATE SEARCH FOR OTHER MEANINGS

The genre of question and answer was thus a stimulus to a flexible commentator to recognize and convey levels of meaning in a biblical text; it was not always appropriate to stay at the level of τὸ γυμνὸν γράμμα: one may have to move to another level to grasp fully the author's meaning. All the Antiochenes constantly warn readers of the Old Testament against its anthropomorphisms; these are simply examples of the concreteness, παχύτης, of scriptural discourse, Chrysostom explains, which should be seen as an effect of divine συγκατάβασις catering to our limitations. Diodore as master in his asketerion admitted in introducing the Psalter that he was open to a further level of meaning beyond the surface meaning:

> We shall treat of it historically and textually (κατὰ τὴν ἱστορίαν καὶ τὴν λέξιν) and not stand in the way of a spiritual and more elevated sense (τὴν ἀναγωγὴν καὶ τὴν θεωρίαν).[56]

His only requirement, we saw, was that continuity ("coherence," in Young's term)[57] be preserved between both senses, "the underlying" and "the more elevated;" he had no patience with those who severed that connection, or developed levels of meaning gratuitously and arbitrarily, as Eustathius had found in Origen, and Theodore and Theodoret would observe in Didymus (and modern commentators on Origen have to explain).[58] To Diodore that lack of conti-

---

[55] *Theodoreti Cyrensis Quaestiones in Octateuchum*, 115, 129.

[56] *Commentarii*, 7.

[57] *Biblical Exegesis*, 176: "What (the Antiochenes) resisted was the type of allegory that destroyed textual coherence."

[58] Robert J. Daly in the foreword to his translation of H. U. von Balthasar's *Origen. Spirit and Fire*, xvi–xvii, concedes that the schema of a threefold sense of Scripture developed by Origen (such as that laid out by H. De Lubac, *Histoire et*

nuity was to be found in allegory, and was anathema;[59] hence in his view Paul was astray in using the term of his legitimate movement from Hagar and Sarah to the earthly and the heavenly Jerusalem in Gal 4, where continuity is in fact preserved. Both the manner of moving with continuity to a further level of meaning and its outcome can be styled θεωρία, Diodore declares, as the opposite, arbitrary movement and outcome are ἀλληγορία: there is a necessary antithesis involved, as likewise ἀλληγορία parts company with ἱστορία and the underlying sense of a scriptural text.[60]

The influence Diodore exerts in this manifesto and his further axiom, "We far prefer τὸ ἱστορικόν to τὸ ἀλληγορικόν," is shown by the adoption by the Antiochenes (and later commentators) of the two terms θεωρία and ἀλληγορία as representing the respective positions of Antioch and Alexandria, and the ongoing Antiochene reservations about recognizing allegory in the Old Testament in particular. When in his third homily on Isaiah 6 Chrysostom wants to document the devil's arrogance, he has to forego any support from another Isaian text (14.14, the words of the king of Babylon), knowing his congregation would resist any such allegorical application of the text, and so he settles for Paul's plain statement to Timothy (1 Tim 3:6):

> If, on the one hand, we cite Isaiah as witness in his words about him, "I shall rise up to heaven, and I shall be like the most high," those not happy to accept allegories will reject our testimony; if, on the other

Esprit, 139–43) is open to criticism on the score of arbitrariness and irrelevance. The scheme is laid out at no one place in Origen's works, unlike Diodore's in his Psalms Commentary. R. P. C. Hanson, *Allegory and Event*, 257, is even more trenchant in his criticism of Origen's method, which he finds "ultimately self-frustrating. In an effort to distinguish objectively between three different senses of Scripture he only succeeded in reaching a position where all distinctions were dissolved in a 'spiritual' sense which was in fact governed by nothing but Origen's arbitrary fancy as to what doctrine any given text ought to contain."

[59] This judgement by Diodore affected Antiochene thinking not only on Scripture but also on Christology, soteriology, morality and spirituality, as we shall see later.

[60] This was the view taken of allegory by A. Vaccari, "La θεωρία nella scuola esegetica di Antiochia," 12: "La essenziale differenza fra teoria e allegoria consiste in ciò, che l'allegoria esclude di sua natura il senso letterale." In the view of P. Ternant, "La θεωρία d'Antioche dans le cadre de sens de l'Ecriture," 136–38, that was also the view of allegory defined by the rhetors, and unfairly applied by Antioch to Alexandria's use of it—though De Lubac is wrong to claim it was never used there in that fashion. "Par θεωρία Antioche entendait signifier sa propre position, et par ἀλληγορία celle de l'adversaire." It was Diodore, Ternant claims, who gave the name θεωρία to the method of finding "les réalités supérieures."

hand, we call Paul to prosecute him, no one will have any further objections.[61]

Theodore predictably will make no attempt to recognize any use of allegory in the two works he comments on (with one explicable exception).[62] In fact, focusing strictly on the ἰστορία of the Psalms and The Twelve, he is loath (we shall see) to recognize a further level of meaning, including texts applied by the New Testament to Jesus or the Church, like Pss 22; 31; 69, Joel 2 and Amos 9.

With the lapse of time, however, and exposure to predecessors of another school, Theodoret in adopting a spiritual approach to the Song of Songs as his first exegetical work claims familiarity with "the norms of allegory"[63] in rehearsing Ezekiel 16 & 17 and, as we have seen, warns about the deadly effect of adherence to the letter. After infringing that latter principle himself in his next work in his fruit-less attempt to vindicate the historical character and prophetic cre-dentials of Daniel, he proceeds in commentary on Ezekiel to engage again with the allegorical presentations of Jerusalem in chs 16 & 17 and also the prophet's use of "the genre of allegory"[64] in ch 23 to present Samaria and Jerusalem as the daughters Oholah and Oholibah. Though in commentary on The Twelve he joins Theodore and Cyril in protesting against those who chose to see Hosea's marriage not as one more prophetic action but as allegorical, he will differ from the former in allowing an allegorical interpretation—with New Testa-ment support—to verses like Hab 3:17 and Zech 4:14; and again

---

[61] SC 277.122.3. Chrysostom makes one other brief essay into allegory, in com-ment on Ps 7:12, where John the Baptist's words (Luke 3:9) about the axe being laid to the root are cited. Chrysostom proceeds: "What, then is the axe? Retribution and punishment. And what are the trees? People. What is the straw? The unwor-thy. What is the grain? The virtuous. What is the winnowing fan? Judgement. Likewise in this verse sword and bow and arrows are punishment and retribution" (PG 55.98). Even Diodore would commend the brevity of the excursus, the sup-port cited from the New Testament, and the continuity of thought.

[62] The exception is Ps 45, which Jewish commentators wanted to refer to Solomon. Theodore rebuts the interpretation: "He also mentions a *queen* (v. 9), by *king* refer-ring to Christ, and by *queen* to the Church composed of the faithful" (*Le commen-taire*, 279). On this psalm he even adverts briefly to the two daughters Oholah and Oholibah in the allegory of Samaria and Jerusalem in Ezek 23, without using the term.

[63] *Praef.* (PG 81.40). Guinot, *L'Exégèse*, 643–44, sees Theodoret accessing the inter-pretation of the Song by Origen through the work of Eusebius (while not being certain that Eusbius himself composed a commentary).

[64] On Ezek 23:18 (PG 81.1040).

under Cyril's influence he is even more amenable to such an interpretation in later work on Isaiah. In coming to the Octateuch,
Theodoret may have been aware that commentators of another school
took much of the material allegorically, as Origen did on Joshua; so
when he opens comment on that book, he adverts to Paul's allegorical use of Hagar and Sarah in Gal 4, probably aware that
Diodore had been uneasy about the apostle's adoption of such a
hermeneutic.

> He wrote this, not to exclude the factual basis (ἱστορία), but to com-
> pare the type to the reality—Abraham to God, the women to the two
> covenants, the sons to the peoples. Here too, therefore, in similar fash-
> ion Moses is to be understood as the Law, and Joshua as the savior
> of the same name. Now, the fact that the Law goes under the name
> of Moses we have already demonstrated by citing the testimonies of
> the divine Scripture: "They have Moses and the prophets" (Luke 16:29)
> and "To this day when Moses is read out, a veil lies over their heart"
> (2 Cor 3:15). So just as when Moses died in actual fact, Joshua led
> the people into the promised land, so after the end of the Law our
> Joshua came and opened the kingdom of heaven to the devout people.[65]

That the continuity has been preserved in "the more elevated sense,"
as Diodore required, New Testament citation confirms; so his readers can rest assured. The same principle applies to interpretation of
the Gen 38 story of Tamar's twins Zerah and Perez (cf. Matt 1:3)
and the crimson thread that established priority for the former:

> This is the reason that Zerah thrust his hand out first, pointing to the
> way of life before the Law. The crimson thread was a pointer to the
> sacrifices of old; those men appeased God with sacrifices—Abel, Enoch,
> Noah, Melchizedek, Abraham, Isaac and Jacob. He next withdrew his
> hand, and Perez came out, the Law being midway between those
> before the Law and those after the Law.[66]

Treatment of Kingdoms and Chronicles does not require application of this hermeneutic, and the commentator does not invoke it.
    Though Diodore had allowed in principle for a further level of
meaning in Old Testament texts beyond the factual under certain
conditions, his general avoidance of it was taken by Theodore to
mean that "spiritual" interpretations were suspect (we saw above in

---

[65] *Theodoreti Cyrensis Quaestiones in Octateuchum*, 268.
[66] *Theodoreti Cyrensis Quaestiones in Octateuchum*, 205.

his comment on Gal 4:24); even the term θεωρία is found rarely in his mouth, in reference to the New Testament's citing texts.[67] Chrysostom, on the other hand, simply accepted the licence allowed in Diodore's principle, which in fact must be applied to make sense of the Bible's use of figurative language. To show how a verse like Ps 115:16 must thus be understood, he cites a similarly anthropomorphic statement in Jer 23:24.

> "Do I not fill heaven and earth? says the Lord." It would have the opposite meaning to this if we were to take the words at face value (κατὰ τὴν πρόχειρον) superficially, and were not to have regard to the fuller sense (θεωρία) contained therein. So what does he mean by *The heaven is the Lord's heaven, but the earth he has given to human beings?* He is employing language out of considerateness (συγκατάβασις).[68]

After commenting on all the verses of the psalm numbered 147 in the LXX (Heb. 147:12–20), he tells his congregation:

> What has been said, then, is adequate for the literal sense (κατὰ τὸν ῥητόν). If, however, you have the desire to take the psalm also in an anagogical sense (κατὰ ἀναγωγήν), we shall not decline to travel that path as well, without doing violence to the historical meaning (τὴν ἱστορίαν)—perish the thought—but along with it adding this as well for the benefit of the scholars to the extent appropriate.[69]

And he proceeds to re-interpret all the verses, accepting the licence while respecting Antioch's hermeneutical priorities and safeguards.

Theodoret's willingness to move to another level of meaning does not need documenting any further. As he adopted a completely spiritual interpretation of the Song of Songs in accordance with "the norms of allegory," he uses the same phrase in giving a spiritual meaning to the ruler of Tyre and to Pharaoh in Ezekiel 28 & 31.[70] Approaches to the Psalms that were either too allegorical or too historical were rejected in favor of a "moderate historicism"[71] that allowed also for another level of interpretation. That further level could often be classed generally as eschatological, the literal referent

---

[67] Theodore will also employ the term (in connection with the term λῆμμα for the prophetic oracle uttered in a state of ecstasy) of the contemplation possible to an ecstatic Nahum (*Theodori Mopsuesteni commentarius*, 239).

[68] PG 55.313.6.

[69] PG 55.483.3.

[70] On Ezek 31:10 (PG 81.1124).

[71] Wallace-Hadrill, *Christian Antioch*, 39.

pointing ahead to a later one—in Theodoret's case to the person of Jesus, the Church, some other New Testament person or event, or an eternal realization such as the heavenly Jerusalem. On Ps 33:6, for instance, Theodoret comments,

> *By the word of the Lord the heavens were established, and by the breath of his mouth all their power.* Effort and time on the part of workers were not required: a word was sufficient for creating on his part; he said, remember, Let a firmament be made, and so it was; Let lights be made in the firmament of heaven, and so it was (Gen 1:6–7,14–15). So the face value of the text conveys the surface meaning of this; it was appropriate for the Jews of old. True theology, on the other hand, gives a glimpse of God the Word with the all-holy Spirit making the heavens and the heavenly powers. Old Testament inspired composition anticipates the Gospel teaching.[72]

That final axiom was not derived from Diodore, who had acknowledged a direct messianic reference in only four psalms (Pss 2; 8; 45; 110), as would Theodore. These men would probably deny that the "true theology" of the Old Testament emerges only from looking ahead to the New Testament; that would represent a reversal of Antiochene priorities, as Chrysostom was at pains to insist above that giving an anagogical sense to LXX Ps 147 should not "do violence to the ἱστορίαν—perish the thought." The basic question to put to Old Testament authors and composition was, Where lies the text's true reality, the truth, ἀλήθεια?[73]

E. Where lies the truth?

The question applies in particular to prophetic material (always prospective for Antioch), whether in the Latter Prophets or in a composer like David. In introducing Joel, Theodore gives David pride of place as a prophet of "what would shortly happen."

> First place among them, as I said before, was held by blessed David, who long ago—in fact, very long ago—and well before the outcome of the events mentioned all that would happen in regard to the people

---

[72] PG 80.1096.

[73] Cf. Schäublin, *Untersuchungen*, 170: "Der Bezug auf die 'Realität', die ἀλήθεια, stellt aber die wohl entscheidende Komponente der antiochenischen 'historischen' Auslegung dar."

at different times. The same thing was done also by the other prophets, who later mentioned what had long before been said by him, and a little before the actual outcome of the events, the purpose being both to remind everyone of what had been prophesied and, by saying what would shortly happen, to disclose the truth of the prophecy.[74]

The events foretold, πράγματα, would "shortly" have their outcome, ἔκβασις, thus proving the truth, ἀλήθεια, of what was foretold. The perspective was not extended into the dim and distant future of the New Testament, let alone the eschaton; even before Jesus a figure like Zerubbabel was a likely candidate, and even before the Roman conquest of Judea or a distant Armageddon, the avenging angel of 701 that annihilated Sennacherib's forces or the Maccabees in battle against Antiochus gave closure to prophecies of future hostilities and ultimate victory. Theodore, we noted, had been instructed by the aphorisms of Aristarchus to "clarify Homer from Homer"[75]—in other words, to look within the Old Testament for fulfilment (ἔκβασις, τέλος) of Old Testament prophecies; the perspective need not be extended indefinitely. That was not to deny that the Lord was responsible for an οἰκονομία in which the Incarnation of Jesus represented the high point, in which context all Old and New Testament realities gained full significance.[76] Theodore sketched just such a scenario in introducing Jonah in the hope of bringing some sense to the "novel and extraordinary things" of that unusual book (imperfectly understood by the commentator, of course).

> For the purpose of making it clear and to prevent it being thought he had at a later stage made plans and decisions in our regard, he conveyed to human beings through other means as well the coming

---

[74] *Theodori Mopsuesteni commentarius*, 79.

[75] Cf. Schäublin, *Unersuchungen*, 159. "Der realen Geschichte Israels in christlicher Sicht ihre Bedeutung zu verleihen, ohne den Texten Gewalt antun und ohne dem Grundsatz, das Alte Testament aus dem Alten Testament zu erklären, zuwiderhandeln zu müssen" (166–67).

[76] Cf. Young, *Biblical Exegesis*, 296–97: "What we do have (in the Antiochenes) is an important stress on the 'reality' of the overarching narrative from creation through fall to incarnation and redemption. The 'reality' of the *oikonomia*, God's providential activity with respect to the world, meant that spiritualising away the body, the material world, the 'flesh' of Christ in the story of his birth, life or passion, or indeed in the eucharist, had to be deemed heretical. The symbolic allegory of Origen seemed to undermine the core by encouraging such spiritualising." In practice not all Antiochenes would see the need to present the "overarching narrative" as extending quite so far, whereas Theodoret (under Alexandrian influence) would at times take it further.

of Christ the Lord so that all Jews might look forward to it from a distance . . . It is obvious from the facts that he chose to employ blessed Jonah and do novel and extraordinary things, for the reason that he intended to present him as a type of the life of Christ the Lord, and so for this reason he was led on by such incredible novelty and proved worthy of belief, displaying in his own person a type of such a great reality.[77]

But it is a rare concession by a commentator embarrassed by his unattractive protagonist in the book and its incredible contents; typology, too, which has no holds no terrors for his Antiochene peers, especially with New Testament support as in this case, is also only infrequently invoked by Theodore. Generally throughout his comment on other members of the Twelve Zerubbabel is found (by a misreading of Haggai)[78] to be a worthy royal successor to David capable of closing the perspective within which the events prophesied will be fulfilled.

The Psalms likewise in his view, with those few exceptions, have such a foreshortened perspective. We have noted that Theodore is not prepared to see a legitimate Christological θεωρία in verses of Pss 22; 31; 69, despite liturgical usage; he had stated his intention on the first of the Psalms, that "we should maintain a sequence of explanation in faithful accord with history." Despite the fact that in all four evangelists there is an implicit citation of Ps 69:21, "They gave me bile for food, and offered me vinegar to drink," Theodore properly warns against seeing reference to such details of the crucifixion as anything more than accommodation: "It is not as though the psalm were referring to these things . . . the use of the citations was inevitable."[79] While this interpretation, developed in the interests of preserving ἱστορία, could with profit have been heeded by those too

---

[77] *Theodori Mopsuesteni commentarius*, 169, 173. Such an overview, found at other places in the work as well, gives the lie to the judgement on reasons for its unique survival in Greek offered by Sullivan and others, that it contained "nothing of Christological import." Simonetti, too, *Biblical Interpretation*, 69, seems to have missed this passage in claiming, "Theodore has a clear idea of the typological interpretation of the Old Testament. Yet, if we move from the statement of the theory to see how and where it is applied in his Commentary, we discover that at no point is Jonah described as a *typos* of Christ."

[78] The LXX misreads an unfamiliar term of Akkadian origins in the Heb. text of 1:1, *pahath*, "governor (of Judah)," as "from the tribe of Judah," which Theodore takes to be a index of royal status.

[79] *Le commentaire*, 455.

willing to forsake it for "spiritual" meanings, Theodore needed to
learn from Theodoret that texts can have "two levels of meanings,"[80]
as the latter demonstrated in frequently finding a sacramental dimension in Old Testament texts.

Having been exposed to other options from the outset of his exegetical career, Theodoret is not prepared to accept Theodore's fore-
shortening of the hermeneutical perspective. He says as much when
he meets it in the latter on the eventual successor to David in Amos
9:11–12.

> Some commentators understood this of Zerubbabel, believing that it
> applied to him as descending from David. They refused to acknowl-
> edge, however, that Zerubbabel's government lasted for a short time
> before being cut short by death, whereas the prophecy contains word
> of eternal good things and the acknowledgement of God by all the
> nations, none of which we find happening in the achievements of
> Zerubbabel. Our Lord Jesus Christ, on the other hand, descended as
> he was from David according to the flesh, fulfilled the promise made
> to David: "the Word became flesh and dwelt among us" (John 1:14),
> assuming the tent from David.[81]

It is a direct rebuttal of the application of Aristarchus to the Old
Testament; the timeline of its ἔκβασις must be extended not only
into the New Testament but beyond, and in particular Jesus must
supersede Zerubbabel.[82] Other Christian institutions must also come
into focus; Theodoret is—for him—scathing in his criticism of fellow commentators (the Ioudaiophrôn in focus but unnamed) for disputing that the description of Jerusalem in Micah 4:2 as the source
of the saving word's dissemination throughout the world refers to
apostolic evangelization.

> Jews, on the contrary, far from wanting to understand it in this way,
> claim it is a prophecy of the return from Babylon. While there is noth-
> ing surprising in their being so stupid as to take it this way, the error
> about this prophecy being all of a piece with their other follies, it
> seems to me intolerable and unpardonable, on the other hand, that
> even some of the teachers of religion insert this interpretation in their
> writings.[83]

---

[80] On Ps 69.25 (PG 80.1409).
[81] PG 81.1705.
[82] Cf. Guinot, "La cristallisation d'un différend: Zorobabel dans l'exégèse de
Théodore de Mopsueste et de Théodoret de Cyr."
[83] PG 81.1760–61. Cf. Hill, "*Sartor resartus*: Theodore under review by Theodoret."

Theodoret was confirmed in this placement of the ἀλήθεια of the Old Testament beyond its own confines when he came under the influence of Cyril in composing his Commentaries on The Twelve and Isaiah. At an appropriate, if late, moment in the Isaiah commentary, the kernel of Third Isaiah's message beginning at ch 60, Theodoret lays out his hermeneutical principles for prophetic material in particular. He states that he is interested particularly in the reality, ἀλήθεια, πράγματα, the anagogical meaning of a text, less so in its ecclesial meaning, and least of all in its historical meaning. As a model to explain this he takes an artist, with original in mind, first doing a rough sketch (σκιά), and then coloring it in (εἰκών, τύπος)—terms he would have found in Cyril; and he says that in reading a biblical—or at least prophetic—text on this model we encounter, in reverse order, the historical meaning, the ecclesial meaning, and finally the anagogical meaning—the ἀλήθεια.

> The prophecy (in ch. 60) contains three themes at the one time: (Isaiah) prophesies as though in outline the rebuilding of Jerusalem that happened under Cyrus and Darius; as though in a picture drawn in stronger colors he also presents the more precise imprint of the reality, the splendor of holy Church; and yet he indicates in advance also the original of the picture, namely, the future life and the way of living in heaven.

To prove his point he then cites Hebrew 10:1, where the author also speaks of those three levels of meaning, σκιά, εἰκών, πράγματα.

> This distinction the divine Paul also drew, "For the Law contains a shadow of future realities and not the picture of the realities:" by "future realities" he refers to that immortal life free from grief, that ageless existence bereft of care; by "picture of the realities" he refers to the way of life in the Church, which in the present life resembles as far as possible the future realities; and by "shadow" he refers to the Law's teaching this more obscurely than the Church. The artists, you see, have the original, and they sketch a likeness of it, firstly doing an outline, then filling in the outline with colors.[84]

Theodoret will repeat this three-fold hermeneutical model in commenting on Leviticus on his *Quaestiones*.

Diodore, Theodore and even Chrysostom would hardly endorse this reversal of Antioch's hermeneutical priorities; it was not the way

---

[84] SC 315.238–40.1.

to find the truth of the Old Testament that was taught in the asketerion in their time, even if of longstanding elsewhere.[85] Their interpretation of it was not that attributed—inadequately—to Cyril:

> Cyril knew no way to speak of Christ than in the words of the Bible,
> and no way to interpret the words of the Bible than through
> Christ . . . Only by relating what is written in the Scriptures to Christ
> who is the 'truth' can the interpreter discover what is 'true' in the
> text.[86]

In his movement from situating Old Testament books, events and
characters within a broadly Christological οἰκονομία, like Theodore,
to finding reference to Jesus in individual verses in the manner of
Cyril, Theodoret was accepting a notion of biblical truth which to
that point had not been current in Antioch. That it was somewhat
exotic, not bred in the bone nor his last word on the subject, is
shown by his subsequent Jeremiah Commentary (in the form we
have it) and the Questions, both vintage Antioch compositions.

Antiochene hermeneutics of the Old Testament has been dismissed
on the grounds that "a strictly historical interpretation of the Old
Testament is anachronistic," and has even been misrepresented as
"killing the word of God and robbing it of saving power."[87] Such
views retain something of the adversarial character of positions reached
on this question of interpretation in those early centuries, as we noted
in statements of Eustathius, Diodore and Theodore in particular. For

---

[85] Of the foreshortened hermeneutical perspective favored by Theodore, Greer,
Early Biblical Interpretation, 182, says it "cut across opinions almost universally held
in the ancient church."

[86] R. L. Wilken, "Cyril of Alexandria as interpreter of the Old Testament," 21,
16. O'Keefe, "'A letter that killeth,'" 96, using terminology of Hans Frei and Eric
Auerbach, makes the claim, "In the end, Antiochene exegesis failed precisely because
it did not appreciate how central a Christ-centered figural reading of the Old
Testament was to its appropriation by the Christian church." One has to wonder,
on the other hand, whether such views take account of Cyril's strong emphasis on
ἱστορία before proceeding to ecclesiological and Christological levels of interpreting OT texts.

[87] Wilken, "Cyril of Alexandria," 21; O'Keefe, "'A letter that killeth,'" 104, (sym-
pathetically) relaying the thought of Leontius of Byzantium. An alternative (and pre-
mature?) judgement was offered by Hatch, *The Influence of Greek Ideas on Christianity*,
82: "It has been one of the many results of the controversies into which the meta-
physical tendencies of the Greeks led the churches of the fourth and fifth centuries,
to postpone almost to modern times the acceptance of 'the literal grammatical and
historical sense' as the true sense of Scripture."

hermeneuts in those times an approach to the Old Testament was associated with theological convictions, whether arising from or giving rise to them, a question yet to be investigated in this volume. For the moment it could be conceded that interpreters of that ancient text of all schools were principally—and commendably—interested in arriving at its "truth." For Antioch the text's factuality, ἱστορία, was basic to that search, if not always the dominating factor; the text was primarily a window for them, not a mirror. It came to be acknowledged that attention to the bare text, τὸ γυμνὸν γράμμα, did not lead to a discovery of the full meaning,[88] and allowance was explicitly made for discernment of other levels, provided these were not arrived at arbitrarily—hardly an "anachronistic" judgement. In Chapter Ten we shall consider whether this relative flexibility in commentators on the Old Testament ensured that Antiochene readers/listeners were thus adequately prepared to share in its "saving power." It is time now to take note of individual theological accents discernible in the works of these commentators.

---

[88] One notes a similar shift in position in the case of Alexandrian interpreters, as for instance by comparing Cyril's Commentry on Zechariah with his predecessor Didymus's. Bardy, "Interprétation chez les pères," 580, concurs: "Des purs alexandrins comme saint Cyrille s'efforcaient de donner une grande place à l'interprétation historique." Cyril's modern commentator, Alexander Kerrigan, *St Cyril of Alexandria, Interpreter of the Old Testament*, Analecta Biblica 2, Roma: Pontificio Istituto Biblico, 1952, 110, thinks Cyril may have read Antiochene works (including Theodore's) in the period before the accession of Nestorius to the see of Constantinople (he could hardly have read Theodoret's exegetical works by then, as Kerrigan also suggests).

CHAPTER NINE

THEOLOGICAL ACCENTS IN OLD TESTAMENT COMMENTARY

The question has yet to be addressed as to whether hermeneutics in Antioch and its biblical commentary in general in the fourth and fifth centuries took their distinctive character under the influence of theological positions and concerns of the age, or vice versa. "The writings of Athanasius," for instance, "make it absolutely clear that the Arian controversy was about exegesis," though "of course, Athanasius cannot admit to a genuine controversy about exegesis."[1] In their Old Testament commentaries none of the principal figures of the school of Antioch admit to any current controversies, either, though Chrysostom (the least controversial in matters of doctrine)[2] occasionally takes indiscriminate aim at a rogues gallery drawn from a couple of centuries, from Mani and Marcion to Arius.[3] Their reticence on theological and ecclesiastical developments, while admirable, can make it difficult to date their works; internal evidence has led commentators to place Theodoret's Commentary on the Song of Songs, for instance, variously in respect of the council of Ephesus in 431 and the Symbol of Union in 433.[4]

Yet all the Antiochene commentators were public figures and pastors, all caught up to some extent in theological and ecclesiastical turmoil, and some the explicit object of fierce polemic, even labeled heretics. Diodore, champion of the faith against Julian and Valens,

---

[1] Young, *Biblical Exegesis*, 30–31. Young proceeds, "For in his eyes any opponent is 'double-minded' and has betrayed the unity of the truth."

[2] Cf. Wiles, "Theodore of Mopsuestia as representative of the Antiochene school," 490: "Chrysostom was the one leading Antiochene scholar of that time to remain free of any suspicion of heretical taint."

[3] Cf. the opening to his commentary on the messianic Ps 110 (PG 55.264–65).

[4] Guinot, "La Christologie de Théodoret de Cyr dans son Commentaire sur le Cantique," 272, for instance, takes account of the reasoning behind the decision of M. Richard, "Notes sur l'evolution doctrinale de Théodoret de Cyr," 268, who places the work after the Symbol of Union, to opt instead for a date around 428 and certainly before the Symbol of Union. But in *L'Exégèse*, 60, he prefers to assign the work to a date after Ephesus.

was awarded for his role at the council of 381 and in the development of its creed an accolade for his orthodoxy by the emperor
Theodosius in confirming the council decrees;[5] yet he came to be
labeled father of Nestorianism[6] and condemned at a synod of
Constantinople in 499. Theodore died as bishop of Mopsuestia in
428 as Nestorius succeeded to the see of Constantinople, and for his
complicity in the latter's education his works were condemned by
the fifth ecumenical council.[7] Even today Theodoret is referred to
by some eastern communities as a crypto-Nestorian,[8] though happily the flames of prejudice did not destroy his works. Church councils of Constantinople, Ephesus and Chalcedon, held in this period,
issued dogmatic creeds and formulas that we find leaving an imprint
on the commentaries without being explicitly cited and without necessarily being in every case to Antioch's complete satisfaction. While
Chalcedon at the end of our period may have been referred to as
"the triumph of Antiochene Christology,"[9] earlier synods were held
under the influence of parties unsympathetic to Antioch's theology.

Leaving aside the question of the relationship between the Antiochene
approach to the Old Testament and any underlying theology, then,
we find it to be to the credit of these pastors that they do not use
their commentaries to develop polemical theological theses. In commenting on Zechariah, for instance, Theodore and Theodoret are
much less obsessed with a range of heretics than is the monk Didymus
in his cell in Alexandria, who frequently locks horns with Arians,
Macedonians, Apollinarists, Ebionites, Docetists, Manichees, Valenti-
nians, Sabellians. It is only under the influence of Alexandrian predecessors that Theodoret in his Isaiah Commentary turns to inveighing
against Arians and Eunomians a dozen times. It is only in common
defense of divine transcendence that all these commentators urge
their readers/listeners to recognize anthropomorphisms as a gesture
of divine considerateness, συγκατάβασις, while being careful not to

---

[5] *Cod. Theodos.* xvi 1.3, cited by J. Quasten, *Patrology* 3, 397.
[6] By Cyril of Alexandria in his *Contra Diodorum et Theodorum* 17 (PG 76.1149).
[7] Cf. DS 425–26, 433–37.
[8] The term is used of Theodoret in the 1990 Agreed Statement of the Orthodox
Church and the Oriental Orthodox Churches meeting at Chambesy, Geneva. Bardy's
view, "Théodoret", 324, is to be preferred: "En réalité, Théodoret n'a pas été
nestorien."
[9] Cf. Kelly, *Early Christian Doctrines*, 341.

misinterpret them. When Chrysostom in Homily 60 on Genesis comes to comment on 35:13, "God left him, ascending at the spot where he had been talking with him," he instinctively feels the need to remind his congregation (not for the first time),

> Ascending and descending, of course, are not properly applied to God; but since it is a particular token of his unspeakable love that for the sake of our instruction he should permit the concreteness (παχύτης) of such words, accordingly he employs such human expressions, since it would not otherwise be possible for human hearing to cope with the sublimity of the message had he spoken to us in a manner worthy of the Lord.[10]

And though we saw him taking occasion of the contrast between the reverence of the seraphim in Isa 6 and the temerity of King Uzziah in 2 Chr 26 to fulminate against Anomean presumption in "examining the unexaminable," the theological aberration was probably not the motive for those six homilies *In Oziam*.

A. Trinitarian accents

Although these Antiochene pastors wrote formal dogmatic works on the Trinity and the Incarnation and various moral treatises, then, most of which have perished, we do not find Diodore, Theodore and Theodoret in their desk commentaries abandoning the Old Testament text for lengthy digressions on these topics.[11] In his pulpit, with his congregation before him, on the other hand, Chrysostom can move from the text of Genesis and the Psalms to discourse on such moral themes as the evils of secular amusements, such as the theatre and the races, and the need for almsgiving and (in relation to Ps 4) "the art of prayer;" perhaps his most powerful passage in the Psalms homilies is his heavy satire of the funerary excesses of the rich in comment on Ps 49:11. But the open text is a discipline

---

[10] PG 54.521.1. We noted the contrast between a lack of sustained theological polemic in Chrysostom's commentary on Gen and the bitter attacks on Arians in particular by his contemporary in Constantinople Severian of Gabala.

[11] In case the more pedestrian style of commentary by these Antiochenes should lead readers to think them less profoundly theological, Maurice Wiles, "Theodore of Mopsuestia," 492, reminds us that "Antiochene exegesis was no less theological (except in the very technical and somewhat misleading use of that word in which it is sometimes employed as a synonym for mystical) than its Alexandrian counterpart."

that brings even the ardent preacher back to the biblical author's theme. It is that text that at times elicits from commentator and preacher some incidental elucidation of a theological nicety that is perhaps the subject of current debate, conciliar decree or simply popular misunderstanding.

Diodore and Theodore are concerned that Christians should not read their own theological distinctions—for example, of the persons of the Trinity—into Old Testament expressions. The former comments on Ps 30:8,

> This expression *I shall cry to you, Lord, and make my petition to my God* Scripture is in the habit of using; such an expression is not an interchange of persons, nor in fact is he speaking of the Lord and God as different, unless one were to suspect that with inspired vision he is hinting at the Father and the Son.[12]

As in his hermeneutics, Theodore is vigorously opposed to our presuming in the Old Testament authors New Testament ideas; they had no notion of trinitarian distinctions, he asserts in commentary on the vision of horses of various colors in Zechariah 1, dismissing the views of Hippolytus, Apollinaris, Eusebius and Jerome that the rider of the red horse is Christ.

> Now, the statement of certain commentators, characterized by extreme error and stupidity, and not innocent of impiety, is to the effect that he saw the Son of God here. It is, in fact, obvious that none of those who lived before the coming of Christ the Lord knew of Father and Son, none knew that God the Father was the father of God the Son, that God the Son was the son of God the Father, being what the Father is in also being from him. While terminology for father and son is to be found in the Old Testament, since God is commonly called father for his care when people are shown attention from that source, and they are called sons in having something more on the basis of relationship with God, yet absolutely no one of those living at that time understood God the Father to be father of God the Son, as I said before, or God the Son to be son of God the Father. You see, the people before the coming of Christ the Lord in their religious knowledge were aware only of God and creation, identifying God as eternal in being and as cause of everything, and creation (to put it in a nutshell) as what was brought by him from non-being to being.[13]

---

[12] *Commentarii*, 168–69.
[13] *Theodori Mopsuesteni commentarius*, 325.

We find in Theodore a similar resistance to recognising in the Old Testament any reference to the Holy Spirit. When the Lord says in Joel 2:28, "I shall pour out my spirit on all flesh," Theodore hastens to comment,

> The people in the time of the Old Testament did not understand the Holy Spirit to be a unit as a person (μοναδικὸν ἐν ὑποστάσει) distinct from the others, being both God and from God; by 'holy spirit' and every other such name at the time they referred to his grace, care and affection.[14]

He is equally insistent in similar terms at another occurrence of "My spirit" in Hag 2:5:

> The people of the Old Testament were unaware of a distinct hypostasis of a Holy Spirit identified as a person (πρόσωπον) in its own right in God, since everyone before the coming of Christ the Lord knew of God and creation but nothing further. The divine Scripture taught this to its readers at that time without having an insight into anything in invisible creation consisting of separate kinds, referring to all the invisible and ministering beings in general as angels and powers, which according to its teaching carried out the divine decisions. Consequently, they were not in a position to know of a Holy Spirit as a distinct hypostasis in God, being unable even to list separate kinds among the ministering beings or to associate with God what could be described as a distinct person (πρόσωπον), since they understood nothing of this sort.[15]

And he proceeds to cite the need of Jesus to inform the disciples of this doctrine through the trinitarian formula in Matt 28:19,

> from which we learn of a distinct person (πρόσωπον) of a Father, a distinct person of a Son, and a distinct person of a Holy Spirit, believing each of them to be of a divine and eternal substance (οὐσία),

something communicated to later Christians (he says) by religious instruction and the baptismal liturgy.

Theodoret in his time, and with his more flexible notion of the boundaries between Old Testament revelation and New, does not resonate with Theodore's insistence on this matter. In Gen 1:26, in fact, he sees the author giving us an insight into both Trinity and Incarnation.

---

[14] *Theodori Mopsuesteni commentarius*, 95.
[15] *Theodori Mopsuesteni commentarius*, 310–311.

By saying, "God said," you see, he indicated the divine nature held
in common, and by proceeding to say, "Let us make," he made clear
the number of persons. Likewise, by saying "image" in the singular,
he brought out the identity of nature: he did not say, in images, but
"in image." On the other hand, by saying "our" he indicated the number of the hypostases: the God of all foresees what is not yet made
as already made, and discerns in advance the enfleshment and Incarnation of the Only-begotten.[16]

Theodoret also takes occasion of Isa 48:16, "And now the Lord has
sent me and his Spirit," to point out (under the influence of Alexandria)
the limitations of both Jewish monotheism and Sabellian notions of
the Trinity:

He clearly conveyed to us something else on God's part, the Spirit's
part, by way of refutation of the Jews and those under the baleful
influence of Sabellius . . . He is obliged to bring out also the particular properties of the persons, of Son and Father in one case, of Father
and Holy Spirit in another.[17]

B. CHRISTOLOGICAL ACCENTS

In the case of Diodore's Commentary on the Psalms, those like
Mariès and Olivier who upheld the attribution of the work to Diodore
had to deal with the objection that this "father of Nestorianism"
could hardly be responsible for a work betraying such an orthodox
Christology, and that it must have been composed in the wake of
Chalcedon.[18] Admittedly, a messianic character to psalms is rarely
conceded, Marie-Josèphe Rondeau remarking on the "effacement du
Christ locuteur chez Diodore."[19] In comment on Ps 45 we saw him
making an exception (if only to resist Jewish claims that Solomon is
in focus); when after an assertion of the central figure's royal and
even divine status v.7 reads, "God your God anointed you with the

---

[16] *Theodoreti Cyrensis Quaestiones in Octateuchum*, 22. Chrysostom in his second sermon on Genesis had simply read the plural verb (a matter "of grammar alone,
without a direct bearing on the meaning," we are told by Speiser, *Genesis*, 7) to
suggest the honor shown humanity (SC 433.184–86).

[17] SC 315.66–68.

[18] *Commentarii*, cv–cvi. For discussion of the authenticity of the work, see Chapter
Six.

[19] *Les commentaires patristiques* 2, 303.

oil of gladness beyond your partners," thus grouping him with other gifted figures, Diodore feels a distinction called for.

> He uses the phrase *beyond your partners* in this way, that while the others who were anointed were anointed with oil of prophecy or priesthood or royalty, he was anointed with the Holy Spirit. Here again he makes mention of the Incarnation (οἰκονομία), or how he was able to call the same person God in one case as in the above verse *Your throne, O God, is forever*, and in another case *God your God anointed you*. In the above case, however, he referred to nature; here he introduces the Incarnation.[20]

He thus distinguishes between equality in nature and the human condition assumed by Jesus, upholding the two natures while denying subordination. We find him resisting an Arian subordinationist interpretation also of Ps 2:8.

Such an interpretation of psalm verses Theodore is also seen resisting. In fact, taking all his Christological statements together from this work, one gets the overall impression of a young if unschooled theologian trying, in the face of Arian and Apollinarian opponents and an Alexandrian response that imperiled the reality of Jesus' humanity, to express the hypostatic union (not a term he employs, of course) in way that clearly distinguishes between the two natures as defined by Nicea and (later) by Constantinople I without giving the appearance of a two sons Christology.[21] Figures occurring in the text of the Psalms, of course, are not always susceptible of precise application to this mystery; v. 8 of that Ps 45 accorded messianic reference by Diodore, "Myrrh, resin and cassia from your garments," proves to be one such in Theodore's unhappy phrasing:

> By his *garments* he nicely referred to the body, in being something put on from outside, while inside there was the divinity on the basis of indwelling.[22]

---

[20] *Commentarii*, 272. In building a case (against Alois Grillmeier) for Diodore's Christology to be seen as truly Antiochene, Greer in "The Antiochene Christology of Diodore of Tarsus" might well have made a reference to the Commentary on the Psalms.

[21] For an insight into Theodore's reputation for orthodoxy in the Syriac Church, and the Greek text of his Commentary on John, "an invaluable source in our efforts to understand his Christological thought," see G. Kalantzis, "Theodore of Mopsuestia's *Commentarius in evangelium Johannis apostoli*: Text and transmission," *Aug* 43 (2003) 473–93. The Syriac version introduced into the text foreign elements that had the effect of "skewing our undertstanding and interpretation of his Christology" (493).

[22] *Le commentaire*, 290.

His good intentions are not sufficient to avoid the impression of an adoptionist Christology, a risk Antioch's two nature Christology always ran.[23] In his next work, on The Twelve, Theodore upholds the homoousion of the Son, without using the term; in denying knowledge of the Trinity to the Old Testament people in comment on Zech 1 (above), he goes on to conclude that even the apostles, on the basis of John 16, did not grasp the divinity of Jesus, either:

> They had heard word of the Father obscurely, taking it in human fashion, but they would truly know the Son when they knew him to be God in his being, coming from him, and one in being with him.[24]

If Zerubbabel is accorded priority to Jesus as a fulfilment of prophecy, it is only on account of Theodore's foreshortened hermeneutical perspective.

Chrysostom wisely decides that the pulpit is not the place for theological elaboration and refinement of Old Testament texts, having learnt the axiom that Theodore recites in his Commentary on John,

> I judge the exegete's task to be to explain words that most people find difficult; it is the preacher's task to reflect also on words that are perfectly clear and to speak about them.[25]

It is perhaps his being content to joust briefly with a bevy of infamous heretics in Pss 110; 144; 145; 148 that denies him the term theologian "au sens strict de ce mot" in Bardy's view.[26] Along with his respect for divine transcendence (seen in his warnings about anthropomorphisms) go frequent accents on the humanity of Jesus and litanies of the deprivations that involved, as in Homily 23 on Genesis.[27] That much-debated Gen 1:26 text leads him in Homily 8 to urge his congregation to hold fast to "the dogmas of the Church" (not a familiar phrase of his).

---

[23] Cf. Kelly, *Early Christian Doctrines*, 305: "It is characteristic of (Theodore) to describe the humanity as 'the man assumed', and occasionally his language seems almost to suggest that the Word adopted a human being who was already in existence."

[24] *Theodori Mopsuesteni commentarius*, 326.

[25] Quoted by Wiles, "Theodore of Mopsuestia as a representative of the Antiochene school," 491.

[26] "Jean Chrysostome," 672.

[27] PG 53.205.6. Cf. Hill, "St John Chrysostom and the Incarnation of the Word in Scripture."

Argue the point in friendly exchange with Jews, on the one hand, showing them that the words have reference not to some one of the ministering powers but to the only-begotten the only Son of God himself; to those holding Arian views, on the other hand, prove from this text the Son's equality (ὁμοτιμία) with the Father.[28]

In the first of his homilies on the obscurity of the Old Testament, in reference to the obscure background of Melchizedek on the evidence of Heb 7:2–3, Chrysostom admits his own limitations:

> While the fact that he was born of the Father I know, how so I do not know; while the fact that he was born of the virgin I understand, the manner even in this instance I do not grasp: the generation of each nature is a matter for confession, and the manner of each is a matter for silence. As in this case of the virgin I do not know how he was born of the virgin but I confess he was born, yet I do not abolish the fact owing to my ignorance of the manner, so too should you also act in the case of the Father: even if you do not know how he was born, confess the truth 'He was born.'[29]

An apophatic approach is better than an anomean.

Bishop Theodoret at his desk, however, cannot afford to be simply apophatic; without seeking controversy (except where Alexandrian influence is felt, as in the Isaiah Commentary), he feels he must, as one who led the oriental bishops at Ephesus and was instrumental in drawing up the Symbol of Union and also in eventually having the council of Chalcedon convened, declare his colors. From his early work on the Song his Antiochene dyophysitism is patent, as is also a certain insecurity in regard to confessing the hypostatic union in Jesus (not an Antiochene phrase). He goes out of his way to interpret Cant 5:15, "His form is like choice incense, like cedars," in an Antiochene fashion:

> Here again she makes reference to the fact of two natures, calling the divine nature *incense* since by the Law incense was offered to God, and by *cedar* referring to the human nature in its not being affected by the rottenness of sin, the cedar of all trees not going rotten.[30]

---

[28] PG 53.73.4.

[29] *Omelie*, 70–72.2. Chrysostom's reluctance to pry further into the birth of Jesus from Mary (unnamed), and the Antiochene commentators' general reticence compared, say, with Didymus on the glories of the θεοτόκος, perhaps arise from the conviction "that the incarnation cannot have involved the impassible Word in any change or suffering" (the view of Nestorius in his *Heracleides* cited by Kelly, *Early Christian Doctrines*, 312).

[30] PG 81.164.

On the other hand, 5:10, "My nephew is white and ruddy," receives the following gloss,

> She mentions *white* first and *ruddy* second: he was always God, but he became man as well, not by abandoning what he was or being turned into a man, but by putting on a human nature.[31]

This twofold pattern appears in all Theodoret's Old Testament commentaries, without swamping them; one feels the commentator needs—with typical conciseness—to remind his readers of crucial dogmas, if not "of the Church" (in Chrysostom's term), at least of the church of Antioch. There is little reason for Christological embellishment of Daniel beyond the Son of Man pericope in 7:13, again presented in typically Antiochene dyophysite terms. The passage from that book to which most lengthy Christological attention is paid is 2:34–35 mentioning "the stone hewn out a mountain without hands being used;" after again rehearsing an arsenal of texts to confute Jewish interpretation, and borrowing the detail of the virgin birth from another source, Theodoret concludes,

> So we learn from Old and New Testament that our Lord Jesus Christ was called *stone*: it was cut from a mountain without hands being used, being born of a virgin independently of marital intercourse.[32]

A phrase, "two natures in one person," redolent of the Symbol of Union, appears in the next work, on Ezekiel, in relating 11:22–23 to the ascension of Jesus, along with other typical expressions. His response to Theodore's commentary on The Twelve involves an insistence that the true fulfilment of earlier prophecies is not Zerubbabel but Jesus; "the one who sent is Lord almighty, and the one who was sent is the Lord almighty, and there is no difference in status,"[33] he says on Zech 2:9.

Theodoret's Psalms Commentary, composed in the 440s as was his *Eranistes*, admits a Christological interpretation of them not found in the earlier Antiochenes, while retaining typical accents. Ps 55 is taken to refer to the passion of Jesus, the realism of the language

---

[31] Cf. Viciano, "Theodoret von Kyros als Interpret des Apostels Paulus", 288: "Er hebt die *unio hypostatica* nicht genügend hervor. Das gilt auch für die *communicatio idiomatum*."

[32] PG 81.1303.

[33] PG 81.1889.

excused on the grounds that "the terms should reflect the reality;" of vv.4–5 Theodoret says,

> It was necessary, you see, for the nature which underwent the passion to be revealed, and the extraordinary longsuffering which the loving God had for our race; he underwent suffering in the flesh, wishing also in this to be involved in our salvation.[34]

Theodoret had reason to know that trouble still loomed both from continuing Arian ideas of subordination of the Word and from Cyril's inadequate terminology for grappling with them. Hence in giving a Christological interpretation to Ps 45:5 he takes issue with both, employing the Nicene talisman ὁμοούσιος that passed into the Constantinopolitan creed of 381 to put paid to Arianism, and rejecting Cyril's description of the union of natures as φυσική:

> Thus he was also anointed in the holy Spirit, not as God but as man: as God he was of one being with the Spirit, whereas as man he receives the gifts of the Spirit like a kind of anointing. Thus *he loved righteousness and hated lawlessness*: this is a matter of intentional choice, not of natural (φυσική) power, whereas as God he has *a rod of equity* as *the rod of his kingship*.[35]

If this style of theology has been styled "fundamentally dualistic,"[36] it also represents a balance in speaking of God made man.

C. Moral accents

Just such a balance, perceivable in the Antiochenes' Christology where this emerges in their Old Testament commentaries, characterizes their thinking also on the moral life, even if it is not morality but the biblical text that is the principal, or at least nominal, focus even of most of Chrysostom's exegetical homilies and sermons.[37]

---

[34] PG 80.1272.

[35] PG 80.1192.

[36] Young, *From Nicaea to Chalcedon*, 274. "Symmetrical" is used with the same intent, initially by Grillmeier and then by K. McNamara, "Theodoret of Cyrus and the unity of person in Christ," 326. In a survey of Theodoret's (non-exegetical) works, M. Mandac, "L'union Christologique dans les oeuvres de Théodoret de Cyr antérieures au Concile d'Ephèse," 96, concludes that Theodoret's Christology is "correcte tout en étant incomplète."

[37] Admittedly, the two short series of Chrysostom's homilies on David and Saul

The careful—if sometimes uneasy—distinction of divine and human natures in Jesus by these dyophysite pastors is replicated in their careful—if sometimes uneasy—balance of the respective roles played by divine grace and human effort in the moral life. Yes, the Fall has happened; but it is a *felix culpa* that ushers in God's healing through the coming of the savior. Human nature and free will have not been impaired by that early reverse ("original sin" not a term of theirs);[38] we are still morally accountable, even if we tend to misquote Scripture to discharge ourselves of accountability—yet natural law[39] and positive law apply without the rigor of a Novatian.[40] Antiochene Christology and morality are thus all of a piece with the rest of their *Weltanschauung*.

Although Augustine felt it necessary to defend Chrysostom against charges by Julian of Eclanum of complicity in Pelagian positions,[41] Antiochene Old Testament commentaries give little comfort to the

---

and on Hannah, though based on the text of the books of Samuel, spend most time on the virtues of the eponymous heroes—gentleness in David's case, prayerfulness in Hannah's, the former to make a point in a time of political crisis (see Chapter Six). Psalms classifed as moral receive a moral development by all the commentators.

[38] In reference to Prov 2:5 in the Commentary on Proverbs, Chrysostom sees Abel "infected in some respect by his father's sin (προγονικὴ ἁμαρτία)"—an early formulation of original sin?

[39] It is in keeping with Antiochene moral reasoning that Diodore should in comment on the first psalm uphold the primacy of natural law (*Commentarii*, 8): "Now, if it mentions *law* (v. 2), it does not oblige us to think only of the written Law but of the innate law, which is not coercive, as the Manichees say, but instructing the person prepared to learn. So do not allow the identity in terms to give rise to misunderstanding: law that is natural and linked to nature is referred to, which cannot be bypassed, like a person's having a sense of humor, having two feet, going grey in old age. It is implanted in all people and in every individual person; it cannot be bypassed or altered, being also called a natural law because by it we can learn and distinguish what is for the better, like knowing that God exists, that it is good to respect parents and not to harm others. It is nature, in fact, that teaches each person this as if giving orders not to do to another what one would not want to suffer from someone else."

[40] Theodoret insists in comment on Ezek 3:20; 18:24 that one sin will not make forgiveness impossible for a repentant transgressor.

[41] Augustine, *Contra Iulianum* 1, 22 (PL 44.655), refutes Julian's claims that some of Chrysostom's statements in his New Testament homilies on infant baptism amounted to a denial of original sin. A. Wenger, "Jean Chrysostome," 336–37, struggles to uphold his orthodoxy, admitting, "Il est vrai toutefois qu'il a davantage insisté sur le rôle du vouloir humain que sur celui de la grace." The view of Bardy, "Jean Chrysostome," 477, is that "il n'y a pas, en tout cela, de théorie précise du péché original."

Pelagians, if only by default in some cases. In what might seem perversity, Diodore—and consequently Theodore—decline to take as referring to David's sin a key text, Psalm 51, the principal one of the early Church's seven penitential psalms, interpreting it instead as the exiled people's cry for forgiveness. Theodore seems aware of some such accusation of perversity by retorting, "At no stage have we given the impression of being dictated to by the titles," this psalm's title making the customary identification. While both Antiochenes thus pass up the opportunity to speak on the topic of the Fall and its effect on human nature, Theodore finds another occasion in Ps 39:5, "Lo, you made my days handbreadths," to imply the mortality consequent upon that transgression:

> God, of course, manages affairs by a certain plan, making our nature subject to a sentence of death once and for all and rendering us capable of lasting for an acknowledged number of years.[42]

While Chrysostom, unfortunately, is not extant on Ps 51, Theodoret may be taken as giving the standard Antiochene position on the question in his commentary on v.5; while suitably vague about the transmission of the sin to later generations, he cites Paul in Rom 5:12, rightly taking the critical phrase ἐφ᾽ ᾧ in a causal sense:

> He means that, by having control over our forebears, sin effected some way or path through the offspring. This is also what blessed Paul says: 'Since, you see, sin entered the world through a human being, and through sin death, because all sinned.'

Theodoret proceeds to see further implications of David's and Paul's thinking:

> We learn from all this that the force of sin is not part of nature (if it were so, after all, we would be free from sin), but that nature tends to stumble when troubled by passions; yet victory lies with freewill (γνώμη), making use of effort (πόνοι) to lend assistance.[43]

Of all the elements of moral behavior in Antiochene thinking one single—but critical—element is missing here: divine grace. In the context Theodoret feels that for the moment he has to uphold other elements under threat: human nature after the Fall, the independence of the will, the individual's contribution, and thus moral

---

[42] *Le commentaire*, 235.
[43] PG 80.1244.

accountability. All of these—and the role of grace—the other Antiochenes also in their commentaries on the Old Testament include. When Chrysostom speaks on Genesis in the Lenten sermons of 386, he speaks of a Fall, but presents it positively; grace outweighed sin; human nature was not impaired by the sin; and so when all of us sinned, as we have, we are accountable.

> While they were the first to sin and thus introduced slavery through disobedience on their part, once it was introduced those who came afterwards ratified it by sins of their own . . . The human being did not sin to the extent that God gave grace, the loss was not as great as the gain, the shipwreck was not as great as the commerce—instead, the good things outweighed the bad . . . I said this lest you think you have been badly affected by the first human beings.[44]

And the sin of these first parents? Indifference, ῥαθυμία, of course, the capital sin; Chrysostom's homilies and sermons in this diagnosis are at one with Theodoret's analysis.

If that is the primal sin—indifference, negligence, sloth—the individual must make efforts, πόνοι, if not to be morally reprehensible. It is all up to freewill, γνώμη, the mindset; no point in sheeting the blame home to some malevolent deity on the grounds of being unaccountable, a tendency of which Chrysostom found his listeners guilty in "mangling the limbs of Scripture" by glibly citing Jer 10:23, "Lord, people's ways are not their own, nor will human beings make progress or direct their own going," or misquoting Haggai 2:8, Pss 10:11,13; 14:1; 127:1, Rom 9:16, 1 Cor 7:8–9. Moral responsibility cannot be abdicated by this lazy ruse: we must do our best, and God will (then) match that effort with his grace. As Diodore comments on Ps 1:3, "Whatever he does will prosper," about the proverbially righteous man, "To such a person everything comes simply and easily, God working and cooperating with him."[45]

There lies a continuing quandary for Antiochene moralists: how does divine grace relate to the necessity for human effort? The human element in meritorious living can no more be downplayed than it can in the person of Jesus, so how leave room for the divine? In introducing Ps 4 Diodore continues in the same vein:

---

[44] SC 433.324–26.3.
[45] *Commentarii*, 10. The LXX here does in fact address simply the "man," eliciting a necessary clarification from Theodoret at this point—though much of his own and the other Antochenes' usage is often exclusive. See Chapter One on the inclusion of women in their congregations and readership.

It is the greatest form of providence that all alike—sinful and righteous—are not granted the identical lot; instead, each benefits from
God's oversight according to individual merit.[46]

It is easy to see how Theodore finds it necessary to amend the text
of Jonah when he finds Nineveh offered conversion and achieving
it simply on a few words spoken by a stranger:

> They could never have believed in God on the basis of this remark
> alone, from a completely unknown foreigner threatening them with
> destruction and adding nothing further, not even letting the listeners
> know by whom he was sent. Rather, it is obvious he also mentioned
> God, the Lord of all, and said he had been sent by him; and he deliv-
> ered the message of destruction, calling them to repentance.[47]

Theodoret in commenting on Romans likewise rewrites Paul to nuance
the gratuity of divine mercy with his own codicil on the need for
human effort,[48] and he rewrites Ezekiel also; Old Testament prophet
and apostle both have too simplistic a notion of the economy of salvation. Faith is certainly not sufficient of itself—in fact, it is the prod-
uct of human initiative; in that Ps 45 where Theodore is prepared
to see the queen representing the Church, he comments on v. 5,

> He rightly calls the Church queen to bring out the high dignity she
> attained from union with Christ, which came to her through faith.[49]

Theodoret in his Isaiah Commentary remarks on 1:23, "Faith does
not suffice for salvation: there is need also for the practice of virtue,"
and he represents the prophet requiring his eighth century audience
to proceed also to "approach saving baptism" and "other forms of
virtue."[50] No, it cannot all be left up to divine grace, the Antiochenes
insist. Kelly, admitting of them only "an intensified emphasis on indi-
vidualism," acquits them of the charge of Pelagianism "unless the
Eastern attitude generally is to be dismissed as Pelagian."[51]

---

[46] *Commentarii*, 21.
[47] *Theodori Mopsuesteni commentarius*, 186.
[48] Cf. Hill, "Theodoret wrestling with Romans." Bardy, "Théodoret," 323, reviews
his stance on these moral matters, including original sin: "On voit sans peine les
insuffisances et les lacunes de cette doctrine. Lorsqu'il s'agit de la grâce et de sa
necessité, Théodoret n'est pas moins incomplet."
[49] *Le commentaire*, 288.
[50] SC 276.178.
[51] *Early Christian Doctrines*, 373. Cf. Hill, "A pelagian commentator on the Psalms?"

Is it only a common position of eastern moralists in this period that the Antiochenes maintain in their Old Testament commentaries? We might need to look at their works on the Gospels and Paul to assemble more evidence of particularity. What does strike today's reader, on the one hand, is the uniformity of their position on morality (beyond a lack of sureness of touch when it comes to stating the balance between grace and human effort, comparable to their infelicitous expressions of the hypostatic union) and the insistence that that human element not be downplayed and, on the other, the consistency of this position with their understanding of the person of Jesus and their Christian worldview as a whole. Terms like "dualistic" and "symmetrical" applied to the Antiochenes' Christology might be thought by some analysts to be applicable to the moral accents in their works as well; others would see simply a carefully developed balance. Pastors tend to accentuate the need both for divine grace and for personal commitment in their flock. We need now to examine whether Antiochene pastors' moral views arising from Old Testament texts catered also for adequate spiritual development.

CHAPTER TEN

PASTORAL AND SPIRITUAL GUIDANCE

Commentary on the Old Testament was but one form of transmission of the faith in the churches of Antioch in the fourth and fifth centuries, a process that was the beneficiary of other traditions as well. In keeping with an educational philosophy that seems to have shown a preference for a "concentration of mind upon observable facts,"[1] whether thereby qualifying as Aristotelian or not, the accent in faith education in the Bible fell upon comprehension; liturgical singing of odd verses from the Psalms, for instance, did not supply for a full grasp of the text. Old Testament books not frequently, if ever, the subject of previous comment, like Ruth and Chronicles, were at this time introduced to readers, at least those able to profit from Theodoret's works, while the Questions genre adopted by himself and Diodore was directed at a grasp of ticklish details in the narratives of a Yahwist, Elohist and Deuteronomist (terms not familiar to the commentators, of course). Appreciation of textual details was also part of Chrysostom's aim in preaching on Genesis; scores of times in his homilies he urges his listeners to note the precision, ἀκρίβεια, of the author, as he does with the adversative particle δέ in Gen 2:20.

> Listen now to the words of Sacred Scripture: "For Adam, however, there proved to be no helpmate of his kind." What is the force of this brief phrase, "For Adam, however"? Why did he add the particle? I mean, would it not be enough to say, For Adam? Let us not be heedless in our anxiety to explore these matters, acting out of idle curiosity; instead, let us act so as to interpret everything precisely and instruct you not to pass by even a brief phrase or a single syllable contained in the Holy Scriptures. After all, they are not simply words, but words of the Holy Spirit, and hence the treasure to be found in even a single syllable is great.[2]

---

[1] Wallace-Hadrill, *Christian Antioch*, 96, 102.
[2] PG 53.1191.1.

Profundity is not requisite; attention to detail will suffice. If such was the attitude of the pastor, however, did it satisfy the needs of the flock and do justice to the richness of Holy Writ? We need to examine whether both preachers in their pulpits and commentators at their desks in breaking the bread of the Word in Antioch went beyond simple explication to apply it to the lives of the faithful and encourage greater depth in spiritual development.

A. The preacher and his congregation

Readers of the Old Testament in Antioch looked to the Scriptures for more than information, and they expected commentators to provide more. A preacher like Chrysostom did not disappoint that expectation. It was his explicit conviction that what was written in the sacred text bore on the lives of the readers, and there were various ways in which the intended beneficiaries could access it. After treating of the first creation story in Genesis, he closes Homily 10 with a recommendation to his congregation to reinforce what he has been saying.

> Any time must be considered suitable for discourse on spiritual topics. If we have a precise realization of this, we will be able while relaxing at home, both before eating and after eating, to take the Scriptures in our hands and gain benefit from them and provide spiritual nourishment for our soul . . . This is our salvation, this is spiritual treasure, this security. If we thus strengthen ourselves each day—by reading (ἀνάγνωσις), by listening, by spiritual discourse (διάλεξις)—we will be able to remain unconquered, and render the snares of the devil ineffectual.[3]

Growth in faith as a result of access to the scriptural tradition of Christianity and the benefit it communicates involves three stages, Chrysostom affirms. None of the processes he lists in this case are private. While Bibles and other Christian books are readily available (we noted in Chapter Four), even the reading of them at home in the family circle is reading out loud, ἀνάγνωσις, like the reading in church during a liturgy of the Word. In both situations attentive listening is required. And the third beneficial process—"saving," he

---

[3] PG 53.90.8. Chrysostom speaks in similar terms in Sermons 7 & 8 on Genesis.

calls it—is spiritual interchange, διάλεξις, that follows upon reading and listening, as occurs in a Bible discussion or prayer group. In this instance he does not refer as a fourth process specifically to his own role as homilist in the way he proudly does in beginning his fourth homily on Isaiah 6 in one of his most sustained and memorable metaphors.

> Since, then, our theatre is full or, to put it differently, the heaving sea is awash with tranquillity or, again, the storm-tossed ocean is steady—come now, let us launch the boat, unfurling our tongue in place of the sail, calling on the grace of the Spirit in place of the breeze, employing as pilot the Cross instead of rudder and oar. While the sea has water that is brackish, here there is living water. There you find brute beasts, here rational souls; there the travelers go from sea to land, here the travelers leave the earth and put in at heaven; there boats, here spiritual sermons; there planks in the boat, here tightly-welded sermons; there a sail, here a tongue; there a breath of air, here a visit from the Spirit; there a human pilot, here the pilot is Christ.[4]

It is a noble image of the homilist in church as an instrument of grace bringing to the listeners the message of Christ to those on their Christian journey. One recalls the image of the the Scriptures as the letters of the emperor delivered by an unworthy emissary in Homily 44 on Genesis:

> If such a man, who is carrying a man's letters and is bearer merely of paper, is welcomed by everybody, so much the more would you be justified in receiving with great attention the sayings sent you by the Spirit by means of us, so that you may gain a great reward for your appreciativeness.[5]

There are thus multiple ways, Chrysostom assures his listeners, for them to gain benefit from the text of the Old Testament mediated to them in church and pondered at home once they comprehend it. It is "spiritual treasure" that brings with it "a visit from the Spirit." The Old Testament offers such a variety of saving material, of a moral and hagiographical nature, as he says in his first homily on David and Saul.

---

[4] SC 277.142.1. Cf. Hill, "St John Chrysostom's teaching on inspiration in his 'Six homilies on Isaiah.'"

[5] PG 54.406.1.

> Let us not simply imprint this on our minds, but also discuss it con-
> stantly with one another in our get-togethers; let us constantly revive
> the memory of this story both with our wives and with the children.
> In fact, if you want to talk about a king, see, there is a king here; if
> about soldiers, about a household, about political affairs, you will find
> a great abundance of these things in the Scriptures. These narratives
> bring the greatest benefit: it is impossible—impossible, I say—for a
> soul nourished on these stories ever to manage to fall victim to passion.[6]

As he said above, profound insights are not of the essence; anyone
can tap into narrative in particular. The story of David offers such
a compelling example of gentleness and clemency under provoca-
tion (virtues an irate emperor in Constantinople in that year 387
might show to his delinquent subjects in Antioch). Likewise, Hannah
offers instruction in godly education and prayerfulness; the seraphim
in Isa 6 are models of reverence for God in contrast to Uzziah and
the Anomeans. And so on.

B. THE COMMENTATOR AND HIS READERS

Clearly, then, readers of the Old Testament in Antioch expected
more from a commentator than observations on textual precision
and documentary hypotheses, and in a preacher like Chrysostom
they received assistance in tapping into the "spiritual treasure." To
judge from Diodore, Theodore and even Theodoret, by contrast,
such assistance was not readily forthcoming in written commentaries;
these pastors clearly did not see—or at least speak of—their pen
fulfilling quite the role that Chrysosom's tongue did, a sail for the
Spirit's breath to carry the believers forward on their journey. It is
not simply that the different genre does not allow for engagement
with the reader to the same extent, though that is a factor: the writers studiously avoid trespassing on the role of a preacher. For one
thing, they rarely if ever moralize; with their focus steadily on ἱστορία,
Diodore and Theodore class only a few psalms (1; 35; 47) as moral,
touching on the situation of all people, and Diodore's editor Olivier
admits that "there are none that deal with individual morality, strictly
speaking."[7] Occasionally they will concede that some sentiments in

---

[6] PG 54.686.7.
[7] *Commentarii*, lxxxi.

other psalms have general relevance; only at the very close of Ps 32, in which Diodore recognizes the πρόσωπον of Hezekiah, does he implicitly admit what his church, in classing it as one of the Pentitential Psalms, already admitted, that it has general relevance.

> What, then, is the purpose of the psalm? *Rejoice in the Lord and be glad, you righteous ones, and boast, all you who are upright in heart* (v.11): aware of this, then, all you who attend to virtue, be full of joy for the reason that God does not close a blind eye to those against us.[8]

The contrast with Chrysostom's pastoral engagement could hardly be starker.

Theodore in commenting on The Twelve, too, concentrates on cognitive aspects of the prophets, "by the grace of God bringing clarity" to them. He does not resonate with the moving calls for social justice he meets in Amos 8:4–6, Micah 3:1–4 and Zechariah 7:9–10 ("one of the finest summaries of the former prophets. It has a strong emphasis on social justice")[9] and invoke a response from his readers, settling instead for a brief paraphrase in each case. He passes up the opportunity to develop a spiritual interpretation of the prophets' message, even when it almost demands it in that distillation of refined Old Testament morality in Micah 6:6–8, with its hierarchy of cultic and moral obligations:

> Has it been told you, mortal that you are, what is good, and what the Lord requires of you, other than doing justice, loving mercy and being ready to walk behind the Lord your God?

An exception is the sermon he delivers against divorce prompted by Malachi 2:13–16, which seems lifted from a common stock and in which for the first time at this late stage he adopts the parenetic tone of a preacher.

Even Bishop Theodoret, in whom the focus on ἱστορία is not so exclusive, and who is ready to see a sacramental reference in a text, is reluctant to apply the words of a prophet to the lives of his readers; it is rare to find an aside like the following in comment on the water flowing from the Temple in Ezekiel 47.

---

[8] *Commentarii*, 185–86. Bardy, "Diodore," 993, can nevertheles commend his subject for his "vie spirituelle et son souci d'apostolat." Cf. Hill, "Diodore of Tarsus as spiritual director."

[9] R. L. Smith, *Micah-Malachi*, 226.

> *At its mouth, in its turning and in its overflowing its shallows will not be healed,*
> *they will turn to salt* (v.11). We see this happening at the present time:
> after growing in number, we are caught up in indifference (ῥᾳθυμία).
> The Lord also forecast a fate in keeping with this, "When lawlessness
> abounds, the love of many will grow cool" (Matt 24:12). So he refers
> to those who are superficial and only have a vestige of the message,
> as is true of most of us, as *shallows*, since shallows are not deep, con-
> taining only water on the surface. So he says that those of this dis-
> position do not receive a cure; yet, he says, they will not be without
> benefit to the others: when corrected, they will prove of further use—
> hence his saying *they will turn to salt*. In other words, not only the
> instructive word but also retribution imposed for sin are accustomed
> to put us on our mettle and fill us with benefit.[10]

Though today's reader would hardly guess it, Theodoret will admit
that there is a pastoral dimension even to the Questions on the
Octateuch; after debating the matter in Q.62 on Genesis of how the
people came to be called Hebrews, he closes debate by conceding,
"No point, however, in squabbling over this: no harm is done to
devotion, whichever way we take it." Twice in the questions on
Leviticus the bishop is tempted by the liturgical nature of the material to slip the limitations of the genre to make a pastoral, even
ascetical, observation, as he does in his long reply to the opening
"question" (a cue for the commentator, of course) on the reason for
laws on sacrifice.

> He orders that all victims be without fault or blemish, different though
> they be and offered in different ways, through this instructing people
> in every walk of life to keep free of fault—those embracing virginity
> to live according to its norms, those choosing the yoke of marriage
> not to impair the conjugal bond in their association with one another,
> and those opting for the ascetical life to observe the norms of perfec-
> tion, and in a word people of wealth, people in poverty, people in
> servitude, people in high places to keep an unblemished and unstained
> record in their particular status.[11]

Such applications by the commentator to the lives of the readers,
however, are very rare.

---

[10] PG 81.1244–45. Cf. Hill, "A spiritual director from Antioch."
[11] *Theodoreti Cyrensis Quaestiones in Octateuchum*, 158.

C. An asceticism without mysticism

And yet the potential of at least parts of Old Testament material for moral guidance, let alone the spiritual direction of its readers, is profound and much celebrated. We have only to observe Didymus in Alexandria at work on a text like Zechariah, that left his Antiochene successors unmoved, to see its possibilities for spiritual development and direction, even if we find that by comparison the historical situation of the prophet and his community is downplayed there, and that much of the spiritual elaboration of the text is gratuitous and arbitrary. Is is true here also, as we have observed about Antioch's hermeneutics generally, that a position is being arrived at in reaction against another elsewhere that seemed only to exploit the text, neglect the intentions of its author and historical reference, and use it as a mirror for commentator and reader rather than as a window on the past?

Or is genre and context a factor once again? Certainly the treatment of the Psalms in Antioch varied at the hands of desk commentators and preacher. Though Diodore and Theodore may concede them some limited moral character of a general kind, they do not see them as spiritual or ascetical compositions, and their readers are not led in that direction. The Psalms may offer the reader (or worshiper) more than historical insights—lyrical expressions of hope and despair, love and longing, trust and abandonment, sin and forgiveness, suffering and relief—all the stuff of spiritual awareness and growth. Diodore, however (and Theodore under his influence), is not willing or not able to approach them at that level. Psalms like 23 ("The Lord shepherds me") and 32 ("Happy are those whose transgressions are forgiven") that express such moving sentiments are generally given short shrift; rare it is for a verse to elicit anything like an insight into intimacy with God, as in comment on Ps 36:9:

> He continues, *Because with you is a fountain of life; in your light we shall see light*: thanks to you it is possible for us both to live and to be enlightened unto piety: *In your light* we see you, as if to say, through piety leading to you we experience you.[12]

Psalm 25 Diodore will claim—against the evidence—to be composed on the part of the exiles; but he soon has to abandon the effort and

---

[12] *Commentarii*, 213.

recognise it as expressing sentiments proper, in the words of Weiser, to "a pensive soul earnest in its piety,"[13] the result being that his commentary degenerates into terse paraphrase.

A preacher like Chrysostom, on the other hand, is predictably capable of responding to the moral and even ascetical elements in the Psalter. Beyond inveighing against the vulgar excesses of the idle rich in comment on Ps 49, he can lecture on "the art of prayer," as he does on Ps 4:

> We are, however, not as aware as we should be of the benefit of prayer, for the reason that we neither apply ourselves to it with assiduity nor have recourse to it in accord with God's laws. Instead, when on the point of conversing with some people of a class above us we ensure our appearance and gait and attire are as they should be, and dialogue with them in this fashion. In approaching God, by contrast, we yawn, scratch ourselves, look this way and that, pay little attention, loll on the ground, do the shopping.[14]

Prayer is an art that can be learnt, he says in comment on Ps 7; it is "medicine, but if we do not know how to apply the medicine, neither will we gain benefit from it." So learn the rules, follow the prescription.

> Being heard happens in this fashion: first, of course, worthiness to receive something; then, praying in accordance with God's laws; third, persistence; fourth, asking nothing earthly; fifth, seeking things to our real benefit; sixth, contributing everything of our own.[15]

While we appreciate the recognition that the Psalms are prayers, we may find the treatment of the topic pedestrian and somewhat mechanical. In comment on some few psalms outside his longer series, as on Ps 42, "As the deer longs for living springs," Chrysostom can rise to greater heights of spiritual intimacy that Theodore and Theodoret will not imitate, as we noted in Chapter Seven; but it is an exception.[16] Antiochene congregations may not even have appreciated the change in tone; they may not have looked to their pastors as spiritual gurus, and none of the commentators assumed that

---

[13] *The Psalms*, 238.
[14] PG 55.41.2.
[15] PG 55.85.4. Cf. Hill, "The spirituality of Chrysostom's Commentary on the Psalms."
[16] Cf. Hill, "Psalm 41(42): a classic text for Antiochene spirituality."

role. Despite submitting the Song of Songs to a thoroughly spiritual interpretation in the Alexandrian style so as to offset charges against it of eroticism, Theodoret only once in the course of commentary allows himself to apply a verse (2:7) to the spiritual lives of his readers.[17]

Why did these pastors in Antioch not feel it incumbent on them to plumb for their readers the spiritual depths of the Old Testament, even in its most lyrical and intimate passages of prayer?[18] Were they reacting against what they perceived as excesses in the approach of another school, as Froehlich remarks of their hermeneutics?[19] There is no question that Antioch's approach to the Bible generally is feet-on-the-ground rather than head-in-the-air, and this realism we have seen to be apparent in other areas of their worldview as well, such as their Christology and soteriology. So it is not surprising to sense a sort of reluctance, if not suspicion, when it comes to instruction on spiritual intimacy, if not mysticism. Louis Bouyer also sees a history behind this reluctance, a reaction which affects "the whole orientation of spirituality." As Bouyer sees it,

> in the school of Origen, the tendency is to find Christian dogma under its most metaphysical aspects, or Christian spirituality under its most mystical aspects (that is, what is connected with the life of Christ in us).

In this tendency Antioch would find elements of "fanaticism" (Bouyer's term), as they would likewise not follow Didymus in the direction of layers of spiritual meanings in Zechariah arbitrarily developed, or Cyril in understanding the Bible only in relation to Christ.[20] Instead, Antioch opted for an "asceticism without mysticism,"[21] if by mysticism is meant intimacy of relationship with Christ; that is something beyond elucidation, an area into which only Anomeans pry. The art of prayer can be acquired by following six clearcut rules, Chrysostom

---

[17] Cf. Hill, "A spiritual director from Antioch."
[18] Cf. Guinot, *L'Exégèse*, 75–76, in reference to Antioch generally and Theodoret in particular: "Cette exégèse reste le plus souvent fermée à la dimension spirituelle et mystique du texte scripturaire: elle ne pouvait donc que souffrir d'une comparaison avec celle d'Origène ou de Grégoire de Nysse, dont c'est là un des attraits et la richesse."
[19] Cf. Froehlich, *Biblical Interpretation in the Early Church*, 20: "There can be little doubt that the hermeneutical theories of the Antiochene school were aimed at the excesses of Alexandrian spiritualism."
[20] Cf. Wilken, *The Theology of St Cyril of Alexandria*, 21.
[21] Bouyer, *The Spirituality of the New Testament and the Fathers*, 436–46.

says, the first being "worthiness" and the final one "contributing everything of our own." Theodore declines to engage with the moving presentation by Hosea 1–2 of the Lord's uniting himself with his people in the intimate relationship of marriage. The spirituality of the Song, Theodoret decides, is best left to individual meditation. "Do you want to learn how Isaiah saw God? Become a prophet yourself."[22] Anomeans, take note.

To judge from the many references to the obscurity and problems (αἰνίγματα) of Old Testament texts made in the works of the Antiochene commentators, and from their promises to bring clarity to such texts, clarification was thought a considerable benefit in its own right, a worthwhile contribution to the transmission of faith of the Antioch communities. From this point of view, it could be said that their work in promoting comprehension was pastoral in itself. Yet the inspired Word offered more to its hearers, at least of a moral and hagiographical nature, as well as providing models of prayer and converse with God and inviting a response. Engaging with his congregations, Chrysostom constantly unpacked this "spiritual treasure," taking occasion to apply it to their daily lives—even if we may demur when claims are made for him as "the precursor if not the initiator of a spirituality for the laity," for whom "he traces the way."[23] That Diodore, Theodore and Theodoret as authors of written commentaries in Antioch did not aspire to do the same at their desks suggests that Antioch did not encourage such a moralistic approach from any pastor not a preacher, and certainly did not support any exploration in the Bible of spiritual intimacy and mysticism of the kind favored elsewhere, where terms like "mystical" came more readily to biblical commentators. Today's readers, accustomed to a per-

---

[22] Chrysostom, Homily Six on Isaiah 6 (SC 277.206.1). Wenger, "Jean Chrysostome," 339, points out that Chrysostom will forsake this agnosticism in his homilies "On the incomprehensible nature of God." He is not accorded a place by D. G. Hunter under a heading "Patristic spirituality" in M. Downey, ed., *The New Dictionary of Catholic Spirituality*, Collegeville: Glazier, 1993, 723–32.

[23] Bouyer, *The Spirituality*, 446; A.-M. Malingrey, "John Chrysostom," in A. Di Berardino, ed., *Encyclopedia of the Early Church*, 441. The latter's description of Chrysostom as "the most illustrious representative of the school of Antioch" may be thought partial and unnuanced; cf. B. Smalley, *The Study of the Bible in the Middle Ages*, 18: "He was by far the best known representative of Antiochene principles in the West and, at the same time, the author who could teach his readers least about Antiochene exegesis."

sonalist approach to spirituality, may find Antiochene commentaries by comparison relatively unspiritual in that sense, though never crass or jejune. If that observation is thought impertinent, it is made in the belief that the commentators of that age are not irrelevant to the interests of ours where the "spiritual treasure" of the Scripture is concerned.

CHAPTER ELEVEN

ASSESSING ANTIOCH'S ACHIEVEMENT

One can only wonder what might have been our estimate of the extent of the achievement of the Antioch commentators of the fourth and fifth centuries, from Diodore to Theodoret, if all their works on the Old Testment were extant like those of the bishop of Cyrus. If Diodore's Questions on the Octateuch had survived in its entirety, that valuable source of Theodoret's, which it seems he disagreed with more often than not, we might have gained a further inkling into the progression of Antiochene exegesis and commentary. If Theodore had in fact written commentaries on the major prophets, despite the silence on this of councils and Greek historians, and if Diodore had also left what he is credited with writing on that biblical corpus, great light would have been shed especially on the hermeneutical perspective of early Antioch. If it were in fact Theodore's work on the Song that Theodoret scorns in his own preface, and if along with it we also had the commentaries written by "Diodore, the noble champion of piety, and John, bedewing the whole world with the streams of his teaching to this very day," as he says were then available, would we have thus been regaled with further commentary upon it "according to the norms of allegory"?[1] Probably not. In any event, the large amount of their work that we do have, including Psalms commentaries by them all, allows us to gain some impression of Antioch's considerable achievement.

A. A COMMITMENT TO PASTORAL CARE

For one thing, it demonstrates these churchmen's commitment to the formation of their flock in the faith by the biblical tradition of Christianity in particular—though we also get some incidental insight into the community's liturgical tradition in the process, such as in

---

[1] Theodoret's claim of his own work on the Song (PG 81.32, 40).

the homilies of Chrysostom delivered in the churches of Antioch proper. Whether the works are now available to us to read or not, they represent an enormous investment in faith formation by zealous pastors, no matter what view we take of the pastoral character of the material or the pastors' aspirations or success as spiritual guides. "All of them put their scholarly techniques to the service of preaching,"[2] Frances Young reminded us. As a corollary, the extant works testify to the esteem in which the commentators held these Jewish scriptures, whose "meaning belongs to us" even if "the books are from them," in Chrysostom's view.[3]

The question has to be asked as to whether (in the case of Theodoret, for one) they gave a priority to laborious commentary on this literature, admittedly Jewish and obscure, because they recognized its divinely-inspired character, because they regarded it as vital to the faith development of their congregations, or because they acknowledged a Christological dimension in the Old and not only in New Testament writings, despite being unwilling to see Jesus there at every hand's turn as had commentators from another school. Unfriendly critics ancient and modern may claim the Antiochenes were "killing the Word of God"[4] in the way they discharged this self-imposed task; but if we can believe Chrysostom's applauding congregations and the repeated requests to a busy man like Theodoret in Cyrus for more and more commentaries, the Antioch faithful believed they were being well served.

It is not as though the work of commentary was an easy burden. The repeated references to αἰνίγματα in Old Testament texts and Chrysostom's formal treatment of the topic show it was uphill labor. Even with the best of exegetical skills and resources at their disposal, today's commentators admit the same about books like the Psalter, the Octateuch and some of the Prophets; yet it is these in particular that received attention in Antioch at that time. The Septuagint version in the form which they received and in which they and private readers read the Old Testament was less than perfect, at times settling for transliteration or omission of difficult Hebrew terms, and

---

    [2] *Biblical Exegesis*, 185.
    [3] Chrysostom, Sermon 2 on Genesis (SC 433.188.1).
    [4] The claim of an unfriendly Leontius of Byzantium in the sixth century, relayed (not unsympathetically) by O'Keefe, "'A letter that killeth'," 104.

often misreading terms and syntax. Alternative versions were credited with being "clearer," like that of Symmachus, if the commentator had access to them or troubled to consult them. But not all
of them did, we noted, and none of them was properly equipped to
supplement the shortcomings of their local text. If they did not have
sound linguistic equipment to qualify them as exegetes strictly speaking, they brought to bear their personal background (like a knowledge of Syriac in Theodoret's case—a mixed blessing in Theodore's
view) and experience. In Diodore's case this experience included
personal acquaintance with Athenian philosophers, as well as with
persecution by tyrants trying to reinstate paganism in Antioch, an
experience that may have embittered him. Their education, if not
strongly philosophical beyond a "concentration of mind upon observable facts,"[5] was rhetorical to the extent of allowing them to imbibe
the literary principles of the academy and hermeneutical principles
that would affect their way of relating the Old to the New Testament
in a way different from students in another school.

B. A BELIEF IN THE OLD TESTAMENT

The upshot of this was that these churchmen brought a mix of atti-
tudes to their approach to the biblical texts they felt Antioch congregations needed to comprehend. One was a conviction that the
Old Testament, Jewish as it may be but interpreted in a non-Jewish
way (unless one were a *Ioudaiophrōn*), had value in itself. It had a
validity of its own, as any work of literature stands alone; it did not
require salvaging by being related to the New Testament; it came
from the same source as the New, even if the latter "talks about
more important things."[6] The same Spirit is at work in both; both
are divinely-inspired, authors and text both. Both testaments represent God's ὁμιλία with human beings, though the text of the Old,
in its language and the concreteness of its expressions (too crass at
times for critics and commentators of another school), demonstrate
more forcefully the divine author's considerateness, συγκατάβασις,
evident also in the sacred history told in its pages.

---

[5] Wallace-Hadrill, *Christian Antioch*, 96, 102.
[6] Chrysostom, *Omelie*, 74.3.

If the story told in those pages is real, where lies the reality, ἀλήθεια—already in those pages and events and characters? or must it be sought for more distantly, in the New Testament and beyond? Is the Old just a mirror of the New? Must everything—events and characters—be seen as pointing forward to Jesus and the New, robbing the Old of continuing validity? or is there operating instead, and discernible by an adequate θεωρία, a Christological οἰκονομία, an "overarching narrative," in which continuity (or "coherence")[7] must be maintained with those historical events and characters? Can the Old be interpreted adequately within the confines of the Old, as Homer was best clarified by Homer? Is that rhetorical adage a more appropriate hermeneutic than a platonic schema in which the historical and the fleshly are discarded (by a Didymus in Alexandria, for example) for the μυστικός, πνευματικός, νοητός?

In opting at least partially for the reality of the Old, for the text as a window onto the past, for the need to retain continuity with what was said and done then, Antioch (even from the time of Paul of Samosata and Lucian before our period)[8] adopted a distinctive style of interpretation. It represented a reaction against another style, and to that extent was adversarial, as can be seen in Eustathius, Diodore and Theodore; if in some respects misinformed (about the nature of allegory and Alexandria's use of it, e.g.), it spoke from experience. But it was not polemical to the extent of airing disagreements at length in public;[9] *cura pastoralis* was not achieved through *odium theologicum* in its view (though ironically it will fall victim to such odium itself).

C. Accounting for Antioch's approach

How account, then, for Antioch's distinctive stance towards the Old Testament? From the outset we have been shying away from the

---

[7] Young, *Biblical Exegesis*, 296, 176.

[8] Cf. Wiles, "Theodore of Mopsuestia," 489–90: "The leading figures of the Antiochene school of biblical scholarship in the fourth century . . . probably stand much closer in approach to Paul and to Lucian than they would ever have been prepared to admit. There is the same emphasis on the biblical text, on historical fact, and on the humanity of Jesus, which we can already detect in the scanty and biased accounts of Paul and Lucian."

[9] Severian, a contemporary and adversary of Chrysostom in Constantinople, would be an exception in this regard, to judge from his few extant works.

question of the relation between Antiochene "exegesis" (applied loosely and used rather in the particular sense of hermeneutics) and the theology held by members of the school. Was it their theology (or at least a particular philosophy of theirs) that led them to treat the biblical text as they did,[10] or rather was it the case that a particular exegetical approach lay behind Antiochene theology? If it is a complex question, which we have to this stage declined to enter, the solution is simple for some; for Vosté, the theological errors into which Antiochene scholars fell (from Diodore and Theodore to Nestorius) can be sheeted home to their exegetical method, to a rationalist approach to the Bible and to Christ.[11] Others come to the opposite conclusion: for Greer it is Judaism that accounts for their exegetical method;[12] others detect an indebtedness to Aristotelian thought or a rejection by Diodore of an allegorical approach in Neoplatonic authors;[13] and we have seen Schäublin tracing the Antiochene hermeneutic to rhetoricians and grammarians like Aristarchus.

Perhaps the outlook of Antioch's commentators is more complex than that. Behind their approach to Scripture in general and the Old Testament in particular lies a worldview that expresses itself also in the Christological accents in their works, as it explains the soteriology and morality we read there, too, as well as the spiritual guidance given by the commentators that has been styled an "asceticism without mysticism."[14] In all these areas of thought and life can be

---

[10] The placement of "'philosophy'/'exegesis'" among "the false disjunctions of modernity" by Sarah Coakley, *Rethinking Gregory of Nyssa*, 2, does not invalidate the relevance of investigating the interrelation of the two in the approach to the biblical text adopted in Antioch and Alexandria.

[11] "La chronologie de l'activité littéraire de Théodore de Mopsueste," 56: "Les germes de toutes ces erreurs se retrouvaient dans le méthode exégètiques de l'École d'Antioche: les trois noms de Diodore, Théodore et Nestorius marquent les étapes d'une même tendance vers le rationalisme biblique et christologique."

[12] *Theodore of Mopsuestia*, 110: "The respective positions of Alexandria and Antioch regarding exegesis developed from Judaism and within the early Church."

[13] Viciano, "Das formale Verfahren," 387–89, 404–405, surveys opinions on the topic.

[14] Bouyer, *The Spirituality of the New Testament and the Fathers*, 439. Thompson, *Writing the Wrongs*, 242–43, similarly sees an allegorical reading of biblical texts arising from a particular ideology: "To construct an allegory or to read allegorically is certainly also to express one's own ideology and worldview in conscious or unconscious dialogue with—or, perhaps, in opposition to—the text from which one's allegory is ostensibly drawn." Diodore sensed such "opposition" frequently occurring in Alexandrian reading and the worldview it represented—hence his hostility to allegory.

seen an emphasis on the human—without denial of the divine—as
if to offset a real danger of its being minimized and obliterated. The
human author of Old Testament texts and his factual situation cannot be bypassed in a process of moving—arbitrarily—to a range of
spiritual meanings; an elevated meaning is permissible in texts on
the proviso that continuity be maintained with the factual; the concreteness of the language of obscure texts and the crassness of the
conduct described there are a necessary implication of the incarnation of the Word in Scripture.[15] The human nature in Jesus is in
no way to be etherealized or downplayed, either; human limitations
are an essential element of the (other) Incarnation, too. Divine gift
though it be, salvation likewise is not simply to be accepted in faith
but striven for by virtuous actions, with the free will of an unim-
paired human nature playing at least an equal part. Spiritual development occurs according to ordinary steps taken in imitation of
biblical figures besides Jesus, like David and Hannah; the art of
prayer can be acquired by well-rehearsed rules, mystical rapture bor-
dering on the anomean and not worth considering.

The Old Testament yields itself readily to commentators, congregations and private readers sharing such a worldview. If this approach
does less than justice to the range of religious sentiment expressed
by the psalmists, it sketches an οἰκονομία in which Jesus himself can
be shown to have participated through his lowly life and passion. If
it is reluctant to interpret the Bible only through the person of Jesus,
it can arguably claim to be Christological in terms of the whole
divine οἰκονομία, or in Paul's term "the mystery of Christ." If it fails
to appreciate apocalyptic scenarios of a prophet, it resonates warmly
with chroniclers and ἱστοριογράφοι, and at least is prepared to grapple with the Octateuch. If it is stronger on the past events of the
οἰκονομία, the New Testament in homilies and commentaries at other
times was available to plot the future—Antiochene works which lie
beyond the scope of this volume. Certainly, Antioch is not "mono-

---

[15] Cyril, Alexandrian himself, at the outset of his Commentary on The Twelve
(in which he seems aware of Theodore's work), has to deal with people (evidently
of his own school, and even acquaintance) who rejected the reality of Hosea's marriage with a prostitute (like Origen, it seems), or who while accepting the reality
could not stomach the distasteful character of the story (Eusebius of Caesarea). Cf.
P. E. Pusey (ed.), *Sancti Patris Nostri Cyrilli Archiepiscopi Alexandrini in XII Prophetas*, I,
15ff.

lithic," and its authors "need separate monographs"[16]—another goal not attempted here. Hopefully, however, common patterns and individual accents within the one school of biblical commentary have been allowed to emerge in the above, all amounting to a significant chapter in the history of Christian exegesis and interpretation.

---

[16] Wallace-Hadrill, *Christian Antioch*, 39; Nassif, "'Spiritual exegesis' in the school of Antioch," 374.

SELECT BIBLIOGRAPHY

A. Modern editions of Antiochene Old Testament commentaries

1. *Eustathius*

Klostermann, E., *Origenes, Eustathius von Antiochien, und Gregor von Nyssa über die Hexe von Endor*, KlT 83, 1912

2. *Diodore*

Deconinck, J., *Quaestiones in Octateuchum et Reges*, Paris: Librairie Ancienne Honoré Champion, 1912
Devreesse, R., *Les anciens commentateurs grecs de l'Octateuque es des Rois*, ST 201, 1959
Olivier, J.-M., *Diodori Tarsensis commentarii in Psalmos, 1 Commentarii in Psalmos I–L*, CCG 6, 1980

3. *Theodore*

Devreesse, R., *Essai sur Théodore de Mopsueste*, ST 141, 1948, 286–421
——, *Le commentaire de Théodore de Mopsueste sur les psaumes (I–LXXX)*, ST 93, 1939
Sprenger, H. N., *Theodori Mopsuesteni Commentarius in XII Prophetas*, GO, Biblica et Patristica 1, 1977

4. *John Chrysostom*

Brottier, L., *Jean Chrysostome. Sermons sur la Genèse*, SC 433, 1998
Dumortier, J., *Jean Chrysostome. Homélies sur Ozias*, SC 277, 1981
Sorlin, H., *Jean Chrysostome. Commentaire sur Job*, SC 346, 348, 1988
Zincone, S., *Giovanni Crisostomo, Omelie sull'oscurità delle Profezie*, Verba seniorum N.S. 12; Roma: Edizioni Studium, 1998

5. *Theodoret*

Fernández Marcos, N., Sáenz-Badillos, A., *Theodoreti Cyrensis Quaestiones in Octateuchum*, Textos y Estudios "Cardenal Cisneros" 17; Madrid: Consejo Superior de Investigaciones Cientificas, 1979
——, J. R. Busto Saiz, *Theodoreti Cyrensis Quaestiones in Reges et Paralipomena*, Textos y Estudios "Cardenal Cisneros" 32; Madrid: Consejo Superior de Investigaciones Cientificas, 1984
Guinot, J.-N., *Théodoret de Cyr. Commentaire sur Isaïe I,II,III*, SC 276, 295, 315, 1980, 1982, 1984

B. Secondary sources cited in the text

Aland, K., Aland, B., *The Text of the New Testament*, 2nd ed., Eng. trans., Grand Rapids: Eerdmans, 1989
Asensio, F., "El Crisóstomo y su visión de la escritura en la exposición homilética del Génesis," *EstBib* 32 (1973) 223–55, 329–56
Augustin, P., "La pérennité de l'Eglise selon Jean Chrysostome et l'authenticité de la IVᵉ Homélie *Sur Ozias*," *Recherches Augustiniennes* 28 (1995) 95–144
Azéma, Y., *Théodoret de Cyr, Correspondance 2*, SC 98, 1964

von Balthasar, H. U., *Origen. Spirit and Fire*, Eng. trans., Washington DC: Catholic University of America Press, 1984

Bardy, G., "La littérature patristique des '*Quaestiones et Responsiones*' sur l'écriture sainte," *RB* 41 (1932) 210–36, 341–69, 515–37; 42 (1933) 14–30, 211–29, 328–52

——, "Théodoret," *DTC* 15, 1946, 299–325

——, "Interprétation chez les pères," *DBS* 4, 1949, 569–91

——, "Diodore," *Dictionnaire de spiritualité* 3, Paris: Beauchesne, 1967, 986–93

Barr, J., "St Jerome's appreciation of Hebrew," *BJRL* 49 (1966) 280–302

Barthélemy, D., *Les devanciers d'Aquila*, VTS 10, 1963

Baur, P. C., *John Chrysostom and his Time*, Eng. trans., London-Glasgow, 1959, 1960

Bouyer, L., *The Spirituality of the New Testament and the Fathers*, Eng. trans., London: Burns & Oates, 1963

Bruce, F. F., *The Canon of Scripture*, Downers Grove Ill: InterVarsity Press, 1988

Bruns, P. "Theodor von Mopsuestia." *TRE* 33, 240–46

Canivet, P., *Histoire d'une entreprise apologétique au Vᵉ siècle*, Paris: Bloud & Gay, 1957

Chase, F. H., *Chrysostom. A Study in the History of Biblical Interpretation*, Cambridge: Deighton, Bell, 1887

Childs, B. S., *Introduction to the Old Testament as Scripture*, London: SCM, 1979

Clark, E. A., *Reading Renunciation. Asceticism and Scripture in Early Christianity*, Princeton NJ: Princeton University Press, 1999

Coakley, S., ed., *Rethinking Gregory of Nyssa*, Oxford: Blackwell, 2003

Crouzel, H., *Origen*, Eng. trans., San Francisco: Harper & Row, 1989

Dahood, M., *Psalms*. AB 16, 17, 17A, 1965, 1968, 1970

——, "Ebla, Ugarit and the Old Testament," *The Month* 239 (1978) 271–76, 341–45

Daley, B. E., "Apocalypticism in early Christian theology," in B. McGinn, *The Encyclopedia of Apocalypticism* 2, 3–47

Di Berardino, A., ed., *Encyclopedia of the Early Church*, Eng. trans., Cambridge: James Clark & Co., 1992

Dorival, G., "L'apport des chaînes exégétiques grecques à une réédition des *Hexaples* d'Origène (à propos du Psaume 118)," *RHT* 4 (1974) 44–74

Doutreleau, L., *Didyme L'Aveugle. Sur Zacharie*, SC 83, 1962

Downey, G., *The History of Antioch in Syria from Seleucus to the Arab Conquest*, Princeton NJ: Princeton University Press, 1961

Fabbi, F., "La 'condiscendenza' divina nell' ispirazione biblica secondo S. Giovanni Crisostomo," *Bib* 14 (1933) 330–47

Fernández Marcos, N., "Some reflections on the Antiochian text of the Septuagint," in *Studien zur Septuagint—Robert Hanhart zu Ehren*, ed. D. Fraenkel, U. Quast, J. W. Wevers, MSU 20, 1990, 219–29

——, *Scribes and Translators. Septuagint and Old Latin in the Books of Kings*. VTS 54, 1994

——, *The Septuagint in Context: Introduction to the Greek Versions of the Bible*, Eng. trans., Boston-Leiden: Brill, 2001

Gamble, H. Y., *Books and Readers in the Early Church. A History of Early Christian Texts*, New Haven-London: Yale University Press, 1995

de Ghellinck, J., *Patristique et moyen age. Etudes d'histoire littéraire et doctrinale, 2 Introductions et compléments à l'étude de la patristique*, Paris: Desclée de Brouwer, 1947

Greer, R. A., *Theodore of Mopsuestia. Exegete and Theologian*, London: The Faith Press, 1961

——, "The Antiochene Christology of Diodore of Tarsus," *JTS* ns 17 (1966) 327–41

——, Kugel, J. L., *Early Biblical Interpretation*. Library of Early Christianity, Philadelphia: Westminster, 1986

Guinot, J.-N., "Théodoret a-t-il lu les homélies d'Origène sur l'Ancien Testament?" *Vetera Christianorum* 21 (1984) 285–312

——, "L'importance de la dette de Théodoret de Cyr à l'égard de l'exégèse de Théodore de Mopsueste," *Orpheus* 5 (1984): 68–109

——, "La cristallisation d'un différend: Zorobabel dans l'exégèse de Théodore de Mopsueste et de Théodoret de Cyr," *Aug* 24 (1984) 527–47

—— "La christologie de Théodoret de Cyr dans son commentaire sur le Cantique", *VC* 39 (1985) 256–272

——, "Les sources de l'exégèse de Théodoret de Cyr", *StudP* 25 (1993) 72–94

——, "L'*In Psalmos* de Théodoret: une relecture critique du commentaire de Diodore de Tarse," *Cahiers de Biblia Patristica* 4 (1993) 97–134

——, *L'Exégèse de Théodoret de Cyr*, Théologie Historique 100, Paris: Beauchesne, 1995

——, "Theodoret von Kyrrhos," *TRE* 33, 250–54

Hamman, A. "Stenografia," in A. Di Berardino, ed., *Dizionario Patristico e di Antichità Cristiana* 2, Casale Monferrato: Marietti, 1984

Hanson, R. P. C., *Allegory and Event. A Study of the Sources and Significance of Origen's Interpretation of Scripture*, London: SCM, 1959

——, "Biblical exegesis in the early Church," *The Cambridge History of the Bible* I, Cambridge: Cambridge University Press, 1970, 412–53

Hatch, E., *The Influence of Greek Ideas on Christianity*, Gloucester, Mass: Peter Smith, 1970

Heine, R. E., *Gregory of Nyssa'a Treatise on the Inscription of the Psalms*, Oxford Early Christian Studies, Oxford: Clarendon, 1995

Henry, R., ed., Photius. Bibliothèque II, III, Paris: Belles Lettres, 1960, 1962

Hill, R. C., "St John Chrysostom's teaching on inspiration in 'Six Homilies on Isaiah,'" *VC* 22 (1968) 19–37

——, "St John Chrysostom and the incarnation of the Word in Scripture," *Compass Theology Review* 14 (1980) 34–38

——, "On looking again at *synkatabasis*", *Prudentia* 13 (1981) 3–11

——, "*Akribeia*: a principle of Chrysostom's exegesis," *Colloquium* 14 (Oct. 1981) 32–36

——, "On giving up the horses for Lent," *Clergy Review* 68 (1983) 105–106

——, "Chrysostom's terminology for the inspired Word," *EstBib* 41 (1983) 367–73

——, "Chrysostom as Old Testament commentator," *EstBib* 46 (1988) 61–77

——, "Psalm 45: a *locus classicus* for patristic thinking on biblical inspiration," *StudP* 25 (1993) 95–100

——, "From Good News to Holy Writ: the share of the text in the saving purpose of the Word," *EstBib* 51 (1993) 145–62

——, "The spirituality of Chrysostom's *Commentary on the Psalms*," *JECS* 5 (1997) 569–79

——, "A pelagian commentator on the Psalms?" *ITQ* 63 (1998) 263–71

——, "Chrysostom's Commentary on the Psalms: homilies or tracts?" in *Prayer and Spirituality in the Early Church* 1, ed. P. Allen, Brisbane: Australian Catholic University, 1998, 301–17

——, "Chrysostom, interpreter of the Psalms," *EstBib* 54 (1998) 61–74

——, "A spiritual director from Antioch," *Pacifica* 12 (1999) 181–91

——, "Theodoret, commentator on the Psalms," *ETL* 76 (2000) 88–104

——, "'Norms, definitions, and unalterable doctrines:' Chrysostom on Jeremiah," *ITQ* 65 (2000) 335–46

——, "Chrysostom's homilies on David and Saul," *SVTQ* 44 (2000) 123–41

——, "Theodore of Mopsuestia, interpreter of the prophets," *Sacris Erudiri* 40 (2001) 107–129

——, "*Sartor resartus*: Theodore under review by Theodoret," *Aug* 41 (2001) 465–76

——, "St John Chrysostom's homilies on Hannah," *SVTQ* 45 (2001) 319–38

——, "Chrysostom on the obscurity of the Old Testament," *OCP* 67 (2001) 371–83

——, "Theodoret wrestling with Romans," *StudP* 34 (2001) 347–52

——, "Orientale lumen: western biblical scholarship's unacknowledged debt," in *Orientale Lumen Australasia-Oceania 2000: Proceedings*, ed. L. Cross; Melbourne: Australian Catholic University, 2001, 157–72

——, *Theodoret of Cyrus. Commentary on the Letters of St Paul*, Brookline MA: Holy Cross Orthdox Press, 2001

——, "Jonah in Antioch." *Pacifica* 14 (2001) 245–61

——, "Old Testament *Questions* of Theodoret of Cyrus," *GOTR* 46 (2001) 57–73

——, "St John Chrysostom, preacher on the Old Testament, *GOTR* 46 (2001) 267–86

——, "Psalm 41 (42): a classic text for Antiochene spirituality," *ITQ* 68 (2003) 25–33

——, "St John Chrysostom as biblical commentator: Six homilies on Isaiah 6," *SVTQ* 47 (2003) 307–22

——, "His Master's Voice: Theodore of Mopsuestia on the Psalms." *HeyJ* 44 (2004) 40–53

——, "Diodore of Tarsus as spiritual director," *OCP* 71 (2005)

Jellicoe, S., *The Septuagint and Modern Study*, Oxford: Clarendon, 1968

Kahle, P., *The Cairo Genizah*, 2nd ed., Oxford: Blackwell, 1959

Kalantzis, G., "*Duo Filii* and the *Homo Assumptus* in the Christology of Theodore of Mopsuestia," *ETL* 78 (2002) 57–78

——, "Theodore of Mopsuestia's *Commentarius in evangelium Iohannis apostoli*: text and transmission," *Aug* 43 (2003) 473–93

——, *Theodore of Mopsuestia. Commentary on the Gospel of John*, ECS 7, Strathfield: St Paul's Publications, 2004

Kannengiesser, C., "The Bible as read in the early church," *Concilium* 1991/1, 29–36

——, *A Handbook of Patristic Exegesis*, BAC 1, 2004

Kelly, J. N. D., *Jerome. His Life, Writings and Controversies*, London: Duckworth, 1975

——, *Early Christian Doctrines*, 5th ed.; New York: Harper & Row, 1978

——, *Golden Mouth. The Story of John Chrysostom. Ascetic, Preacher, Bishop*, Ithaca NY: Cornell University Press, 1995

Kerrigan, A., *St Cyril of Alexandria, Interpreter of the Old Testament*, AnBib 2, 1952

Leroux, J.-M., "Johannes Chrysostomus," *TRE* 17, 118–27

de Lubac, H., *Histoire et Esprit: L'intelligence de l'Ecriture d'après Origène*, Théologie 16; Paris: Aubier, 1950

McDonald, L. M., Sanders, J. A., edd., *The Canon Debate*, Peabody MA: Hendrickson, 2002

McGinn, B., ed., *The Encyclopedia of Apocalypticism*, New York-London: Continuum, 2002

McGregor, L. J., *The Greek Text of Ezekiel*, Septuagint and Cognate Studies 18, Atlanta GA: Scholars Press, 1985

McKane, W., *Jeremiah 1–25, 26–52*, ICC, 1986, 1996

McNamara, K., "Theodore of Mopsuestia and the Nestorian heresy," *ITQ* 19 (1952) 254–78; 20 (1953) 172–91

Malingrey, A.-M., "John Chrysostom," in A. Di Berardino, ed., *Encyclopedia of the Early Church* 1, Eng. trans., Edinburgh: Clark, 1992

Mandac, M., "L'union Christologique dans les oeuvres de Théodoret antérieures au Concile d'Ephèse", *ETL* 47 (1971) 64–96

Marcowicz, W. A., "Chrysostom's sermons on *Genesis*: a problem," *TS* 24 (1963) 652–64

W. Mayer, "The dynamics of liturgical space: aspects of the interaction between John Chrysostom and his audiences," *Ephemerides liturgicae* 111 (1997) 104–115

——, "John Chrysostom: extraordinary preacher, ordinary audience," in M. Cunningham, P. Allen, edd., *Preacher and Audience: Studies in Early Christian and Byzantine Homilies*, Leiden: Brill, 1998, 105–37

——, Allen, P., *John Chrysostom*, The Early Church Fathers, London-New York: Routledge, 2000

Meeks, W. A. and Wilken, R. L., *Jews and Christians in Antioch in the First Four Centuries*, SBL Sources for Biblical Study 13, Missoula, Montana: Scholars Press, 1978

Nassif, B., "'Spiritual Exegesis' in the School of Antioch." in B. Nassif, ed., *New Perspectives in Biblical Theology*, Grand Rapids: Eerdmans, 1996.

Norris, R. A., *Manhood and Christ. A Study in the Christology of Theodore of Mopsuestia*, Oxford: Clarendon, 1963

O'Keefe, J. J., "'A letter that killeth': Toward a reassessment of Antiochene exegesis, or Diodore, Theodore, and Theodoret on the Psalms," *JECS* 8 (2000) 83–104

Pirot, L., *L'Oeuvre exégètique de Théodore de Mopsueste*, Roma: Pontificio Istituto Biblico, 1913

Pusey, P. E. (ed.), *Sancti Patris Nostri Cyrilli Archiepiscopi Alexandrini in XII Prophetas*, 2 vols, Brussels: Culture et Civilisation, 1965

Quasten, J., *Patrology*, Westminster MD: Newman, 1950, 1953, 1960

Reuling, H., *After Eden*. Church Fathers and Rabbis on Genesis 3:16–21, private printing, 2004 208, C.: *Diodore of Tarsus*. Commentary on the Psalms 1–51, WGRW 9, 2005

Richard, M., "Notes sur l'évolution doctrinale de Théodoret de Cyr", *RSPT* 25 (1936) 459–481

——, "Le commentaire de Saint Jean Chrysostome sur les *Proverbes de Salomon*," in Συμπόσιον. *Studies on St. John Chrysostom*, Ἀναλέκτα Βλατάδων 18, Thessaloniki: Patriarchal Institute for Patristic Studies, 1973, 99–103

Rondeau, M.-J., *Les commentaires patristiques du psautier IIIᵉ–Vᵉ siècles*, 1 *Les travaux des pères grecs et latins sur le psautier. Recherches et bilan*, 2 *Exégèse prosopologique et théologie*, OCA 219, 220; Rome: Pont. Inst. Stud. Orient., 1982, 1985

Schäublin, C., "Diodor von Tarsus," *TRE* 8, 763–67

——, *Untersuchungen zu Methode und Herkunft der antiochenischen Exegese*, Theophaneia: Beiträge zur Religions- und Kirchengeschichte des Altertums 23; Köln-Bonn: Peter Hanstein Verlag, 1974

Simonetti, M., "Le 'Quaestiones' di Teodoreto su Genesi e Esodo," *ASE* 5 (1988) 39–56

——, *Biblical Interpretation in the Early Church*, Eng. trans., Edinburgh: Clark, 1994

Siquans, A., *Der Deuteronomiumkommentar des Theodoret von Kyros*, ÖBS 19, 2002

Smalley, B., *The Study of the Bible in the Middle Ages*, 3rd ed., Oxford: Blackwell, 1983

Smith, R. L., *Micah-Malachi*. Word Biblical Commentary 32, Waco TX: Word Books, 1984

Speiser, E. A., *Genesis*, AB 1, Garden City NY: Doubleday, 1964

Sullivan, F. A., *The Christology of Theodore of Mopsuestia*, Analecta Gregoriana 82. Roma: Gregorianum, 1956

Sundberg, A. C., *The Old Testament of the Early Church*, Cambridge MA: Harvard University Press, 1964

——, "The Protestant Old Testament canon: should it be re-examined?" *CBQ* 28 (1966) 194–203

——, "The 'Old Testament': a Christian canon," *CBQ* 30 (1968) 143–55

Ternant, P., "La θεωρία d'Antioche dans le cadre de sens de l'Ecriture," *Bib* 34 (1953) 135–58, 354–83, 456–86

Thiselton, A. C., *New Horizons in Hermeneutics*, London: Harper & Collins, 1992

Thompson, J. L., *Writing the Wrongs. Women of the Old Testament among Biblical Commentators from Philo through the Reformation*, Oxford-New York: Oxford University Press, 2001

Vaccari, A., "La θεωρία nella scuola esegetica di Antiochia," *Bib* 1 (1920) 3–36

van de Paverd, F., *The Homilies on the Statues. An Introduction*, OCA 239, Rome, 1991

Vawter, B., *Biblical Inspiration*, Theological Resources, London: Hutchinson & Co, 1972

Viciano, A., "Theodoret von Kyros als Interpret des Apostels Paulus", *TGl* 80 (1990) 279–315

——, "Ο ΣΚΟΠΟΣ ΤΗΣ ΑΛΗΘΕΙΑΣ. Théodoret de Cyr et ses principes herméneutiques dans le prologue du Commentaire de Cantique des Cantiques", in *Letture cristianae dei Libri Sapienziali. XX incontro di studiosi dell'antichità cristiana*, Roma 1992, 419–435

——, "Das formale Verfahren der antiochenischen Schriftauslegung: ein Forschungsüberblick," in *Stimuli. Exegese und ihre Hermenutik in Antike und Christentum*, Festschrift für Ernst Dassmann, *JAC* 28 (1996) 370–405

Von Rad, G., *Genesis*, Eng. trans., rev. ed., OTL, 1972

Vosté, J. M. "La chronologie de l'activité littéraire de Théodore de Mopsueste." *RB* 34 (1925): 54–81

Wallace-Hadrill, D. S., *Christian Antioch. A Study of Early Christian Thought in the East*, Cambridge: CUP, 1982

Weiser, A., *The Psalms*, Eng. trans., OTL, 1962

Weitzman, M. P., *The Syriac Version of the Old Testament* (Cambridge: CUP, 1999)

Wenger, A., "Jean Chrysostome," *Dictionnaire de spiritualité* 8, Paris: Beauchesne, 1974, 331–55

Wiles, M. F., "Theodore of Mopsuestia as a representative of the Antiochene school," in P. R. Ackroyd, C. F. Evans, edd., *The Cambridge History of the Bible* I, Cambridge: Cambridge University Press, 1970, 489–510

Wilken, R. L., *John Chrysostom and the Jews. Rhetoric and Reality in the late Fourth Century*, Berkeley: University of California Press, 1983

——, "Cyril of Alexandria as interpreter of the Old Testament," in T. G. Weinandy, D. A. Keating, edd, *The Theology of St Cyril of Alexandria: a critical appreciation*, London-New York: T&T Clark, 2003, 1–21

Young, F. M., *From Nicaea to Chalcedon. A Guide to the Literature and Its Background*, Philadelphia: Fortress, 1983

——, *Biblical Exegesis and the Formation of Christian Culture*, Cambridge: CUP, 1997

Zaharopoulos, D. Z., *Theodore of Mopsuestia on the Bible. A Study of his Old Testament Exegesis*, New York: Paulist Press, 1989

Ziegler, J., *Duodecim Prophetae*, Septuaginta 13, Göttingen: Vandenhoeck & Ruprecht, 1943

——, *Jeremias, Baruch, Threni, Epistula Jeremiae*, Septuaginta 15, 3rd ed., Göttingen: Vandenhoeck & Ruprecht, 1976

——, *Ezechiel*, Septuaginta 16/1, 2nd ed., 1977

——, *Susanna, Daniel, Bet et Draco*, Septuaginta 16/2, 1954

Zorell, F., *Lexicon Hebraicum et Aramaicum Veteris Testamenti*, Roma: Pontificium Institutum Biblicum, 1963

C. English translations of Antiochene Old Testament commentaries by R. C. Hill

Diodore of Tarsus. Commentary on the Psalms 1–51, WGRW, forthcoming

Theodore of Mopsuestia. Commentary on Psalms 1–81, WGRW, forthcoming

——, *Commentary on the Twelve Prophets*, FOTC 108, 2004

St John Chrysostom. Homilies on Genesis, FOTC 74, 82, 87, 1986, 1990, 1982

——, *Commentary on the Psalms*, Brookline MA: Holy Cross Orthodox Press, 1998

——, *Old Testament Homilies*, 1 *Homilies on Hannah, David and Saul*, 2 *Homilies on Isaiah and Jeremiah*, 3 *Homilies on the Obscurity of the Old Testament, Homilies on the Psalms*, Brookline MA: Holy Cross Orthodox Press, 2003

——, *Eight Sermons on Genesis*, Brookline MA: Holy Cross Orthodox Press, 2004

——, *Commentary on Job*, Brookline MA: Holy Cross Orthodox Press, forthcoming
——, *Commentary on Proverbs*, Brookline MA: Holy Cross Orthodox Press, forthcoming
Theodoret of Cyrus. Commentary on the Psalms, FOTC 101, 102, 2000, 2001
——, *Commentary on the Song of Songs*, ECS 2, 2001
——, *Commentary on Daniel*, WGRW, forthcoming
——, *Commentary on Isaiah*, WGRW, forthcoming
——, *Commentary on Jeremiah, Lamentations, Baruch*, Brookline MA: Holy Cross Orthodox Press, forthcoming
——, *Commentary on Ezekiel*, Brookline MA: Holy Cross Orthodox Press, forthcoming
——, *Commentary on the Twelve Prophets*, Brookline MA: Holy Cross, forthcoming
——, *Questions on the Octateuch*, LEC, forthcoming
——, *Questions on Kingdoms and Chronicles*, LEC, forthcoming

GENERAL INDEX

INDEX OF BIBLICAL CITATIONS

INDEX OF MODERN AUTHORS